ATLA Monograph Series
edited by Dr. Kenneth E. Rowe

LUTHER'S CATECHISM COMES TO AMERICA:

Theological Effects on the
Issues of the Small Catechism
Prepared In or For America
Prior to 1850

by
ARTHUR C. REPP, SR.

ATLA Monograph Series, No. 18

The Scarecrow Press, Inc.
and
The American Theological
Library Association
Metuchen, N.J., & London
1982

Library of Congress Cataloging in Publication Data

Repp, Arthur Christian, 1906-
  Luther's catechism comes to America.

  (ATLA monograph series ; no. 18)
  Bibliography: p.
  Includes indexes.
  1. Luther, Martin, 1483-1546. Kleine
Katechismus--Influence. 2. Lutheran Church--
United States--Education--History.
3. Lutheran Church--United States--Creeds and
catechisms--History. 4. United States--
Church history. I. Title. II. Series.
BX8070.L8R37   238'.4173   82-5453
ISBN 0-8108-1546-X   AACR2

ACKNOWLEDGMENTS

Historians are particularly indebted to the painstaking efforts of others. This is true especially in reference to the libraries and their staffs who, often without appreciation, search out the caverns of their depositories in the hope that they may be of assistance to the researcher. This has been my experience and I have benefited greatly from their search. I herewith acknowledge my indebtedness to the scores of libraries who participated in my quest. A complete list of libraries and archives would be much too lengthy, but I must make special mention of Lucille Hager, former librarian of Concordia Seminary, St. Louis and now librarian at Christ Seminary--Seminex. I would also like to thank Frederick S. Waiser, formerly archivist associated with the library at the Lutheran Seminary at Gettysburg, Pa. Similarly, my appreciation goes to the libraries and staffs of the Lutheran Seminary at Philadelphia, the German Society of Pennsylvania, and the Library Company of Philadelphia, all of whom were of significant help to me in locating copies of Luther's catechism.

The most kind Foreword by Martin E. Marty calls for a special note of thanks. I sincerely hope that his high praise will not become a source of embarrassment to him in the future.

One of the hard facts of research is the cost involved, especially when it spread over a broad geographic area. I am therefore especially grateful to the Aid Association for Lutherans for its grant to finance the final stage of research: the preparation of the manuscript for publication.

Colleagues have a way of showing their interest and giving encouragement over the long years of searching out the sources and this must not go unrecognized. This was true in a special way of my colleagues at Christ Seminary and more particularly of Robert Bertram and John H. Tietjen, who read the manuscript and made valuable suggestions which I have incorporated in this work.

iii

CONTENTS

EDITOR'S NOTE

Since 1972 the American Theological Library Association has undertaken responsibility for a modest dissertation series in the field of religious studies. Our aim in this series is to publish two dissertations of quality each year at a reasonable cost. Titles are selected from studies in a wide variety of religious and theological disciplines nominated by graduate school deans and directors of graduate studies. We are pleased to publish Arthur C. Repp's study of Luther's Catechism in America as number 18 in our series.

Following undergraduate studies in Concordia Collegiate Institute, Bronxville, New York, Professor Repp studied theology at Concordia Seminary in St. Louis and took the doctorate in education and history at Washington University in St. Louis. The holder of two honorary degrees, Dr. Repp has held teaching and administrative posts in the Concordia Seminary and more recently in Christ Seminary in St. Louis. For more than twenty years he has been a member of the Board of Governors and President of the Concordia Historical Institute. A former editor of the Concordia Historical Institute Quarterly, Dr. Repp has published a study of Confirmation in the Lutheran Church and has contributed articles to a number of periodicals and encyclopedias.

Kenneth E. Rowe
Series Editor

Drew University Library
Madison, New Jersey

ix

FOREWORD

"We know of a thousand different doctrines and a
thousand great men. Let us study together the religious
practices and faith of a whole people." That plea, one
might almost call it a cry, is by the French sociologist
Gabriel Le Bras. He spoke up for what is needed in America as much as in France: attention to the ordinary lives
of believers. "We need a history of religious practices as
much as, or more than, a history of religious theory, doctrines, theologies, and dogmas."*

In this book Arthur Repp gives us something of the
two worlds of religious history. Although not many of his
book's men are "great" (perhaps a Count Ludwig von Zinzendorf or a pioneer church founder like Henry Melchior Muhlenberg might qualify for a kind of greatness), he does write
about "a thousand different doctrines." These are doctrines
propounded not in the formal theology of a Jonathan Edwards
or a Paul Tillich but in humble little books of religious instruction employed by Lutheran pastors, teachers, and parents for two centuries up to 1850. Through these books one
has access to important issues of dogma and theology.

Repp's book will be remembered, however, chiefly
for the way it corrects imbalances and talks about "religious
practices" of ordinary people on frontiers of Pennsylvania
and Tennessee and wherever Lutheran immigrants wandered
in early America. It is the history of those practices that
most scholars have overlooked--with good reason. The story
of dogma and bureaucracy is easy to find. Important people
see to it that it gets recorded in leatherbound books, and
sealed in archives. But Arthur Repp, with amazing energy
and diligence, has gone past those formal treatises and dug
up books that were actually used--so much so that most of
them wore out or were thrown away in tatters--by people
who leave few formal records.

---

*From an article written in 1954, quoted in Henri Desroche
Jacob and the Angel: An Essay in Sociologies of Religion
(Amherst: University of Massachusetts Press, 1973), p. 22.

Few institutions have done more to shape the American ethos than the Sunday School. Yet after two centuries we have only one fine but small and jaunty history of them and one large but a bit plodding bureaucratic history of their leadership. Whoever has made a passage through such schools to adult Protestanthood knows that religious images, the primal impressions, came from Sunday Schools more than from sermons or books of theology.

So it is with the schools of instruction that used Luther's Small Catechism. Whether such schools were the churches themselves, or "stay-after" Christenlehre sessions, or home-study sequences, they succeeded in stamping in the minds of children and reinforcing in the heads of their parents and tutors the deepest concepts of their faith. As a product of such catechismal instruction in the 1930's, I can testify that the little book was a constant companion, its every page subjected to memory, its lines cough-upable at the behest of pastors or elders. I can still smell the publisher's paste, remember the way I practiced my signature inside the cover, and recall how we underlined the passages assigned. Several decades of graduate theology have not succeeded in supplanting in my mind a view of the structure of the universe and of the faith that Luther's book, with its "Chief Parts," provided. Even the theology section of my library is still catalogued to follow its sequence. If that was so of people in the 1930's, think what it meant in the largely bookless world of the frontier 1730's and 1830's.

Each faith has its scriptures, and most faiths have their glosses and commentaries on those scriptures. Lutherans have a big fat Book of Concord about which they have been discordant for four centuries. But Lutheran people, and most Lutheran pastors, do not know the Book of Concord or its "Augsburg Confession." They know one script from the book, the Small Catechism. When they undertake to convert a new generation of the baptized to knowledge of this faith, they doll up the catechism once more and lure the young. When they ship the message overseas, they equip missionaries and catechists with--what else?--the Catechism.

Repp's book should have something for Lutherans, Protestants, Christians, religious people, and librarians, as well as students of shipping, migration, the frontier, community-building, education, the family, the congregation, and doctrine. That is quite a varied company, and they may need a bit of cajoling to see what is in it for them.

For one thing, there are a few places in which, for the sake of reference, Repp simply prints lists of versions. These are to me as interesting as the "begats" in the Bible, but they have their place. For another, most of the cast of characters will be unfamiliar even to the most devoted members of all the companies mentioned at the beginning of this paragraph. Yet their obscurity is part of their charm: catechism publication and revision was often a part of entrepreneurship. "You gotta have a gimmick," someone must have told many of these editors. They must have thought they had a better idea, that they could make the book most palatable and memorable, that they could improve on their competitors. Some of them acted out of a sense of ecclesiastical responsibility. A few of them were chartered by jurisdictions, and were then predecessors of the more impersonal and bureaucratized boards that put out religious instructional materials nowadays.

Surprises abound. Most newcomers to the subject probably would bring the expectation that here is merely a history of bindings, of the transmission of texts. Somehow the "pure" Catechism, Lutherans seemed to think, dropped down intact from the hands of the reformer Martin Luther and served as the custodial receptacle of truth and meaning for Lutherans ever after. Anything but that. Repp's is a kind of miniature history of heresy. One meets here whole companies of rationalists and a few posses of rationalist-hunters. He does not set out to censor--though his own theological presuppositions do show quite frequently--but he does successfully smoke out a thousand improvisations that do not square with Luther's own teaching. Thus many catechism writers equated Bible with Word of God, something that Luther and the Bible did not do. They had particular trouble with sacramental teaching. A few of them offered hilarious twists on Christological and Trinitarian teaching. Codification and orthodoxy tended to come later, not earlier in this story. Repp's is not a history of a fall after purity but of adaptations to America, its frontier, its Lutheran sectarian life--and gradual efforts to recover what the heart of the tradition was.

In this history one learns again the importance of language and the ways it relates to faith. Technically, it deals with German and English books, since catechisms by and for Swedes, Finns, and Indians had only their moments under the early American sun. But the subtleties of the German and English need ferreting out, and Repp is tireless in doing so.

As far as Repp pushed his work past existing frontiers of research, so one wishes he could have pushed further, or that someone now will take up his task in other directions. Thus the reader cannot help but be curious about how these books were used. We read that one version went through seventy-three editions, and even obscure ones saw numerous printings, while others give no evidence of having been put to work by anyone. Recent research on the Germany in which Luther's catechism first appeared is showing that the Lutherans had to resort to the State to stuff the teaching down the throats of children. The people did not come running to hear and teach this Gospel. How was it in an America where religion was a voluntary matter? Who saw to it that the wrigglers wrestled with the text? Did they resist memorizing? Did they welcome the teaching? What did they think of the teachers?

Those are all questions of "religious practices" for another day. Arthur Repp, a constant teacher (he was my own at seminary a third of a century ago) has pushed much further than anyone else the border of our access to the mentality of ordinary believers by showing so much about the books they used. I hope his is an encouragement to Catholics, Calvinists, Methodists, and Mormons to engage in similar kinds of work. A composite of such histories would throw a much different light than any we've known until now on the story of believers in the bygone days of America.

Martin E. Marty
Fairfax M. Cone Distinguished
    Service Professor of the History of Modern Christianity
The University of Chicago

INTRODUCTION

The history of the Christian Church or any of its denominations is incomplete when limited to its geographical expansion or to such external phenomena as the theological changes among the professional theologians and the consequent controversies that emerged from such changes. Even the ecclesiastical realignments that took place at the structural level in the church during the course of history may not always be of prime significance. Of equal or even greater importance is to understand what happened among the rank and file church members while the theological issues were being disputed among the professionals. What did the men and women in the pews believe? What were they taught as catechumens? What was the day-to-day working theology of the parish pastor or the frontier missionary? This important phase of church history has frequently been overlooked or given only minimal treatment.

One aspect of this concern is to learn the extent Luther's Small Catechism was taught to the youth and in what context they learned it. Since the Small Catechism is generally regarded as a criterion for confessional Lutheranism, its use or disuse during a given period should give us some indication what the theological climate among the laity was. The kind of text used may, to be sure, not be conclusive, since the personal influence of the instructor was an important factor and his theological tendency could either weaken or strengthen the confessional witness made during the catechization period. However, since there were few ecclesiastical restrictions during the early period of American Lutheranism dictating what text he was to use, the instructor's choice of catechism may already tell us something of his stance and what he taught the youth in his care.

At the time when Lutherans have just observed the 450th anniversary of Luther's two catechisms, it should be of special interest to learn to what extent and in what context his Small Catechism was used and what part it played

in the development of Lutheranism in America during its
earlier period, prior to 1850. This study will limit itself
primarily to the Luther catechisms issued in and for America during that period, bearing in mind that most catechisms
in use at first were those brought by the immigrants from
the homeland. When the diversity of catechisms from the
variety of consistories in Europe made their common use
impractical, a need was felt to prepare new catechism texts
for Lutherans in their new environment.

The introductory chapter of this work deals primarily
with the meager circumstances surrounding whatever catechetical instruction the several Lutheran European-language
groups first maintained after their arrival. The chapter is
intended to provide a background or the setting to help understand the circumstances under which Lutheranism struggled
to maintain its confessional identity. The subsequent chap-
ters will describe in greater detail the wide variety of catechisms produced in this country as Lutheranism assumed its
place in American denominational life.

The year 1850 was chosen as a convenient cutoff date
because at about that time the Lutheran Church in America
entered into a new stage of development. It roughly marked
an era that brought with it a number of new synodical bodies
and new alignments, each struggling to meet the theological
issues of old and new Lutheranism, the needs of an almost
overwhelming number of new immigrants, the challenge to
communicate in the languages of the homeland and in the
language of the new generation, while at the same time trying to adjust to a churchlife in a democracy. All this had
a profound effect on the contents of the many new and old
catechisms that were prepared to instruct the youth of the
church. Therefore, it appeared to the writer that the catechisms after 1850 had a story of their own to tell.

Chapter I

CATECHETICAL INSTRUCTION AMONG EARLY
LUTHERAN SETTLERS IN AMERICA

THE SWEDES AND FINNS

The first Lutheran congregation within the present
limits of the United States was established by the Swedes
and Finns who came to trade and settle along the Delaware
River and its tributaries. [1] Their purpose was to establish
a permanent colony under the name New Sweden. They had
come to the New World during March 1638, under the leadership of Peter Minuit, setting up a trading post in an area
claimed both by the Dutch and the English. Since the Dutch
were preoccupied in the Hudson River valley and the English
in Virginia to the south and in Massachusetts to the north,
neither country at first interfered with the Swedes and Finns,
particularly since at no time were their numbers threatening, never exceeding a few hundred persons. [2]

The Rev. Reorus Torkillus (1608-1643), who came on
the second expedition in 1640, was the first Lutheran pastor
to serve in the American colonies. Public worship was conducted at first in one of the houses built by Minuit but later,
in 1642 or 1643, in their own chapel. [3] Since the Swedes
and Finns had come to New Sweden primarily for economic
reasons the interests of the soldiers and settlers in religion
was dependent on the individual colonists. Many of the settlers during the early period were in fact minor lawbreakers
who had "volunteered" to come to New Sweden. Among them
were poachers, deserters, breakers of forest ordinances,
and small debtors. [4] Nevertheless Johan Printz, the first
governor appointed in 1643, was instructed to see to it that
spiritual care was given to the colonists.

> Above all things, shall the Governor consider and
> see to it that a true and due worship, becoming
> honor, laud, and praise be paid to the Most High

3

God in all things, and to that end all proper care
shall be taken that divine service be zealously performed according to the Unaltered Augsburg Confession, the Council of Uppsala, and the ceremonies
of the Swedish Church; and all persons, but especially the young, shall be duly instructed in the
articles of their Christian faith; and all good church
discipline shall in like manner be duly exercised
and received. 5

Likewise the governor was obligated to see that the
Indians were "instructed in the truths and worship of the
Christian religion."6

As a matter of fact, however, during the entire period of Swedish rule support of the spiritual life of the colonists was sporadic. The few Lutheran pastors, in turn, who
were commissioned to New Sweden came, at least in their
own minds, on a temporary basis, hopefully awaiting a call
to a more permanent position in the homeland. Under the
circumstances of widely separated forts and settlements along
the Delaware and its tributaries, it became quite difficult for
the few pastors who were there to instruct the children on a
regular basis. The responsibility fell therefore chiefly on
the parents. They in turn were dependent on their own interests and instruction, in many cases a limited ability to
read, together with a scarcity of Bibles, hymnals, catechisms and devotional books. Among the few catechisms
known to have been available was Johan Rudbeck's catechism
of 1628. 7 Later settlers brought along the Luther text of
Laurentius Paulinus Gothus' edition of 1641. 8 Both Gothus
and Rudbeck were prestigious church leaders representing a
conservative Lutheranism.

Johan Campanius (1601-1683) was the second Lutheran
pastor in New Sweden. He arrived in February 1643, and
soon replaced Torkillus upon his death on September 7, taking over his congregations on the Christina Creek and up-
stream on the Delaware. During his five years of service,
Campanius showed a lively mission interest in the Delaware
Indians, learned their language and finally translated Luther's
Small Catechism into their language. Unfortunately it remained unprinted for another 50 years when it finally appeared
in 1696, at the personal expense of King Charles XI of Sweden, under the title, Luther's Catechism Translated into the
American Virginian Language. 9

The catechism had an introduction of 14 pages followed by the translation, often a paraphrase, accompanied by
explanatory questions and answers, followed by a Swedish
version. At the close of the catechism there was a 28-page
vocabulary of the Delaware Indian language.

Unfortunately by the time the catechism appeared in
print, interest in mission work among the Delaware Indians
had declined. Only in a few cases did pastors find the energy and time to work among the Indians. [10] Anders Hesselius was one of the few exceptions, and he served the Indians during his period of ministry, 1713-1722. [11] Hence
the publication of this catechism is more of a historical
footnote than a contribution in the use and influence of
Luther's catechism among the Indians.

The Rev. Lars Karlson Lock came in 1647 and succeeded Campanius when the latter returned to Sweden in
1648. Lock served some 40 years on the Delaware, for the
most part the sole Lutheran pastor and one of the few to
make his ministry more than a transient one. During his
time the Dutch finally arrived in 1655 to make good their
claim over the area. Though this meant the close of Swedish domination, most of the settlers nevertheless remained.
The Dutch permitted them to conduct Lutheran services,
primarily because they were too involved with their own af-
fairs in the Hudson River valley. However, only one Lutheran pastor, Lock, was allowed to remain; the other two,
Matthias Nertunius and Peter Hjort, were sent back to Sweden. [12] But the territory was much too large for Lock, and
as a result the teaching of the young people was seriously
neglected. In turn the total number of people scattered over
this primitive area was very small. In July 1654, just before the arrival of the Dutch, Governor Riding reported a
total population of only 370 persons, including a few Dutch
families in the area. [13]

A second political change came in 1664 when the English made good their claim and put an end to the Dutch rule.
Their arrival gave the colony more permanent assurance
that Lutheran worship might continue if some help would
come from the mother country. That year marked the arrival of the last large number of Finnish immigrants, some
104 in number. [14]

A number of years prior to his death in 1688, Lock

was so badly crippled that his ministry virtually came to an
end. His ministry was the last colonial link with the Church
of Sweden. Even when Lock was at the height of his strength,
the work, as previously stated, was beyond the capacity of
one man. The few years of help he received from the Rev.
Jacob Fabritius, a Dutch-speaking German who in 1672 came
from New York, was shortlived. At first Fabritius could
preach only in Dutch. In time he mastered Swedish sufficiently for him to minister to the Swedes. He was able to
preach his first sermon on Trinity Sunday, 1677. But this
too came to an end in 1683 when he became blind. He died
in 1693 or shortly thereafter. [15]

        The years of the single ministry of this large area
took a serious toll on the spiritual life of the people. With
the death of Lock, only reading services could be conducted
and these were never popular considering the effort it took
to come to such a service. Two such reading services were
conducted, one by an old man, Anders Bengston, in Tenakong
near Wicaco (Philadelphia) and the other by a newcomer, Karl
Springer, at Christina or Tranhook (now Wilmington). [16]

        In the meantime all contacts with the mother country
had virtually come to an end. At least two attempts were
made to have a clergyman come from Sweden but the colonists received no answer. In 1691, a letter was sent through
some New York merchants appealing to the Amsterdam Consistory for help. But this letter, too, went unanswered.
Help seemed to be in the making through William Penn who
had been impressed by some of the Swedish merchants with
whom he came in contact in Philadelphia. Immediately on
his return to London in 1683/84, Penn applied to the Swedish
Envoy Extraordinary for assistance in obtaining for the Delaware Swedes one or more clergymen and books from Sweden.
Penn assured the envoy that he would take care of the books
and have them forwarded from London. Penn himself sent
the Swedes a box of catechisms and other books, together
with a Bible in folio for use in church, though all the books
were in English. The books were not further identified. [17]
Nothing else seemed to have come of the colonists' appeal.

        A more promising interest was stimulated about this
time by Anders Printz, a nephew of the former governor.
He had traveled to America and on his return to Sweden related his experiences to Jonas Thelin, postmaster at Gothen-
burg. Thelin was so moved by the account that he in turn
appealed to King Charles XI in behalf of his countrymen living

abroad.   The king encouraged Thelin to write a letter in
1692, inquiring of the needs of the Lutheran colonists, as-
suring them of the king's readiness not only to furnish ministers, "but also all sorts of religious books in both languages," i.e., Swedish and Finnish.   Thelin further asked
for a list of names of the colonists since all contacts had
been lost.   In passing he mentioned Penn's attempt to get
aid some eight or ten years earlier, but said he did not
know what had happened to the request.[18]

Karl Springer, the layreader mentioned above, who a
few years earlier had come to America, answered Thelin's
letter, May 31, 1693.   He requested that two Swedish ministers be sent,

> who are well learned and well excercised in the
> Holy Scriptures, and who may well defend both
> themselves and us against all the false teachers
> and strange sects by whom we are surrounded, or
> who may oppose us on account of our true, pure,
> and uncorrupted service to God and all the world....
> It is also our humble request that we may have sent
> to us twelve Bibles, three copies of Sermons, and
> forty-two Manuals, one hundred Hand-books and
> Spiritual Meditations, two hundred Catechisms, two
> hundred A B C books.[19]

The colonists promised to support their ministers and
pay for the books sent.   Springer's letter was replicated by
many copies and circulated from hand to hand in Sweden.
Enclosed with Springer's letter was the requested list of
Swedes still living in the colonies.   It included the names of
188 families comprising 942 persons who were living along
the Delaware River in 1693.   Of these, 39 were born in
Sweden.   A few of the 942 names were in fact Hollanders,
probably related by intermarriage, but who regarded themselves as one people.[20]

Under a royal directive of July 15, 1696, the King of
Sweden sent the books requested by the colonists as his personal gift.   Among them were 100 copies of Svebilius' catechism, bound in blue paper and 300 copies of Luther's Small
Catechism, bound in boards or wooden covers.   The catechisms were those written by Olof Svebilius (1624-1700),
Archbishop of Sweden (1681-1700), titled Simple Explanation
of Luther's Small Catechism Arranged According to Questions
and Answers.[21]   This catechism had originally been prepared

by Svebilius and Haquin Spegel (1645-1714) but met with vio-
lent opposition from the Orthodox element in parliament in
1686 because of its Pietistic overtones.   Consequently the
king commissioned Svebilius alone to bring out a revision.[22]
It was finally published in Uppsala by Henrich Keyser in
1689, the same year the catechism received the approval of
the clergy.   It remained the official catechism of the Church
of Sweden until 1810, when it was revised by Archbishop Jacob Lindblom in favor of the theology of Enlightenment.

     The same ship that carried these books also brought
500 copies of Campanius' translation previously prepared for
the Delaware Indians.   In addition to the books, two Lutheran
pastors, Andreas Rudman and Ericus Tobias Björk, appointed
by Archbishop Svebilius, were sent.   A third pastor, Jonas
Auren was sent by the king to make a survey of the colony
and to report back to him.   After considerable delay the
ship arrived at Wicaco on June 30, 1697, and on July 2, at
Christina (Tranhock).[23]

     The importance of the books given to the colonists
may be seen from a letter written by Björk from Christina
soon after his arrival.

>   I cannot mention, without astonishment, but to the
>   honour of these people, that we hardly found three
>   Swedish books; but they were so anxious for the
>   improvement of their children, that they lent them
>   to one another, so that they can all read tolerably
>   well.   None of the books that his majesty graciously
>   gave us are now out of use; they are distributed
>   among the families.[24]

     Now finally after a long period of neglect divine serv-
ices, catechetical instruction, and to a degree, church life,
were restored.   Rudman became the pastor in Wicaco and
Björk ministered in Christina.   One of the first measures
taken at each location was to build a more permanent house
of worship since both buildings were in sad disrepair.   The
southern group joyously dedicated its new granite church in
May 1699, and the northern settlers theirs in July 1700.   The
former was called Trinity and the latter Gloria Dei.   Both
are now known as Old Swedes Church.

     In accord with the old Swedish Orthodox custom, though
tempered somewhat by Pietism, catechetical preaching and instruction were again developed.   Acrelius described the services in Wicaco as follows:

On Sundays there were two sermons delivered. The
first was between the first and second ringing of
the bells, when a morning hymn was sung, or "O
God vi lofve tig" ["We praise Thee, O God"]. Then
a sermon was preached upon a portion of the Catechism, and the service was ended with a prayer
and a hymn. The second bell was then rung for
the second sermon, when the Teacher [i.e., the
pastor] went through the aisles and repeated his
sermon, and also examined the people upon what
had been said before. This was done in summer-
time. In winter, when the days were short and
the congregation could not come together so generally, in the morning service one chapter of the Old
and one of the New Testament was read and explained. High mass was performed according to
the Church Ordinance. The catechization was at
first performed in the church; afterwards, for
greater convenience, in private houses, for which
purpose the congregation divided into certain sections. 25

Such examinations in the homes were described by
Acrelius from personal experience:

The congregation was divided into certain sections,
the Provost [i.e., Acrelius] visiting each in order
to hear the Catechism and to make explanations.
This was done in the following manner: The beginning was with some passage of Scripture, which
was explained and adapted to the Order of Salvation;
after this the recitation [of the Svebilius catechism]
was attended to, and a suitable exposition was given
of both the Law and the Gospel, and the use of the
Sacraments, especially of the worthy receiving of
the Lord's Supper, inasmuch as a most unjustifiable
neglect had prevailed in that respect. Some fruit
thereof was perceived, but by no means as much
as had been desired and expected. Both the old
and the young were encouraged to give an account
of their knowledge and faith in answer to questions
proposed, and with most of them a greater acquaint-
ance with the plan of salvation was manifested than
had been expected.... The young were afterwards
taken by themselves to read their parts of Christian
doctrine either in Swedish or in English; for, from
the want of Swedish schools, the young learn mostly

in English, until they become more intelligent, and
then they use the Swedish Catechism.[26]

Conditions stabilized for a while, but the coming and
going of different pastors--punctuated by yearlong vacancies--
continu' ' to hurt the scattered preaching places. Pastor
Gabriel .aesman, who came in 1743, found conditions different from what he had anticipated. New sects had en-
croached on the leaderless Lutherans. Followers of George
Whitefield found adherents among those who were looking for
an English speaking ministry. Also Moravians under the
leadership of Zinzendorf had worked their way in among the
Swedish Lutherans. While working among these and other
hindrances, Naesman during his seven-year ministry tried to
restore the Swedish Lutheran practice of catechetical sermons
followed by an examination in the aisles and urged "that the
people should be assembled several times a year in their
sections and without delay present their children for baptism
and become acquainted with their catechisms" [that is, be
prepared for the Lord's Supper].[27]

Further relief for some of the southern parishes came
in the appointment of Jonas Sandlin who was assigned to the
Racoon and Pennsneck congregations. He arrived in 1748.
The mother church sent along with him 200 copies of Svebilius'
catechism and 200 of Luther's Small Catechism.[28] The joy
at Sandlin's arrival after a five-year vacancy was ended
abruptly, however, for he died after six months, in August
1748.[29]

Actually the Pennsneck congregation had not joined in
the call to Sandlin because it was now mostly English. They
wanted services but only in the English language. Since this
was not forthcoming by Lutheran pastors they had decided
already in 1741 to turn to the Church of England for further
ministry.[30]

Each new pastor who came from Sweden to the Delaware valley naturally served the parishes in his mother
tongue. But with each year the English language made inroads among the parishes. Where pastors would not or could
not minister in English, the people turned to the Anglican
Church or to the English-speaking sects. Here and there
pastors did try to master English to stem the exodus. In
fact in a few cases Lutheran pastors were even able to
preach in Anglican parishes when they had vacancies, but
these were rare.[31]

When Israel Acrelius came to Christina in November 1749, he found that many of his parishioners could express themselves better in English than in their mother tongue. [32] In fact he heard so many requests for English services and reminders of how well his predecessor, Peter Tranberg, had served the English generation that, more out of disgust, Acrelius learned English well enough to preach, much to the delight both of the English-speaking Lutherans as well as some of the Anglicans in the area who were without a pastor. But this soon had to be kept at a minimum because the Swedish-speaking Lutherans complained that they never got to hear their pastor on Sundays since he was on the road so much preaching in English. Some adjustments were made but preaching in English was limited at Christina to one Sunday per month. [33]

In time Swedish lost out entirely since support from the motherland gradually came to an end. The Anglicans for the most part took over the English-speaking Lutherans and in time even their houses of worship. On the other hand, some of the laymen who remained firm in their Lutheran confession, joined hands with the German Lutherans, who had similar language problems, though at first to a lesser degree. As will be seen below, the introduction of an English translation of Luther's catechism among German Lutherans was stimulated and even made possible by Swedish Lutherans living in the Philadelphia area.

THE DUTCH

The earliest Lutheran congregation to assemble for public worship in North America was established by the Swedes and Finns on the Delaware River in 1642-1643, but Lutheran settlers came from The Netherlands to the Hudson River area somewhat earlier, probably as early as 1624 and 1625. The Dutch had discovered the Hudson River in 1609 and by 1614 had established Ft. Orange (near the present Albany) to protect Dutch fur traders in that region. But the Dutch had more in mind than setting up trading centers. They planned to settle and establish major permanent commercial enterprises. Approximately 40 families came to Ft. Orange in 1624, and in the following year some 200 persons came to New Amsterdam, the present New York. [34]

While the majority of the Dutch were Reformed, there was a sizable number of Lutherans in The Netherlands, es-

pecially among the German and Scandinavian merchants who
were directly involved in the expansion of Dutch influence in
America. After many years of stress, the Lutherans had
finally been accorded freedom of worship in The Netherlands
and had organized a number of churches, mostly in the larger
cities, the acknowledged head being in Amsterdam. These
Lutherans were confessionally conservative, reflecting the
period of staunch Orthodoxy of their homeland churches. As
such they maintained strong ties with the church in Hamburg
and later, with Holy Trinity Church in London (Old Hamburg
Church), which had been established as early as 1618.

Though conservative in doctrine the Dutch Lutherans
were strongly influenced by their Calvinistic neighbors in
their forms of worship. These were largely non-liturgical,
emphasizing chiefly the sermon. Due to the nature of the
political situation, however, their form of church government
was "free church," that is, congregational, the authority being placed with the local church council rather than its total
membership.

The Dutch in colonial New Netherland were more re-
strictive than they were in the homeland. They took a strong
stand against all those who did not profess the Reformed
faith. Only the Reformed were permitted to assemble for
public worship, teach, and administer the sacraments. However, at first this order was not strictly observed. In fact
the number of Lutherans in 1643 was sizeable enough to be
noted as a distinct group. Father Isaac Joques, a Jesuit
missionary who had been rescued by the Dutch from the Iro-
quois Indians, mentioned them together with Roman Catholics,
English Puritans, and Mennonites.[35] As the number of Lutherans grew the strictures were tightened so that many Lutherans were arrested and fined for assembling in homes for
worship.[36]

Nevertheless as early as 1649 the Lutherans in New
Amsterdam and Ft. Orange regarded themselves as a congregation and consequently petitioned the Amsterdam Consistory for a pastor. After several years of correspondence,
petitioning, sporadic resistance on the part of the Dutch both
in Europe and America, and the unavailability of a candidate,
the call of the congregation was finally honored in the person
of John Ernestus Goetwater (Gutwasser), who arrived in July
1657. But the action of the Lutherans proved premature as
far as the Reformed leaders were concerned. The Reformed
in New Amsterdam stoutly resisted the Lutherans in their

plea for freedom of worship and Goetwater was finally forced
to return in June 1659 without having been able to minister
to his congregation.

The continued growth of the number of Lutherans was
no doubt a contributing factor to the resistance on the part
of the Reformed.   The Lutherans claimed around 150 families
in New Netherland in 1653, about equally divided between Ft.
Orange and New Amsterdam. [37]

During the period when they first regarded themselves
as a congregation in 1649, and when they finally gained their
freedom of worship in 1664 (at which time the English took
over the rule from the Dutch and granted the Lutherans freedom), many of the Lutherans remained in a loose relationship with the Reformed out of sheer necessity, especially in
reference to the rites of baptism, marriage and burials.
True, the Lutherans did object to the wording of the baptismal rite which requested the parents and sponsors to acknowledge the doctrine taught "here in the church, " as the correct
one.   But their objections were overruled even when the
West Indian Company interceded in their behalf by pointing
out that the "here" was not in the older forms of baptism in
use in The Netherlands. [38]

Some Lutherans, of course, attended public worship,
called upon as they were to observe the Reformed faith in
public, and no doubt a number of these were lost to the Lutherans. [39]   Others assembled in private and when caught
paid the fines or suffered imprisonment.

With the English in control the colony, now called New
York, accorded the Lutherans and others freedom of worship.
The Lutherans again petitioned for a pastor.   Finally, in
1668 Jacobus Fabritius (d.1696), a refugee pastor, accepted
the call.   He was a Silesian by birth and had been a pastor
there.   Fabritius arrived in New York in February 1669.
With little delay he took charge of his flock.   After the congregation had elected its officers, he entered on an active
ministry.   Already by April 25, he reported to the Amsterdam Consistory that he had baptized a Negro of about 50
years.

> Furthermore, thanks be to God, I am also instruct-
> ing some Indians and heathen, which among our op-
> ponents causes partly amazement and surprise and
> partly hatred, envy and slander. [40]

Fabritius was optimistic about the "future success of the Holy Gospel, except that we lack catechisms and hymnals." He asked for 100 hymnals and small Lutheran catechisms.[41]

That Fabritius was a man of vision may be seen in the fact that though just beginning in his ministry, he asked that

one or more students be sent over, who can easily support themselves here by teaching (but they must first be examined by your reverences and be provided with a Testiminio Examinationis), in order that they, or one of them, in case of my death, might be proposed to the congregation.

Even more than that, he saw a need for a printer too.

Should there also be a printer who could supply us with a small collection of type to print A B C books and catechisms, together with some good samples of reading and writing, he could earn a living to his ample satisfaction. Should we wish to employ him as a precentor, I cannot sufficiently say what high benefit the country might derive therefrom.[42]

Had it been possible to honor either or both of these requests the direction of the New York church might have taken a different course.

Fabritius organized the two Lutheran groups in New York and Albany into two congregations[43] and introduced the Service Book of the Amsterdam Church Order which the congregations adopted for their own use. The Service Book (Kerckenagenda) had originally been prepared by the Antwerp Lutheran Church in 1567 and adopted by the Amsterdam Church when it was organized. It expressed the strict confessional stand of Lutheran Orthodoxy and as such determined the stance of the Dutch Lutherans in the New York area at this time. Nevertheless the Service Book revealed the Calvinistic influence on public worship. Instead of a Lutheran liturgical emphasis, it stressed the use of Psalms and centered on the sermon. Only in the case of the celebration of the Lord's Supper was a liturgical form proscribed.[44]

The bases for the instruction of both children and adults were set forth to be:

The Small Catechism of Luther.
The Small Corpus Doctrinae by John Ligarius.
Questions and Answers on the Catechism, by
    Adolph Visscher for those who are admitted
    to the Lord's Supper.
Questions and Answers on the Catechism
    [Attributed to Luther].
The Augsburg Confession.
The Passion Narrative. 45

John Ligarius, the author of the book mentioned, had
been pastor at Wörden. While he was there he revised the
Corpus Doctrinae of Matthew Judex, printed in Wesel in 1564,
for his congregation under the title, Little Corpus Doctrinae.
The book had been widely used in The Netherlands. The
questions and answers of the Corpus were based on Luther's
Small Catechism. 46

The Questions and Answers on the Catechism by Adolph
Visscher (Fischer) was first published in 1601. The Questions
and Answers together with Luther's Small Catechism had been
prepared both for those being instructed in the faith and for
those who were preparing themselves for the confession of
sins. 47

The appendices included the Small Corpus Doctrinae
of Ligarius in 63 questions and answers in dogmatic order
and a series of questions on the catechism for those who
would go to the Lord's Supper. 48

In spite of Fabritius' vision and organizing ability he
was a disappointment to his congregation. He was despotic,
quarrelsome, lacking necessary tact and discretion, and was
somewhat eccentric. He got into trouble with the civil authorities both in New York and Albany, as well as with his
congregations so that by 1671 he was forced to leave and set
out for the Delaware River region where he took charge of
congregations in Philadelphia and Tinicum. 49

Under existing conditions it was most remarkable that
a replacement came soon after Fabritius' departure. Already by August 1671, Bernhard Arnzius (also called Arenius
and Arnzen) arrived in New York as the next pastor. Arnzius
had been pastor in Medemblick, North Holland. Though he
had a ministry of some 20 years in New York, until his death
in 1691, little is known of him except that he was a devoted
and beloved pastor. During his ministry the Dutch again oc-
cupied New York and the Hudson valley (1673-1674), which

revived disturbances for the Lutherans with the Reformed, in addition to creating serious teaching interruptions. All this added considerably to the burdens of Arnzius. The resumption of English rule and the continuous political uncertainties brought about a sharp decline in immigration from Germany and the Scandinavian countries. Some shifts also took place among the Lutherans in the surrounding region. Their number declined in Albany, many of them going to Loonenburg (Athens). Others moved from the New York area and crossed over to New Jersey or scattered along the Hudson valley. All this sharply depleted the parish in New York.

With the death of Arnzius in 1691, the same year that Fabritius was compelled to resign in Pennsylvania because of ill health and blindness, a serious dearth of pastors was experienced by all Lutherans in America. As Tappert observed, during the six years that followed there was not a single Lutheran minister in all of continental America.[50]

As already mentioned earlier, the Swedes received help when Andreas Rudman and Eric Björk came to the Delaware valley in 1697, but the Hudson valley Lutherans had to wait another five years when Rudman, forced to resign due to illness, agreed to come to New York in 1702, before returning to Sweden. However, as might be expected his pastorate was shortlived by illness, this time due to yellow fever. He finally resigned in 1703.

But there was one compensating factor in all this. Rudman was instrumental in persuading Justus Falckner (1672-1723) to accept a call to New York and Albany to replace him. Falckner was born in Reinsdorf, Saxony. He had studied for the ministry at the University of Halle under August Hermann Francke and Christian Thomasius. Not certain of his vocation, Falckner wandered among various odd jobs, including teaching in Lübeck, Rostock, and Schleswig-Holstein. Finally he joined his brother Daniel in Pennsylvania to go into the land business with him.[51]

Justus arrived in 1700, where Rudman in time got to know him. Now that Rudman no longer could minister, he persuaded Falckner not only to enter the ministry but to accept the call to New York. After much prayer Falckner accepted and on Nov. 24, 1703, was ordained by Rudman, who served as suffragen bishop for the Church of Sweden. He was assisted by Anders Sandel, who had come to Pennsylvania in 1702, and Eric Björk. This was the first Lutheran ordination in America.[52]

When Falckner took over the pastorate in New York, he found that not only had the membership declined but those who were left were poor both spiritually and economically. As soon as he was able, he explored the outlying districts of his parish--Hackensack (Teaneck), N.J., the Raritan parishes, Loonenburg, Claverack, and Albany. The latter was especially desolate since only a few lived in the city, the rest were scattered on farms over a radius of some 25 miles. [53]

Falckner's work was cut out for him and his deep spiritual piety proved a source of enormous strength. As the first Halle pastor in America, his Pietism had matured and moderated during his stay in Pennsylvania. What he had seen there among the German sects had sobered him against any extremes, had he been so inclined. [54] His past experiences had in every way prepared him for the overwhelming task ahead of him.

The first thing Falckner needed to do was to learn the language of his parishioners. Perhaps his years in northern Germany facilitated this task, for by June 1704 he could write Francke at Halle, "I learned the Dutch language in a short time, so that I now at times actually preach thrice a week." [55]

Another problem for Falckner was the need of books if he was to instruct his scattered congregations. He turned to the Amsterdam Consistory for help. His members, he wrote, especially the young people, were "ignorant on account of the lack of Bibles, Catechisms, Psalm and Hymn Books." [56]

But there was one need that bothered him especially. The long association of the Lutherans and Reformed had erased the confessional consciousness of his people. So he added the petition,

> It would be of great service here to have a booklet in which, by means of short questions and answers, the difference between the Lutherans and the so-called Reformed opinions were exposed, every point thus concluding, "Therefore the Lutheran opinion is the better one." [57]

What happened to the request for books at this time is not known. Certain it is that the request for a book of questions and answers that Falckner had in mind for his particular situation was not answered.

But the idea persisted with Falckner for he could not counteract the overpowering influence of the Dutch Reformed on his small band of Lutherans. It would not be enough for him to be their spokesman when discussions arose concerning doctrinal difficulties. His members needed to know for themselves and to have ready answers. Discussions with his people made it clear that they would welcome such a book. In the house meetings the people were actually asking the questions that needed to be answered and soon Falckner began jotting them down so that he could formulate answers which would set the minds of his people at ease.[58]

Soon Falckner set about writing such a book himself. During the winter of 1707/1708, he began the task and by the end of March it was completed and sent to the printer. The translated title read, in the ponderous manner of the day,

> Fundamental Instruction upon Certain Points of the
> True, Pure, Saving Christian Teaching; Founded
> upon the Apostles and Prophets, of Which Jesus
> Christ is the Chief Corner Stone; Set Forth in
> Plain but Edifying Questions and Answers; by Justus Falckner, Saxon German, minister of the Protestants, so-called Lutheran Congregation at New
> York and Albany. Ps. 119, v. 104. "Through
> thy precepts I get understanding, therefore I hate
> every false way." Printed at New York by William
> Bradford. 1708.[59]

The book was not based on Luther's Small Catechism, primarily because the author had a polemical purpose in mind. It was a catechism, however, in the sense that it dealt with the fundamental Christian doctrine and in fact was intended to prepare candidates for Holy Communion. Clark describes it as follows,

> The book was divided into twenty-one chapters
> whose titles followed the usual course of Christian
> instruction. It was intended not merely to give an
> answer to Calvinists, but also to give a brief but
> complete presentation of Christian doctrine, suitable
> for the preparation of a candidate for confirmation.
> It began with a chapter on Holy Scripture. This
> was followed by others on God, Creation, Angels,
> and God's Foreknowledge. A little further on came
> chapters on Man, Free Will, Sin, and God's Universal Mercy. There followed the discussion of

Christ, Justification, Regeneration, and Good Works.
After this were the Sacraments, the Church, Governments (Family, State, and Church). The closing
chapter dealt briefly with the "Last Things": Death,
Resurrection, Judgment, the End of the World,
Everlasting Damnation, and Everlasting Blessed-
ness.

At the back of the book was a rhymed version
of the creed and two hymns (probably of Falckner's
own composition), entitled "Voor de Predicatie"
(before the sermon). [60]

The book's soundness as a Lutheran book of instruc-
tion is not disputed. Valenti Ernst Loescher, a prominent
Lutheran theologian, commended it highly as an "anti-
Calvinistic compendium of doctrine. "[61]

Fundamental Instruction is the first book printed by a
Lutheran clergyman in America, but one book does not fill
all the needs. Falckner continued to request books from the
Amsterdam Consistory. In response to such a request the
Consistory sent "a large folio Bible, 50 Psalters, 50 Para-
dijshofkens [Paradise Gardens], and 50 Haverman's prayer
books. "[62] Apparently no catechisms were included.

Speaking of this gift, Falckner referred to it as "a
blessed present, "

for so blessed has it been that many members of
the small scattered congregations, who were as good
as asleep, yes, dead, have through these books become awake and alive and found renewed zeal and
courage to remain within the obedience of our Holy
Church and to exercise themselves in the true faith
and in godliness, whereas heretofore some thought
that we were forgotten by the community at large,
as one forgets the dead, and that we had become
like a broken vessel; yes, they hardly dared openly
to confess their faith, as almost no books thereof
are seen here and none can be obtained here. [63]

Falckner's deep pastoral concern for each individual,
stimulated no doubt by his healthy approach to Pietism, may
be seen in his personal concern for those to whom he ministered. When he recorded the baptism of a person in the
church record, he added his personal prayer. Similarly for
those whom he confirmed and married. As the number of

baptisms increased, he included them all in a special prayer
at the close of the year.[64]   Such a prayer for the newly
confirmed of 1707, read,

> Lord Jesus Christ, should Satan seek to sift as
> wheat one or the other of these members of thy
> congregation, then do Thou pray for them to Thy
> heavenly Father that their faith may not cease, for
> the sake of Thy holy merit.   Amen.[65]

About this time a migration of Palatinates arrived from
Germany, via London.   The Palatinates had left their homeland because of the French invasion in 1707, and, soon thereafter, because of the bitter winter of 1708/1709.   During the
Thirty Years War Lutherans and Calvinists had fought and
suffered side by side.   Now with the invasion, they became
common refugees as they emigrated to England.   Too numerous to settle there, some 2000 came to New York to settle
along the Hudson River.

The first contingency of 41 persons arrived in New
York on Dec. 31, 1708, under the leadership of the Rev.
Joshuah Kocherthal.   Fifteen of these were Lutherans and 26
Calvinists.[66]   They soon left for a site on the Hudson River
to the present Newburgh.   Thereafter a larger contingency of
nearly 3000 arrived, the first ship reaching New York in
June 1710.   Most of these continued up the valley and settled
on both sides of the river some 90 miles north.   Later due
to some dissatisfaction with the area a large number migrated
to the Schoharie and Mohawk valleys in upstate New York.
A few went directly to Pennsylvania and North Carolina.

Joshuah Kocherthal (1669-1719) was the pastor for the
Lutherans among the settlers.   He was born as Joshuah Harrsch
in Fachsenfeld, Swabia, in the valley of the Kocher River.   For
some reason, still not determined, he later adopted the pseu-
donym of Kocherthal.   Little is known of his youth except
that he matriculated at the University of Jena in 1695, and
wrote his dissertation at the University of Tübingen.[67]   Both
universities at that time reflected Orthodox Lutheranism.

The Palatine Lutherans had suffered spiritually over
the years.   A common enemy often drove the Lutherans and
Reformed together.   As a consequence they had lost much of
their confessional sensitivity.   Sheer necessity because of
poverty and outside pressures made them share their houses
of worship and, in time, even their pastors.   Their pluralistic

community often supported a union church, one building for two congregations. This became a model later for the Germans in Pennsylvania.

Kocherthal's confessional theology had a wholesome influence on these German Lutherans. While not influenced by Pietism, as far as can be determined, there seemed to be a touch of it in references to new communicants. Though the title page of his Church Record used the older expression "New Communicants to the Altar" for what Pietists called confirmation, [68] the heading on the register read,

> With Jesus, Author and Preserver of his church. Register of the New Communicants through whose admission to our membership the number of members to our church has been increased, pray with me in your heart Reader, that they all may be and remain living and true members. [69]

There were two columns on the page, one for the Lutheran youth and another for those who were added from another faith. The reference to the "New Communicants" as having been admitted "to our membership" certainly reflected a Pietistic view, though here Kocherthal may have used it because of those who came from another denomination. At best it was somewhat ambiguous.

Kocherthal settled at New Town (West Camp), N. Y. by 1711, with four congregations of his Palatinates under his care. He served them faithfully until his death in June 1719. [70]

Meanwhile, Falckner's parishes were expanding beyond his limitations. He continued to ask the Amsterdam Consistory for books to serve his Dutch constituency. During 1715, he acknowledged the receipt of 24 psalters and two service books to be used among his new congregations. [71]

In addition to his own ten congregations in New York and New Jersey, Falckner inherited the four served by Kocherthal after his death. By 1722, the work had grown so burdensome that he could no longer visit all his congregations though his travel log indicated that he made a valiant effort to do so. [72] Under such circumstances it was natural that his teaching ministry suffered. Falckner died a valiant hero of faith toward the close of 1723.

Through one of its members who was going to Europe,

the congregation of New York appealed to the Amsterdam Consistory late in 1723 for a replacement of Falckner.   No candidate being available, the Consistory urged the member to
apply for a candidate in Hamburg since he was going there
anyway.   The Hamburg Consistory was able to recommend
Wilhelm Christoph Berkenmeyer (1687-1751), who subsequently
accepted the call.[73]   Berkenmeyer was born in Bodensteich
in the duchy of Lünenburg, near Hanover.[74]   He was a graduate of the University of Altdorf.   Thus by training as well
as background he was strongly committed to the Orthodox
emphasis.   After some delay due to illness, Berkenmeyer
was interviewed by the Consistory and finally ordained May
25, 1725.[75]

     Young Berkenmeyer must have been dismayed when he
arrived in New York.   During the vacancy strife had broken
out about the call procedure.   The Albany and Hackensack
congregations felt that they had not been consulted in advance
of the call and had therefore made no commitment.   The
precipitous action of New York was finally explained and a
severe reprimand from the Amsterdam Consistory brought
some degree of peace.[76]

     With that settled, Berkenmeyer became acquainted with
the farflung borders of his pastoral field.   He had inherited
the entire area served by Falckner and Kocherthal, except
the Raritan region where Daniel Falckner, the brother of
Justus, had been called.

     At home in New York there was much to be done.
Berkenmeyer's own words to the Amsterdam Consistory tell
the story clearly.

> If you, Right Reverend and Most Noble Patrons,
> will permit, I will now add some information about
> the conditions of my Congregation.   As before stated
> in numbers our Congregation is but few, and several
> among them live over two German miles from the
> town.   The Church has no income except that of the
> collection bag with the bell [Kling Beutel]....
>   The church, we fear, will not only be demolished
> by the first heavy storm, but looks more like a
> grain barn than a house of God: it has only two
> windows, one near the pulpit and the other directly
> opposite.   As the church is not paved, but merely
> floored with loose boards--some long, others short--
> one cannot pass through it without stumbling.

The preparations for divine worship are so bad,
that I doubt whether greater confusion exists in any
heathen temple.
    The people are not capable of singing a hymn
properly, and upon several occasions they have
stuck in the middle of a hymn, and I have had to
go thus to the altar or ascend the pulpit, although
I permit the precentor to sing whatever he likes,
and what they have been accustomed to sing.   And
now if the seventy-three-year-old one dies, they will
have hardly anyone in the entire congregation who
is capable of acting as reader. [77]

Speaking of books needed for worship and teaching he
wrote in the same report, "Otherwise there is a universal
complaint about the scarcity of hymn-books, catechisms, and
Bibles.... They know little of catechisms; Bibles are found
with the older families, but the new families have to borrow
one from another. "[78]

The conditions the following year in Albany were no
better.   Speaking of the need for a school Berkenmeyer wrote,

What could be more necessary and beneficial?
The grown-up people know nothing, as they cannot
read; therefore, they cannot teach the young.   They
only hear a preacher one-half of the year and during that half-year it often happens that they cannot
even come, especially as those are easily prevented
who are not eager to come. [79]

Two years later he again wrote about the situation in
Albany,

For the youth in this country are not being looked
after and could not be looked after either, because
the people dwell far apart and, moreover are mixed
as to nationality, as well as many different religions.
When I asked the children [and young people] from
20 to 30 years [of age] about the short [i.e., Small]
Catechism, the parents asked whether even a Domine
[pastor] could know that.   Through God's blessing I
have on week days and Sundays, also in the woods,
brought as many as care to come so far that they
take a different view. [80]

At Berkenmeyer's urgent request the Amsterdam Con-

sistory sent a number of books for use in the congregations.
They arrived in New York during November 1726. Among
the books were 30 copies of Elias Taddel's

> Catechism of Dr. Martin Luther, confirmed and
> clearly explained by the declarations of the Holy
> Scriptures, with some questions serving to a bet-
> ter understanding of the same. Amsterdam: 1649.[81]

The same shipment included also 20 copies of Lodewijk
Dögen's Principal Doctrines of the Christian Faith (1725).[82]
In addition there were several copies of Paulus Cordes, Bib-
lical Catechism for the School, Amsterdam: 1719.[83]

Books continued to trickle across the ocean. Berkenmeyer received 30 copies of Luther's Small Catechism in
1729, and 24 copies of Lambertus de Lange's

> Essential Beliefs and Points of Doctrine connected
> with the Knowledge of True Religion, set forth
> clearly and explained briefly after the order of
> Luther's Catechism and confirmed by the Holy
> Scriptures. In the form of Questions and Answers
> for the exercise of the growing youth, but especially
> for the use of those who desire the Lord's Supper.
> Very useful for all Christian families. Amsterdam:
> 1724.[84]

Not all these books served Berkenmeyer's purpose for
a dozen copies of Dögen's catechisms were returned for
credit in 1729.[85]

Because of the constant need throughout all the Dutch
congregations for copies of Luther's Small Catechism, as
well as explanations of the same, it is surprising that besides Falckner's Fundamental Instructions no American reprints of Luther's catechism were authorized during all these
years. If copies were printed by Lutherans in New York,
no record of this has as yet been found.

Berkenmeyer was a man of great organizational talent.
It wasn't long before he persuaded the Amsterdam Consistory
and others to provide him with assistance so that he could
divide the territory in a more manageable way. During
March 1732, Johannes Spaller landed in New York intending
to go to Pennsylvania to become a pastor. He had received
his credentials from Friedrich Ziegenhagen of the Royal

Chapel in London.   Soon after his arrival Berkenmeyer man-
aged to get him the call to Rhinebeck in central Hudson valley area, which he promptly accepted. [86]

During the same year Michael Christian Knoll (born
in Schleswig-Holstein in 1696), a graduate of the University
of Kiel, came to Hamburg.   He was assigned to New York
and the nearby New Jersey stations.   This permitted Berkenmeyer to take over the Loonenburg congregation together with
some of the nearby stations, including Albany. [87]

Somewhat later in 1743, Peter Nicholas Sommer (1709-
1795) also came from Hamburg and assumed the stations in
the Schoharie and Mohawk valleys. [88]   When Daniel Falckner
resigned from the Raritan parishes in 1743 due to illness,
he was replaced by Johannes August Wolf of Lebegin.   He,
too, was recommended by Hamburg.

As the several parishes now had more consistent care
not all were happy about what might be expected of them as
committed Christians.   After having informed his congregations of their responsibilities to which they had given apparent
consent, Spaller wrote,

> I took two elders or, where I thought this un-
> necessary, one elder, with me and made a house
> to house visitation, which, if God will grant me
> life and health, I shall repeat each year.   I exam-
> ined old and young as to their family life and con-
> duct; also, in how far they were instructed in
> reading, praying and the catechism.   In so doing I
> found people who either knew nothing at all, or
> who could hardly recite the Lord's Prayer and the
> Apostles' Creed, and just as ignorant as they were,
> were also their children, so that there was not
> much more there than natural life et cognitio Dei
> tantem generalis [and a kind of general knowledge
> of God].   Some had never, others only many years
> ago, attended the Lord's Supper; some people's
> children were so ignorant and wild that they asked
> what the pastor was, whether he was a human be-
> ing or not.   Others, large and small, ran away
> from me into the woods or hid themselves else-
> where.   But I also found a few, whose parents
> brought a good education with them from Germany,
> who had some information.   Eighteen persons, mar-
> ried as well as unmarried, I instructed for three

> weeks, as I had not time enough left before Pente-
> cost, daily for several hours at my house, con-
> firmed them by the laying on of hands and admitted
> them to Holy Communion. [89]

The letter continued with the plea for proper books.

> There is a lack of Bibles, prayer-books, hymnals
> and catechisms. I wish particularly that we might
> have the Nassau-Idstein one, of which several
> copies, in small format, from that country are in
> the hands [of the congregation]. [90]

It should be noted that Spaller was speaking of con-
firmation and the laying on of hands in connection with it.
This reflected his Pietism.   It also explained why he and
Berkenmeyer did not continue on the best of terms.   Ber-
kenmeyer was known for his outspoken anti-Halle views.
After serving in the Rhinebeck area for about four years,
Spaller resigned because he could no longer take the pres-
sure required under Berkenmeyer's authority. [91]

Soon after Wolf's acceptance of the call to the Raritan
congregations serious trouble began to erupt between pastor
and people.   All attempts to solve the matter at the local
level failed.   It soon became apparent that some type of ar-
bitration was needed on a broader level.   Berkenmeyer called
an assembly of pastors and parish representatives for August
20, 1735.   The assembly met in the Raritan parish at the
Old Mountain church, near the present Pluckemin.   Before
addressing himself to the problem that precipitated the meeting, Berkenmeyer presented a constitution for their approval
and adoption.   The proposed constitution had been modeled
after the Amsterdam Church Order [Kerkelijke Ordinantie]
with such modifications which local conditions might demand. [92]
Confessionally it reflected Orthodox Lutheranism, binding
pastors and congregations to the Bible and the Lutheran Confessions in all their teaching and preaching and requiring that
they "shall not introduce or use any phrases not found in
them. "[93]

Because of the frequent practice of bringing children
for baptism to the nearby Reformed church when there was
no Lutheran pastor available, the proposed constitution ad-
monished parents to refrain from the practice:

> Our Christians should beware of being witnesses

at baptism in other denominations or of bringing
the children to baptism in other denominations,
since it is more advisable to commend them in
prayer to God and to rest on the infinite mercy of
Christ than to burden the conscience of the parents.
Part I, chapter 3, Article VI. [94]

Obviously due to the prevailing clericalism no one was
prompted to suggest that a lay baptism might be performed
under such circumstances.

Innovations in reference to the rite of Baptism, absolution, the Lord's Supper and marriage were forbidden
upon penalty of censure or dismissal. [95]   This may have been
directed in part against a growing Pietistic influence which
had already introduced a rite of confirmation with an emphasis on the renewal of the baptismal covenant, the laying on
of hands and the need of giving evidence of the Christian life.
Pietists had made confirmation a prerequisite for first Communion.   Among the Orthodox there was no specific rite prior
to first Communion, the emphasis being primarily on the instruction in the catechism.   This procedure was in fact described in the section on Holy Communion, Article III:

The young people who have not yet gone to the
Lord's Table or have not been sufficiently instructed
in the Christian doctrine, and likewise such as have
had burdens of conscience should be earnestly ad-
monished that they should come to the preacher
during the week to be examined in the Catechism
and the chief parts of the Christian doctrine and to
be instructed in, and comforted from, the Word of
God; and private absolution shall not be denied them
who desire it. [96]

Preparation for first communion was described by such
general expressions as "to bring the young into union with the
church through catechization, "[97] "catechetical instruction, "[98]
"catechization, "[99] "instructing the catechumens, "[100] or simply "teaching the catechism. "[101]

With the constitution adopted and signed, Berkenmeyer
addressed himself to the controversy between Wolf and the
Raritan parish.   The charges against Wolf were numerous and
among them was the allegation that Wolf had neglected the
teaching of the young.   What the representatives of the congregation had in mind is of special interest because it tells

much about the kind of teaching the people seemed to have
been accustomed to.   Instead of being satisfied with rote
memorization of the catechism, as was done in the past,
Wolf evidently asked the children questions from his own
book of notes and required Bible passages to be learned after
he had explained them.   This angered some of the people
maintaining that these "cannot possibly be answered by little
children."   Because Wolf at times introduced a different order in explaining the Christian doctrine the people concluded
that he had rejected Luther's <u>Small Catechism</u>. 102

    Berkenmeyer, of course, rejected these charges
against Wolf, as well as some others.   The upshot was that
the congregation was asked to retain Wolf and to settle the
other matters in a peaceable way.   Evidently this was not
acceptable to the lay leaders back home who remained ada-
ment in their view that a pastor "who rejects the catechism
of the sainted Doctor Martin Luther, who refuses to teach it,
much less explain it, cannot be considered an Evangelical
[Lutheran] pastor. 103

    The quarrel between Wolf and the Raritan parishes
continued to fester for several years.   Each side became
more obstinate and Wolf's personal life more offensive.

    Realizing that they would receive little help from Ber-
kenmeyer the members finally turned to Mühlenberg in Pennsylvania.   He declined their first two invitations in 1743 and
1744 because he felt that this would be considered an inter-
ference into Berkenmeyer's authority.   Finally he did accept
a third invitation in 1745, with Berkenmeyer's knowledge,
who however declined to serve on the special committee. 104

    It took considerable doing and six weary days but fi-
nally Wolf agreed to resign provided he received a considerable amount of back pay, much more than he had at first requested. 105

    Mühlenberg was invited to return to Raritan some
months later.   In spite of the distance he accepted "expect-
ing to spend about two weeks there."   In his report he later
wrote,

> I gathered the youth together, instructed twenty-four
> older young people, and confirmed them, amid evi-
> dence of sincere emotion.
> The young people were well versed in the chief

parts of the Catechism; though they had learned it
in the Dutch language, they were also able to understand German and give correct answers.   I ad-
ministered the Lord's Supper in both congregations,
which had not been done for many years.   Those
who went to Communion were, for the most part,
those who had no connection with Mr. Wolf, having
come to the country after the troubles had begun.
But the older members of the congregation who
communed first gave Wolf what was due him and
became reconciled with him.   O there were many
tears of joy shed among the older people as they
witnessed the confirmation of their children.   The
spirit revived as did the spirit of Israel, and they
said, "it is enough if only our children, who have
been wandering like lost sheep, are found and
brought back again."[106]

During these years a more widespread problem came
to the fore, the manner in which it would be handled would
have far reaching effect on the teaching of the youth.   In
practically all the New York and New Jersey churches, Dutch
was still the dominant language in the church even though
immigration from The Netherlands was minimal.   A large
number of Low German speaking immigrants found the transition to Dutch to be only a minor inconvenience.   Their Low
German or Plattdeutsch was quite similar to the Dutch.   The
other German Lutherans, however, accepted the situation with
great reluctance.   They simply stayed away, or defected to
the Anglicans, especially if the children could speak neither
Dutch nor German.   By 1742, the Germans asked Knoll to
preach in German as well as Dutch, but he opposed the move.
"The Germans could easily learn Dutch if they attended services regularly," was his argument before the council.   As a
concession it was agreed, nevertheless, to have a preparatory service in German.   This satisfied only a few.[107]

The language conflict continued to simmer in the council until a split occurred in 1749 and a new congregation was
formed as Christ Church.   Finally, at Berkenmeyer's advice,
German was placed on an equal footing in the mother church
late in 1749.[108]

The end of the Orthodox period was at hand.   In October 1751, Berkenmeyer died and with him a chapter in
American Lutheranism came to a close.   Signs of a new
period were beginning to appear.   The spirit of Pietism had

already come to the Raritan and the upper Hudson valley
churches. It was to find a firm place, American version,
in New York.

THE GERMANS

        The German Lutherans were the last of the three ma-
jor national groups to come to America. In number, however, they eventually became the most important and the
most influential among all Lutherans in colonial America.
Different than the Swedes and the Dutch, the Germans were
at no time encouraged by their several territorial governments to emigrate. The German immigrants of the 17th
century were in fact non-conformists who came chiefly for
religious reasons. Among them were the Quakers, Dunkards,
and Mennonites. They established the first German settlements in America in 1683 in Germantown, Pennsylvania, now
a part of Philadelphia.

        The tide of German immigrants grew substantially in
the 1720's and 1730's, reaching a peak during 1735 and 1745.
These Germans differed from the earlier ones in that they
came largely from the established churches: Roman Catholics, Lutherans and Reformed. None of these, except the
Salzburgers in Georgia (1734), came for religious reasons.
They came not only from the Palatinate, but also from Hesse-
Darmstadt, Alsace (Elsass), Württemberg and, to a lesser
extent, from other German states. The large majority came
to America for economic reasons, a few for political or
military reasons. Their destination was largely Pennsylvania,
with some spill-over (or directly in the case of the later immigrants) into Maryland, the Carolinas, Virginia, and Georgia.
Some Germans, as stated above, migrated to New York.
During the earlier years they assimilated largely with the
Dutch. As their numbers increased in the forties and fifties,
they retained their national identity and in time became an
important linguistic element also in that area.

        The great majority of the immigrants, though nominally
associated with a church in the homeland, became churchless
as the social and religious pressures were no longer felt on
the frontier. Only a small portion retained a live interest in
the church. Among the Protestants these represented the
broad spectrum of Moravians, Reformed and Lutherans. Even
among the latter the degree of uniformity was minimal. Many
were confessionally weak, especially among the Palatinates,

who in their homeland had frequently shared their houses of
worship and sometimes even their pastors with the Reformed.
Since both were scarce in the colonies a similar arrangement
prevailed even on a larger scale, often erasing all confessional consciousness beyond the mere name Lutheran or Reformed.   In turn, the few Lutherans that were confessionally
conscious of their identity were sometimes divided among
themselves, either as Pietists or as Orthodox.

Lutheran pastors often came long after a German settlement had been established and where a "make do" worship
or a "make do" theology was already in practice.   Under
such circumstances, together with a scarcity of pastors and
teachers, the congregations were an easy prey to the blandish-
ments of the various sects as well as to the troups of so-
called vagabond preachers.   A few of these self-styled pastors
were no doubt well intentioned, but most of them were either
discredited preachers from elsewhere or were outright char-
latans eager to pick up the stipend that came from preaching
or celebrating the rites, even though they lacked authoriza-
tion and training.

While over the years the Dutch and Swedish Lutherans
maintained some ties with the mother church, the German
Lutherans never enjoyed such bonds with the homeland.   The
several State churches generally regarded the German emigrants with disapproval for having left the homeland.   Hence
they received minimal support from the consistories of the
various German states.   On the other hand considerable support did come from the University at Halle, especially in the
1740's, and to a lesser extent, from the University of Helmstedt.   Consequently both centers exerted considerable influence upon those whom they supported.

Pennsylvania

The beginning of many of the Lutheran churches in
Pennsylvania during this period is unclear.   The first Ger-
man Lutheran congregation was organized in 1703 by Daniel
Falckner (1666-c.1741) in Falckner's Swamp (New Hanover).
Beginning in 1717, Anthony Jacob Henkel (1663-1728) preached
for some time in this congregation.[109]   The Palatinates, who
originally had settled in New York, turned to Pennsylvania in
1712 when conditions went sour on them.   They settled in
Tulpehocken, in Lebanon County, and in Womelsdorf, near
Reading.   The church records of Trappe (Providence) and

Lancaster go back to 1729, of New Holland to 1730, and of
York to 1733.[110] It is known, too, that Anthony Jacob Henkel preached in Germantown before 1726.

In Philadelphia the German Lutherans enjoyed an occasional sermon from the Swedish pastors nearby. John
Christian Schultze brought an organization into being in
1733/34. John C. Stoever (1707-1779), the younger, succeeded him for a short time in 1734-1735. After that only
occasional services were held, though the Swedish pastor
John Dylander (1709-1741) of Gloria Dei preached to the Germans with some degree of regularity from the time of his
arrival in 1737 until his death in 1741.[111]

Fearing that a new heathenism would overtake the Lutherans in Pennsylvania, the congregations at Philadelphia,
Trappe, and Falckner's Swamp were persuaded by Schultze
to unite into a single parish. The United Congregations, as
they were called, further agreed to send a commission of
two laymen to accompany Schultze in 1734 to London and Germany, there to enlist Ziegenhagen and G. A. Francke in obtaining a pastor and hopefully some financial help.

The commission's visit was followed by a series of
frustrating delays due to a variety of reasons, especially one
that concerned itself with the specific salary commitment the
United Congregations could or would make. When, however,
it became known in Halle that von Zinzendorf was personally
active in Pennsylvania in 1741, and was successful in bringing many Moravians, Lutherans, and Reformed under his influence as a single denomination, Francke and the other authorities in Halle were moved to act in spite of some of their
unresolved concerns. Francke succeeded in persuading Henry
Melchior Mühlenberg to accept the call in 1741, during a brief
visit in Halle.

Mühlenberg (1711-1787) was born in Hanover and had
studied theology at the University of Göttingen. In 1738, he
taught at the Halle orphanage during which time he came under the influence of Francke. The following year, after he
received a call to Upper Lusatia (Silesia), he was ordained.
While serving there, he accepted the call to the United Congregations in Pennsylvania.

Mühlenberg had subscribed to the Lutheran Confessions
without reservations at the time he was ordained. Though he
was influenced by Francke's Pietism, he tried to make these

compatible with one another throughout his ministry. Unlike
many traditional Pietists of a later period, Mühlenberg placed
great stress on the faithful use of the sacraments and was
deeply concerned that catechetical instruction was maintained
even under the adverse conditions that he was to experience
in the colonies. [112]

Already in London, while on his way to Pennsylvania,
Mühlenberg discussed with Ziegenhagen (Friedrich Michael,
1694-1777), the court preacher, what catechisms were available. Mühlenberg later reported on this meeting:

> I showed him what I had on the Catechism and the
> Rev. Court Preacher also had a great number (I
> believe almost all that had been published) but he
> complained that none of them suited him especially
> as concerns the article of Christ and the arrange-
> ment of the material. [113]

During the discussion, Ziegenhagen dictated several examples
of how he would desire to have it. [114]

A few days later, while Mühlenberg was awaiting his
departure by ship, the subject concerning the catechism was
brought up, "which convinced me the more how necessary
for our church was a correct and thorough catechism."
Ziegenhagen observed also,

> that if we once had a correct one, as it ought to
> be, then a different or new one would not be made
> so often and in every city or town. I wished that
> the Rev. Court Preacher himself had the time and
> strength to make one, which in our time may very
> well happen. [115]

In addition to all the other difficulties Mühlenberg experienced upon his arrival in Pennsylvania were those in connection with the day-to-day teaching of the youth. With the
general low level of religious life, he soon found out the
hard fact that the youth could not be taught over a long period
of time, nor learn the catechetical books by heart. "We have
to be satisfied if they understand the most necessary things
in outline," he reported. [116]

Due to the lack of teachers and the limited experience
in teaching the catechism among the few that could be found,
much of the teaching in the parishes he visited became Müh-

lenberg's responsibility. To help the teachers he loaned
them books for background purpose, often Johann Jakob Rambach's sermons on the catechism. He even suggested that
they memorize one of them in the event that they were called
upon to preach. [117]

A further problem that he found in teaching the catechism was the number of different catechisms the children
used for their instruction. This was a hindrance unique
among the Germans. True, the Dutch children used a variety of catechisms also but their number was small by comparison and they were all channeled through the Consistory
of Amsterdam. The Swedes were spared much of this difficulty since the Svebilius catechism was later the only official catechism permitted by the mother church.

Speaking of the need for the German churches to have
a special catechism prepared for them, hopefully by Ziegenhagen, Mühlenberg wrote in his report to Halle as late as
November 17, 1745,

> A catechism is as much a necessity for us as our
> daily bread. For in the schools the children ought
> to be well grounded in the truths of the Catechism,
> and to do this, it is important to have a uniform
> set of phrases. If our hopes that our beloved
> Father Ziegenhagen will help us in this matter
> should fail us, then we shall have to use another
> regular catechism as the basis of our instruction.
> If one pastor adopts his own plan, and another uses
> the Württemberg Catechism, a third that of Giessen,
> and a fourth the Holstein Catechism, confusion will
> be the result. I have, therefore, both with heart
> and voice, continually expressed the hope that His
> Reverence, the Court Preacher, would furnish us
> with a catechism. [118]

As Mühlenberg travelled among the United Congregations and especially on his periodic visits to congregations
without pastors, he found that brief presentations of doctrine
were more useful than an extended text. He found the simple Small Catechism of Luther, without further explanation,
an ideal epitome. Another was an order of salvation known
as the Hymn of Faith (Glaubenslied). [119]

Orders of salvation were brief summaries of doctrine
introduced by the Pietists presenting systematically the suc-

cessive stages of the way of salvation. They were drawn up in a variety of forms, either in hymns, a series of brief statements, outlines, or a brief series of questions and answers. Their original purpose had been for the instructor to lead the catechumen inwardly through the individual steps along the way to salvation until he by conversion, experienced a breakthrough to the new life, so that he was ready to make a vow to live alone for God. Such a vow became a part of the confirmation rite. Accordingly, Pietists regarded Baptism as marking merely the beginning of the Spirit's activity while confirmation instruction was the culminating process of regeneration. With this in mind the orders of salvation were developed alongside of Luther's catechism, often to the neglect of the latter.[120]

The Hymn of Faith was Mühlenberg's favorite order of salvation, alongside of the Small Catechism. He made frequent references to its use in his Journals. Even though he prized the Hymn of Faith highly, he did recognize that it was deficient in its exposition of the sacraments. However, he feared to make any changes or additions to the hymn, lest he damage it.[121] In 1747, he translated the order in rhymes into English, and thus prepared it for a 16-year-old girl who did not understand German.[122] Still later, in 1752, he even translated the Hymn of Faith into Dutch,[123] and subsequently had the congregation in Hackensack (Teaneck), N.J. sing it.[124]

During his early ministry, Mühlenberg and his co-worker Peter Brunnholtz (d. 1757) were under the impression that the Hymn of Faith had been written by Ziegenhagen but this was not the case.[125] Later they realized that it was actually prepared by Christoph Starcke (1684-1744), pastor near Leipzig, and had appeared in his Six Concise Orders of Salvation in 1743, and there called The Order of Salvation in Verses.[126]

In 1744, during Brunnholtz's visit with Ziegenhagen while on his way to Pennsylvania to become Mühlenberg's assistant, the two revised the Hymn and, as Mühlenberg later wrote, "brought it to the point where it more nearly served its purpose, though the poetry was, by any valid standard, somewhat rough."[127]

According to Mühlenberg the Hymn of Faith was already in Pennsylvania by 1747, and was widely used not only among the Lutherans but was "bought and read by all denominations, because it was unsectarian and bears no name."[128]

German Lutherans in the
Southern Colonies

A number of Palatinates migrated to North Carolina
at an early date.   How many of them were Lutherans cannot
be determined.   In the late 1730's the spillover of German
Lutherans was felt in the central and western parts of the
colony.   However, no pastors served them on a regular basis until 1773, when Adolph Nüssmann (1739-1794) came on
the recommendation of the Consistory of Hanover.[129] No Lutheran pastors served in South Carolina prior to 1775.[130]

The arrival of Lutherans in Virginia was somewhat
earlier.   Lutherans from Württemberg arrived in 1717, and
settled near Fredericksburg.   Later they moved to Hebron
in Madison County and organized a congregation there.   In
time others spilled over from Pennsylvania and settled in
Hebron and in a number of places along the Shenandoah Valley.[131]

The proximity of Maryland to the southeastern part of
Pennsylvania provided Lutheran colonists places for welcome
farmlands.   They settled near the present Hagerstown.   Those
who preferred an industrial center moved to Baltimore soon
after it was founded in 1730.   Itinerant missionaries served
these Lutherans until the 1760's.   The first resident pastor
came to Baltimore in 1765, with the arrival of John Caspar
Kirchner.[132]

The first German Lutherans to settle in Georgia came
from Salzburg, in present day Austria.   They were unique in
several respects.   In the homeland they had been vigorously
persecuted by their Roman Catholic overlord.   The persecu-
tions were climaxed by the "Emigration Patent" of October
31, 1731, which ordered all Protestants to leave the country
on the penalty of confiscation of their property and imprisonment, unless they renounced their faith.   Some 3000 persons
were eventually forced to flee to other parts of Germany as
well as The Netherlands and Sweden.   The Salzburger's plight
became known in England where through the intervention of the
Society for the Propagation of Christian Knowledge, they were
offered free passage to the newly chartered colony of Georgia.

The first contingency of Salzburger's to accept the offer to emigrate to Georgia left Germany via Amsterdam the
last day of October 1733.   By March 18, 1734, they arrived
in Charleston and a few days later, March 23, they pitched

their tents near Savannah.[133]   Others soon followed this first
migration, all told about 300.   The new settlement was called
Ebenezer.

Besides emigrating for religious reasons, the Salzburgers were unique in another respect.   Not only were they
tied by the strong bond of persecution, they came to Georgia
well supplied with Bibles, hymnals, catechisms, and devotional literature.   What is more, they were accompanied by
two pastors, John Martin Boltzius (1703-1765) and Israel
Christian Gronau (d. 1745), both trained at Halle.   These
men proved to be outstanding leaders as well as pastors.
Consequently the Salzburgers were spared many of the uncertainties that pursued their fellow German Lutherans elsewhere.

Already prior to their leaving Germany, a constitution
had been agreed upon.   It had been prepared in 1733 by pastors Samuel Urlsperger, Frederick Ziegenhagen, and Gotthilf
August Francke.   The constitution was fitted for conditions
prevailing in an English colony and in many respects similar
to the constitution of the Savoy congregation in London, which
in turn was based on the Amsterdam Church Constitution.
The latter was the same one on which Berkenmeyer had
based his constitution for the Dutch Lutherans in New York
in 1735.[134]

One of Boltzius' major pastoral concerns was the instruction of the children of the two congregations into which
the Salzburgers had organized themselves, one in the village
and the other among the plantations.   Both pastors in fact
taught religion in the schools.

The Salzburgers maintained also daily vesper, or
prayer services after the day's work and the evening meal.
Some of the services were used to discuss the chief doctrines.
The pastors reported that this helped the people toward a better understanding of "the doctrines of the Gospel and the order of salvation," and increased their seriousness for the
faith.   Because of these blessings they decided to set aside
about two months each year with the children and the adults
in a study of Freylinghausen's Compendium.[135]

Luther's Small Catechism played a vital role in the
ongoing ministry of the pastors.   On January 13, 1736, they
reported, "We have started to base evening prayers on Luther's small catechism, and we pray to God to honor this

simple work on young and old with His blessing." They described the method as follows:

> after the singing of a short hymn, the chief subject
> of the previous prayer hour is briefly repeated.
> Then the children recite several times, loudly and
> clearly, the part of the catechism under considera-
> tion, which also recalls the words of the catechism
> to the adults. This passage is catechized briefly,
> and its real meaning is explained and applied to the
> practice of godliness. The entire prayer service
> is scheduled to last only one half hour; and for that
> reason we must be brief.[136]

The Sunday sermons too were used to explain the catechism.

> During the sermons we quote from Luther's Small
> Catechism and use its words to explain and elaborate
> the matter under discussion. Thus the congregation,
> young and old, become familiar with the words and
> the meaning of the catechism.[137]

Some of the other Germans who lived nearby also attended these services. These were further made acquainted
with the catechism when they wished to commune. Of them
it was reported,

> Some of our listeners intend to come to the Lord's
> Table with us next Sunday. For their preparation
> they are visiting us this week every noon, and we
> awaken them to worthy readiness with brief and
> simple instruction from Luther's catechism.[138]

Some time later a similar reference was made concerning those who also were not Salzburgers and who intended
to go to communion. They too were examined to see whether
they were familiar with the words of the catechism.

> For, among both old and young who had already at-
> tended Holy Communion in other places, I hardly
> found any who could recite the five chief parts with-
> out explication.[139]

Unique among the Georgia Lutherans also was Boltzius'
frequent contacts with the homeland, particularly with Halle.
During May 1742, for instance, he received a case of books,

medicine, and other supplies for the pastors and the people. Included for the latter was a supply of catechisms. As would be expected the books were Pietistic oriented.[140]

The Salzburgers of Georgia were isolated from their fellow Lutherans not only by distance but also by their theological leanings. As a Pietist, Boltzius was averse to Berkenmeyer and his Orthodox tendencies. The same isolation was maintained toward many of the Lutherans in Pennsylvania for what he regarded as their superficial Lutheranism. Not until Mühlenberg's arrival, with whom he felt a kinship, did he show an interest in them.

Chapter II

GERMAN CATECHISMS ISSUED PRIOR TO THE FIRST OFFICIAL CATECHISM, 1744-1785

The first German catechisms printed in America are of interest not merely for the sake of their priority but for the far reaching influence a number of these had in the development of Lutheran catechisms in this country. Of the seven catechisms issued between 1744-1785, four belong to a single family, three of which are revisions of a fourth. These four are of great significance since they shaped to a large extent the first catechism authorized by an American Lutheran church body, namely the catechism of the Pennsylvania Ministerium. This catechism in turn was not only the most influential German catechism in its own right, covering the span from 1785 to 1857, but it in turn influenced many others that were published privately, both in German and English, during the same period.

The span of time covered in this chapter straddled the period of the American Revolution. The upheaval naturally had far reaching consequences also on the Lutherans, cutting off communication among the colonies and with the homeland and severely restricting the number of immigrants. At the time of the Revolution there were less than 15,000 Lutherans in about 133 congregations, served by some 33 pastors in the colonies, about three fourths of which were in Pennsylvania. It is natural therefore, that all the catechisms published during this time were printed in that colony. [1]

ZINZENDORF'S CATECHISM (1744)

While Mühlenberg was looking to Ziegenhagen to produce a catechism for the German Lutherans in Pennsylvania, a catechism was issued from an unexpected source. By a strange turn of events the first American edition of Luther's Small Catechism was published not by a Lutheran but by a

Moravian, one who posed at times as a Lutheran but who was strongly resented by the Lutheran pastors in Pennsylvania. He was Count Nikolaus Ludwig von Zinzendorf (1700-1760), or as he preferred to be known among the colonists, Ludwig Thürnstein.

As stated earlier, it was Zinzendorf's presence in Pennsylvania that had finally prompted a favorable response on the part of Halle to the plea of the United Congregations for a pastor. The call to Mühlenberg was authorized because of the confusion that Zinzendorf's presence among the Lutheran congregations was creating.

Zinzendorf had a strange history. He had been brought up a Lutheran and early in his life came under the influence of Philip Spener's school of theology. In fact Spener was his godfather. Zinzendorf attended Halle for a short time and studied law at Wittenberg. A man of unbounded enthusiasm and drive, touched with a spirit of mysticism, he strove to free the Lutheran Church in Germany of its theological re-strictions, especially those that engendered polemics. To a point of over-simplification he pressed the major articles of faith into a narrow christological mold.[2]

Early in his career Zinzendorf became interested in the Moravians, the followers of John Huss. He purchased an estate for them in East Saxony and transferred them there. He joined them in their ministry and soon became one of their bishops, professing all the while still to be a Lutheran. He purposed to draw Christians from all persuasions into a sort of confederacy to instill in them a new spirit of life, the personal experience of salvation and a concern for others. He came on the scene at a time when the Lutheran Church was plagued with indifference and was suffering from the weariness of party strife. As such he was a welcome voice in many parts of Europe, though strongly opposed by Halle. He was in fact expelled from Saxony in 1736. Eventually he established his own church. He and his followers desired to be known as The Family of the Augsburg Confession (Augs-burgische Confessionsverwandte), though they were better known as Unity Brethren (Unitas Fratrum), or Moravians.

From a number of sources Zinzendorf had heard of the neglect of the German Lutherans in Pennsylvania and the toll it was taking there. He saw it as a fertile field for his ideas, not only among the Lutherans but hopefully also among the Reformed as well. He arrived in Philadelphia, via New

York, on Dec. 10, 1741, and soon made an extended trip
through the rural areas in Pennsylvania. He announced himself not as Count Zinzendorf, but as Herr von Thürnstein,
fearing that his title might be a handicap. [3]

Through a series of eight conferences, which Zinzendorf called synods, he gathered members of a variety of denominations together--Baptists, Lutherans, Reformed, Seventh-
Day Baptist, and Mennonites--hoping to unite them in a
church union without necessarily creating a new denomination.
While these conferences were going on he imposed himself
on the Lutheran congregations in Philadelphia and assumed
the title of Evangelical Lutheran Inspector and Pastor at
Philadelphia.   However, not all accepted him there and a
serious struggle followed.   The upshot was that Zinzendorf
withdrew with the majority and founded his own church.

In many ways Zinzendorf was an enigma, theologically
and personally.   He wanted to be a Moravian and a Lutheran
at the same time.   He had a high regard for the Augsburg
Confession and Luther's Small Catechism, yet he was eclectic
in what he pursued and what he ignored.   No doubt he was
sincere in his much needed emphasis on the Christian life
over against a mere profession of doctrine, yet his zeal mis-
led him to the point where in fact he was an imposter to the
Lutherans and a disturbing factor in the already meager
church life in the colony.

Mühlenberg arrived in Pennsylvania in time for a con-
frontation on Dec. 8, 1742, just prior to Zinzendorf's departure for Europe.   The result was that Zinzendorf surrendered the records of the church, though not without a struggle and the threat of legal action. [4]   On Jan. 11, 1743, Zinzendorf preached his farewell sermon in Philadelphia and left
for New York on his way to Europe. [5]

Under these circumstances it is marvelously strange
that the first American edition of Luther's Small Catechism
should be issued by a person such as Zinzendorf.   Written
during his visit in Pennsylvania, it was not published until
1744, after his return to Germany.

> The Small Catechism of Dr. Martin Luther, with
> Explanations Issued for the Use of the Lutheran
> Congregations in Pennsylvania.   Germantown:
> Printed by Christoph Saur, 1744. [6]

While the catechism purported to present and explain

Luther's catechism, the author at the very outset reminded
the reader that, as with all human writings, the catechism
was not perfect. "Luther," he wrote, "often speaks of certain matters in a way which in other of his writings, previously or subsequently, he did not say." Zinzendorf begged
the Lutheran congregations to use the book with blessing, for
he had prepared the explanations with the many sects of the
land in mind. He asked the reader to put aside all prejudices
and, if they did that, then he with them would rejoice before
the throne of the Lamb "that I was able to sustain you in
Pennsylvania in the Lutheran religion" (pp. 3-4).

The catechism included the Six Chief Parts of the catechism, also the Office of the Keys, but omitted the Confession of Sins, the prayers and the Table of Duties. After
each subsection of the Chief Parts, he explained and elaborated the text with a series of questions and answers. Bible
passages or references were added as proofs or further explanations of the text. Similarly he frequently quoted from
one of Luther's hymns to make a point.

Zinzendorf's narrow christological emphasis came
through in a number of instances. Without denying the Trinity,
he nevertheless epitomized the concept of God primarily in the
person of Christ. Thus the first question and answer following Luther's explanation of the First Commandment, had

> What is God?
> Ask ye, Who is this? Jesus Christ it is, of
> Sabbaoth Lord, and there's none other God.

There was no further elaboration on this point (p. 6).

Similarly in the First Article, Zinzendorf attributed
the creation to Jesus Christ through the following series of
questions:

> Who made all things?
> God. Heb. 3:4.
>
> Whom does Luther call thus?
> The Creator of all creatures who took on our na-
> ture, and did not despise a poor woman to become
> man in her body.
>
> How does Luther arrive at that?
> He spoke what he knew and bore witness of what he

had seen.
John 3:11.

How did he know that?
That all things were made through the Word that
had become flesh and without him nothing was made
that was made, is said in John 1:3.

What more did he find in the Scriptures?
That in Him all things were created, in heaven and
on earth, visible and invisible, whether thrones or
dominions or principalities or authorities--all things
were created through Him and for Him.   Col. 1:16.

To the question, "How does it then happen that one
refers to the Father as the creator?", he had a threefold
answer, one of them being, "Because our God and His Father
are one.   John 10:30" (pp. 26-27).

Again in connection with the introduction to the Lord's
Prayer, Zinzendorf referred "Father" primarily to Jesus,
though he did state at the outset that Jesus had His heavenly
Father in mind.   To this response, he presented the question,

I thought the Lord Jesus was actually the eternal
Father?
That He is.   Is. 9:6.

Is it the same when one entrusts something to the
Father or to the Son?

To this he answered that there was no difference, citing the
prayers of Jesus, "Father, into thy hands I commit my
spirit, " Luke 23:46, and of Stephen, "Lord Jesus receive
my spirit, " Acts 7:58, because He is the Father and the
Father is in Him.   John 14:10 (p. 40).

In other doctrinal statements Zinzendorf reflected at
times a Lutheran stance and at other times a Reformed one,
without becoming polemical.   He did accept Luther's enumeration and order of the Ten Commandments primarily because
he did not wish to encourage the extreme iconoclasm of Cal-
vinism.   He dismissed the whole problem because he believed
that the controversy raged more for its own sake than for
the practical reality of what Scripture taught (p. 7).

Interestingly enough, Zinzendorf made no reference

either to a Sabbath or a Sunday observance. He did not change Luther's wording as some did later, from "Thou shalt sanctify the holy day," to "Remember the Sabbath Day to keep it holy." He placed the full emphasis on preaching and the Word.

Zinzendorf's tendency to spiritualize was seen especially in the Fourth Petition where "daily bread" was interpreted to mean primarily the Word and only secondarily the necessities of life. This in spite of Luther's own explanation.

Under Baptism, Zinzendorf set forth some interesting views. He did not believe that a child needed to be instructed before becoming a disciple of Christ, as did many of the sects in Pennsylvania. He cited the Old Testament example of circumcision. He further cited the unborn John, who while in his mother's womb leaped for joy before the living God. This, he said, was the work of the Spirit. Then in an odd twist, he cited Peter, who was to have said to such persons, "Can any one forbid water for baptizing these people who have received the Holy Spirit just as we have?" (Acts 10:47). Whereupon the catechism asked the question, "Are the children of believers regarded as unclean?" "No, but holy," was the answer, citing 1 Cor. 7:14.

According to the catechism the sequence was as follows. Children by nature were not holy, but "in their mother's womb they were cast upon the Lord to be their trust and He will keep them at their mother's breasts. Ps. 22:10.11 [9.10]." Thereupon the Lord sanctified them through the washing of regeneration and renewing of the Holy Spirit. Titus 3:5. Following that they were to be brought up in the discipline and instruction of the Lord. Eph. 6:4 (pp. 56-57).

In the section on the Lord's Supper, Zinzendorf had at first only a passing reference to the sacramental presence of the Lord's body and blood, though he did not deny it. He asked,

> What is received in the Lord's Supper?
> The blessed bread which we eat has communion*
> with the body of Jesus and the cup which we bless
> has communion with the blood of Jesus. 1 Cor.
> 10:16.

The asterisk explained this word to mean, "ist vermenget,"

i. e., "is mingled" with the body and blood (p. 68).   Therefore, he said, only Christians partake of the sacrament in a
worthy manner, others eat it to their judgment.

In the section in which Luther asked, "How can bodily
eating and drinking do such great things?" Zinzendorf rejected the idea that Luther had implied that only a spiritual
eating and drinking took place in the sacrament.   Here he
made a clear case for the sacramental or real presence.
He cited as evidence a stanza from a hymn attributed to
John Huss and translated by Luther:

> As His pledge of love undying
> He, this precious food supplying,
> Gives His body with the bread
> And with the wine the blood He shed [p. 72]. [7]

He further quoted from Luther's hymn of thanksgiving after
partaking the sacrament:

> O Lord, we praise Thee and adore Thee,
> In thanksgiving bow before Thee.
> Thou with Thy body and Thy blood didst nourish
> Our weak souls that they may flourish;
> May Thy body, Lord, born of Mary,
> That our sins and sorrows did carry,
> And Thy blood for us plead
> In all trial, fear, and need [p. 73]. [8]

Parenthetically it should be stated that during his stay
in the colony, Zinzendorf prepared a catechism also for the
Reformed as a substitute for the Heidelberg Catechism.   He
had this catechism published under John Bechtel's name, a
pastor of the Reformed Church in Germantown.

Although there was an urgent need for a catechism
among the Lutherans, Zinzendorf's edition could hardly be
said to have been well received among the bulk of them, even
though it was intended for the use of Lutheran congregations
in Pennsylvania.   This was particularly the case since, after
his departure, Lutherans became more established under the
leadership of Mühlenberg and became more aware of their
own identity.   What influence or use his catechism had was
likely limited to such Lutherans, and perhaps even some Reformed, who had become associated with the Moravians.

BRUNNHOLTZ'S CATECHISM (1749)

Mühlenberg's hope that Ziegenhagen might be instrumental in preparing a catechism for the German Lutherans
in America was never realized. During the years of wait-
ing for some action, the situation in Pennsylvania became
still more confused. Mühlenberg's report in 1747 graphically
described the situation.

> Another great hindrance is that now in Germany,
> in nearly every town and village, a distinctive Cat-
> echism and an altered hymnbook is to be found,
> and yet all are called Lutheran. I could find in
> my congregations more than fifty different cate-
> chisms and hymnbooks which the people have brought
> with them. We rejoiced and comforted ourselves
> for some years in the hope of the Catechism of
> which our reverend father, Court Preacher Ziegen-
> hagen, once promised us, ... But, as we have now
> little hope of having a Catechism prepared for us,
> we shall be at last compelled to prepare one as
> best we may, and have it printed for our use. [9]

Peter Brunnholtz, who had become pastor of the congregations in Philadelphia and Germantown in 1745, was the
one who finally put the new catechisms together for the printer. Brunnholtz joyously reported the event in a letter to
Ziegenhagen and Francke, April 11, 1749.

> Since a regular [German] printing shop has now
> been established here in the city, which the resi-
> dent English printer and postmaster, Mr. Franklin,
> has purchased and has placed a German printer in
> charge, we have the opportunity to have anything
> printed that is desirable and necessary. Since the
> printer, who is a Lutheran, wished to publish Lu-
> ther's Small Catechism to be sold for children, and
> requested me to prepare the same, I have done so.
> It can now be used for the instruction of the young.
> The first edition is almost completely sold out. [10]

Since no copy of this first edition is now known to exist, we cannot be certain of its exact title or its contents.
However, a second edition appeared already that same year,
1749. As Brunnholtz reported, the first edition had almost
completely been sold out by mid-April. Either Brunnholtz or

his fellow pastors in the United Congregations, as the Pennsylvania Ministerium at first referred to itself, apparently
felt constrained therefore to reprint the catechism as soon
as possible. Assuming that the few months which elapsed
between the first and second printing did not allow much time
for a major revision and since it was printed at the same
printery, we may assume that the two were essentially the
same. The title of the second edition was,

> The Small Catechism of the Blessed Dr. Martin
> Luther, together with the Usual Morning-, Table-,
> and Evening Prayers. To which are added for the
> use of the older youth: The Orders of Salvation in
> a hymn, known under the title Hymn of Faith and
> In Brief and Simple Questions and Answers. For
> profitable use in schools and children's instruction
> classes. Second edition. Philadelphia: Benjamin
> Fränklin and Johann Böhm, 1749.11

The catechism opened with a one-page introduction
called Brief Explanation (Kurtze Erläuterung) in the form of
a rhyme. Its purpose was apparently to remind the learner
of the importance of the Ten Commandments because in them
God Himself, as it were, speaks to the heart of every person. In accord with the tenor of the times, Luther's radical
interpretation of the Decalog, especially in the Third Commandment, was lost somewhat in this explanation. There we
read,

> The Sabbath hold thou precious, I myself have given
> it, for your true welfare and the life of your soul
> [p. 2].12

The catechism contained the following major parts:
Luther's Small Catechism, the Hymn of Faith, the IV Order
of Salvation (Brief and Simple Questions and Answers), Application of the Catechism, A Brief Summary of the Christian
Doctrine, and a Jesus Hymn.

As the individual parts are considered it will become
evident that the catechism was not intended to be a text for
all the catechumens but rather it was a manual containing a
number of sources that could be used independently or in
combination with one another, depending on the interest of
the teacher and the previous instructional experience of the
catechumens.

Some of the pastors may have followed J. Jakob Ram-

bach's suggestions. According to Rambach, Luther's catechism could be taught successfully only after 1) some simple
preliminary instruction about God; 2) a short order of salvation; and 3) a brief account of Biblical history. Thus one
or more of the orders of salvation were a convenient addition
in the new catechism. [13]

Time, too, might be an important factor in the choice
of the material. If the teacher had only a week in his pastoral visit to some outstation to prepare a group for confirmation, he might feel compelled to choose one of the shorter
forms. If he was a resident pastor, he might select Luther's
catechism in his first course and the IV Order of Salvation
for the second course, or vice versa. Conceivably many of
the catechumens using this book were not taught Luther's
catechism but very possibly taught on the basis of one or
more of the orders of salvation. So for instance, Mühlenberg on one occasion catechized the children on Luther's
catechism, a short explanation of the Ten Commandments in
verses, the Hymn of Faith, the Order of Salvation in Statements, and the penitential psalms. [14] But he might limit
himself at another time to a two-hour examination on the
Order of Salvation in Tables with proof texts. [15] With adults
he might be satisfied with "the catechism and the order of
salvation. "[16]

As schools developed the catechism was intended to
serve children at different levels with material suitable to
their needs.

The catechism text does not, therefore, tell us what
was taught in the congregations in a given instance but rather
the material that was available where this particular catechism
was in use. This was even more the case in the later revisions of Brunnholtz's catechism when additional material was
added.

As was customary the major stress in almost all cases
was placed on the memorization of the material selected. [17]
It must further be remembered that the catechumen classes
frequently represented a wide age range, especially in the
preaching stations that were not served on a regular basis.
Once Mühlenberg instructed a group of 35 persons ranging in
age from 13 to 28, at least one of whom was married. He
instructed them for several days and then examined them on
the Five Chief Parts of Luther's Catechism, the Hymn of
Faith, and the Order of Salvation in Sentences. [18]

Luther's Small Catechism

It is important to note that the manual did not include an exposition of Luther's catechism. It simply contained his text without the addition even of the usual Bible references intended as aids to the teacher and the catechumens.

Interestingly enough, the Luther text did not include some of the later additions ascribed to Luther and customarily found in the traditional versions. Thus it did not contain The Office of the Keys, popularly ascribed to Luther but actually taken from the Nürnberger Kinderpredigten of 1533, composed by Andreas Osiander and Dominicus Sleupner.[19] It omitted also the doxology of the Lord's Prayer which originally came from the Nürnberg Catechismus of 1558. It additionally omitted Luther's Confession of Sins.

On the other hand the catechism did contain the Christian Questions and Answers, which were composed not by Luther as frequently stated, but by his friend Johann Lange of Erfurt.[20]

Luther's prayers were interspersed with Bible passages and hymn stanzas to help parents enrich their home devotions with the children.

The Hymn of Faith (Das Glaubens-Lied)

As already stated The Hymn of Faith, frequently used by Mühlenberg especially when the time of instruction was limited, had been reworked by Ziegenhagen, perhaps with the help of Brunnholtz. It was a summation of the chief parts of the Creed. It did not treat the sacraments individually though it made it clear that the Spirit worked through Word and sacraments. Though prized by Mühlenberg he felt it to be deficient because it made no further reference to the sacraments. However, he feared to make any additions lest he damage the structure.[21] In its altered form The Hymn of Faith was lengthened from eight stanzas to eleven. Starcke had previously suggested it to be sung to the melody of "Ob sey dem allerhöchster Gott,"[22] but the new catechism suggested the melody, "Nun jauchtzet dem Herrn all Welt."[23]

The major changes pertained to the work of Jesus as Savior which was enlarged from two stanzas to three and to the person and work of the Holy Spirit, to which four stanzas

were devoted instead of two.   Actually Starcke did not tie
repentance directly with the work of the Holy Spirit and thus
in effect had only one stanza for the Third Person.   The final stanza of The Hymn of Faith in each case was a prayer.
However, Starcke's rendition was addressed to Jesus while
the revision directed itself to the Father for acceptance
through the Son and by the renewal of the Spirit.   The revision was in every way an improvement although it, too,
did not give sufficient emphasis to the sacraments.

The Bible references inserted in the text were changed
in some instances as well as enlarged, as required by the
extension of the text.

The Hymn of Faith was followed by a two stanza question and answer called "Necessary Self-Examination according
to the Chief Parts of the Creed by a True Christian" (p. 37).

IV.   Order of Salvation in Short and
Simple Questions and Answers

This order of salvation has often been incorrectly ascribed to Johann A. Freylinghausen. [24]   It was, however,
taken from Starcke with only minor changes. [25]   As in the
case of the other orders the Bible passages, including some
from the Apocrypha, were usually printed out by Starcke,
while the catechism cited merely the Bible references.   The
order comprised 169 questions and answers and probably was
used at times as an exposition of Luther's catechism.

However, the order had some serious weaknesses.   It
helped perpetuate for Lutherans in America the confusion
concerning the Biblical meaning of the Word of God, a confusion that had plagued the Lutheran Church for some time,
in fact one that it had inherited from pre-Reformation times.
Though the Bible used the term "Word" to designate either
Jesus Christ or His message, the Gospel, this order of salvation continued to foster an alien meaning, or at best a
secondary meaning of the term by equating "Word of God"
with the Bible.   To be sure, the Bible contains the Word,
but it should not be equated with it without further explanation, if one is to be faithful to New Testament terminology.
To question 87, "How does the Holy Spirit call us [to faith]?,
the order correctly answered according to New Testament
usage, "When we hear God's Word the Holy Spirit calls us
from sin and the power of the devil back to God again.   Acts

26:18." Later, the order continued with the same use of the term by answering question 101, "How can such a deliberate sinner again be sanctified?" with "Through the Word of God he can again be sanctified." But then, without further ado the order shifted the meaning of this term to include more than the Gospel, when in the next question, "What then is the Word of God?" it responded, "The whole Bible or the Holy Scripture is God's Word," adding the Bible reference 2 Peter 1:21, which does not refer to the Bible at all but to the preached message of the apostles and prophets.

By equating "Word of God" with the Bible and thereby extending the New Testament meaning, these early Lutherans continued to remain vulnerable to serious misunderstandings and a variety of false concepts. This misunderstanding reflected already in the first catechism produced by Lutherans in America was not merely an unfortunate inconsistency but the forerunner of a troublesome problem that still haunts Lutherans in America to the present time.

The above error was compounded with a train of thought that led up to an answer that allowed man to play a role in his conversion.

> Q. 111. Of what must one repent if he would convert himself? [wenn er sich bekehren will?]
> A. He who would convert himself must heartily
> a) acknowledge, b) repent, and c) hate his sins.

It was then that God worked faith in him.

The order's treatment of the sacraments and the church as a fellowship of believers was minimal. On the other hand considerable emphasis was placed on repentance, the Christian's personal life, and prayer. As one might expect, this emphasis made the order a popular one among Lutherans influenced by Pietism and so found its way into many of the later German catechisms published in America. This order was translated and included in some of the later English catechisms also.

The Traditional Confessional Prayer
(Das Gewöhnliche Beicht-gebät)

This was taken from the Württemberg Kinder Examen with minor changes, and The Application of the Catechism for the Strengthening of the Faith by Reviewing the Treasures of Salvation (Anwendung des Catechismi, Zur Stärkung des Glaubens in Vorhaltung der Schätze des Heils) followed the IV Order of Salvation. The latter, written in outline form with Bible references, was drawn up according to the three articles of the Creed. It was simply an enumeration, without further comment, of the rich spiritual treasures the Christian has received from the Holy Trinity. No references were made to the fellowship treasures that the Christian had with other believers. The emphasis was wholly on the gracious personal relationship with God.

A Brief Summary of the Christian Doctrine (Kurtzer Begriff der Christlichen Lehre)

This was a one-page summary written as a single paragraph interspersed with Bible references. It was probably intended as a convenient review for the children and was no doubt memorized by many of the catechumens. Its source is not known.

Jesus Hymn

The catechism concluded with the 12-stanza Jesus Hymn "Wer ist wol wie du, Jesus, süsse ruh?" by Johann A. Freylinghausen. This hymn too was interspersed with Bible references.

While Brunnholtz's catechism does have some Pietistic overtones, it was restrained and in general conformed to the Lutheran Confessions. Luther's catechism was faithfully produced and was given the major emphasis. Because, however, it was placed among the orders of salvation, it was natural that it, too, was taught as an order, though this concept was foreign to Luther's intent. He had drawn up his catechism with the baptized child in mind who knew himself to be a child of God. In the years to come his viewpoint was to be lost completely in most catechisms produced by Lutherans in America. This will become more evident as we trace the history of the catechisms during the next century.

ENLARGED AND REVISED EDITIONS OF BRUNNHOLTZ'S CATECHISM (1752-1784)

The next known edition of Brunnholtz's catechism ap-

peared early in 1752, greatly enlarged and with some revisions of the earlier text.   However, no copy with that year
on the title page is known to exist.   There are two undated
editions, differing only in minor details, that carry the line
"Philadelphia, March 6, 1752" on page 127.   If Philadelphia
here refers to the place where the manuscript was printed,
then the undated editions may have been printed later, for
they came from the Christopher Saur press of Germantown.
If, however, Philadelphia refers to the place where the manuscript was written, one of the undated editions may be the
first copy of the enlarged catechism.   Six similar printings,
all dated on the title page, appeared between 1762 and 1782.
They, too, carried the Philadelphia, March 6, 1752, date
and place on page 127.   A similar catechism from 1784 by
Carl Cist of Philadelphia omitted this date and simply repeated the date and place of the title page on its page
127.

This confusing problem of dates and various editions
will face us through the next century.   Apparently any pastor, in most cases presumably with the authority of his congregations, might take his favorite catechism to a nearby
printer, perhaps indicate a few changes and additions that
he found helpful, and have it printed for his own use.   To
add to the confusion, he or perhaps his printer, might further indicate that it was the seventh or eighth edition, depending on the copy on which the proposed edition was based.
Since he or the printer might not be aware of any other catechisms printed in the meanwhile, the enumeration would
not necessarily relate to the facts in the case.   The Pennsylvania Ministerium, just recently organized (1748), but
dormant between 1754-1760, could not concern itself as yet
with publications and was too weak to exercise any jurisdic-
tion in this respect.   Even when in 1785 it did authorize its
first German catechism, it could only express the hope
that some uniformity might be practiced.   But pastors
still continued to print catechisms on their own, either
the authorized catechism or one of their personal preference.   In time they even made changes and additions in
the "official" version, as that seemed to be warranted
by the theological climate of the day.

The following is the title of the enlarged edition of
the Brunnholtz catechism and a listing of the known reprint-
ings of this edition.

The Small Catechism of the Blessed Dr. Martin

Luther, together with the Usual Morning-, Table-, and Evening-Prayers. To which are added the Orders of Salvation in a Hymn, in Short Sentences, in Questions and Answers, in a Table and also the Contents of the Holy Scriptures set forth in Verses. For the use of the Youth. Together with an Appendix including the Seven Penitential Psalms, a Spiritual Hymn, and the One Times One. Germantown: Christoph Saur, n. d. [1752 ?][26]

Germantown: Christoph Saur, n. d.

Philadelphia: Anton Armbrüster, 1762.

Philadelphia: Anton Armbrüster, 1764 (5th and enlarged ed.)

Philadelphia: Anton Armbrüster, 1766 (6th and enlarged ed.)

Germantown: Christoph Saur, Jr. and Peter Saur, 1777.

Lancaster: Francis Bailey, 1778.

Lancaster: Francis Bailey, 1782.

Philadelphia: Carl Cist, 1784.

Philadelphia: Klein und Reynolds, 1784.

Whether Brunnholtz or someone authorized by him or his congregation prepared the enlarged edition of his catechism is not known. Mühlenberg gave no hint that a major revision had been made though it is clear that he approved of the current catechism. Presumably he was speaking of the 1752 print, when he wrote a friend in Germany, Sept. 12, 1753, "A catechism has been compiled by us, and printed here in Philadelphia, which is used in nearly all our united congregations."[27] Even later after another revision had appeared in 1770 and 1774, Mühlenberg still seemed to prefer this enlarged edition which was more commonly in use. In 1778, he asked his daughter in Philadelphia, Margaretha, the wife of the Rev. John C. Kuntze, to send him a dozen of the catechisms reprinted by Saur, presumably that of 1777.[28]

With the enlargement, the catechism was also restructured into four main sections: I. Luther's Small Catechism; II. Four Orders of Salvation; III. The Holy Scriptures Sum-

marized Briefly in the Form of a Hymn; IV.   Appendix and
the Application of the Catechism.

The enlarged catechism reflected a much more Pietistic influence than the original one, not only with the insertion
of several orders of salvation and applications that had strong
Pietistic leanings but also in the revisions made in the parts
retained.

With the number of additions made to the enlarged
catechism, the book became even more a resource book for
the pastor and the catechumens.   It could be used in a wider
variety of circumstances with different theological emphases,
rather than as a text to be used in a fairly uniform manner.
Apparently it too was to be used in the schools.

Luther's Small Catechism

A number of changes were made in this catechism.
Bible references were added in profusion throughout the text
to serve as proof passages and as a guide for the instruction.   It did include the Office of the Keys, but not in its
widely used traditional form.   Instead it simply set forth
three pertinent Bible passages: Luke 10:16; Matt. 16:19;
and John 20:22.23 with no further explanation.   This became
a fairly standard pattern for later catechisms.   It further
included Luther's Confession of Sins which had been omitted
in the earlier rendition.

Four Orders of Salvation

These were all taken from Starcke.   In addition to
The Hymn of Faith and the so-called IV Order of Salvation
(In Short, Simple Questions and Answers), the new edition
included the Order of Salvation in Nine Brief Sentences and
the Short Table.

The Order in Nine Brief Sentences was radically altered from its original in Starcke.[29]   The original had been
written in nine double statements, the second enlarging on
the thought of the first statement.   The altered form con-
densed the two into one statement and supplemented it with
a considerable number of Bible references to serve as proof
and as further illustrations of the text.   Starcke's eighth
statement which had allowed room for synergism was recast

into a more acceptable form.   These statements were found
also in some form in later English catechisms.   In their
original form they sometimes served as a basis for a series
of sermons. [30]

The Order of Salvation as a Short Table was a synopsis showing how the Christian articles of faith were related
to one another. [31]   Except in one instance, the catechism
took Starcke's synopsis over with only minor changes.   The
major variation was in connection with man's powers in his
natural state of sin.   Starcke had, "The remaining strengths
are able to attain nothing for salvation.   1 Cor. 2:14.   The
natural man perceives nothing."[32]   The altered form had, "The
remaining strengths are not adequate for salvation.   1 Cor.
2:14," thus leaving room for synergism. [33]   Whether Brunnholtz made the change or whether he unknowingly adopted an
altered form cannot be established.   The altered text found
its way later into the first authorized catechism of the Pennsylvania Ministerium in 1785, and was retained in the second
authorized catechism of 1857. [34]   In the English translations,
at least as early as 1795, and thereafter, the wording was
further changed to allow for the natural man to cooperate in
his conversion. [35]

Three further points in Starcke's order are of special
interest.   First, the means of grace are said to be "the
Word of God, or Holy Scripture" and the sacraments.   Thus
this order not only employed an alien meaning for "Word of
God," but took a further step by referring to Scripture as a
means of grace.   In fact, the text explicitly stated that both
Law and Gospel of Scripture are included in the means of
grace (p. 80).   Secondly, under aids to repentance are listed
the cross, explained as all manner of suffering which God
gives to his children, and prayer.   Thirdly, persons who
accepted the grace of God are called the church and in the
church there are three stations or classes: the teaching order, the ruling order (the Bible reference is Rom. 13:1-7),
and the family order (p. 81).   This was the only reference
to the church.

The Holy Scriptures Summarized Briefly
in the Form of a Hymn

This comprised the third section.   It was a book by
book summary of the Bible in the form of a hymn, comprising 62 stanzas, to be sung to the tune, "Now thank we all

our God." One can hardly imagine children being expected
to memorize the wooden "poetry," to say nothing of its extraordinary length.

Appendix and the Application of the Catechism

This fourth section contained a variety of helps to assist the pastor or the teacher in applying the catechism in
the lives of the children.

The first help was the Brief Explanation to the Ten
Commandments which had served as an introduction in the
earlier catechism. This was followed by the Treasury of
Salvation, also in the earlier edition. The next was an addition called A Renewal of the Baptismal Covenant. This
was intended especially for those who were being prepared
for confirmation and the reception of the Lord's Supper. A
distinction was made here between the promise made at the
time of one's baptism and the promise or covenant made by
God at that time. The latter was firm and enduring forever.
Yet because it was assumed that the catechumen had broken
his promise, he was instructed to pray, "Receive me again
in your grace ... ," the assumption being that he had fallen
away with the breaking of his vow. This, of course, reflected the strong Pietistic emphasis at the time, one that
has prevailed in some instances to the present.

In addition to the confessional prayer for the adults,
the enlarged catechism added one specifically for children.

Another hymn was added called a Conversion Hymn
(Erweckungslied), "Jesus sinners will receive,"[36] referred
to as a hymn for true contrition and a living faith. Apparently the hymn was intended also as a basis for extensive
class instruction since it was liberally sprinkled with Bible
references at the end of the eleven stanzas.

In a new category the catechism added a hymn for
children about to be confirmed and prepared for a worthy
use of the Holy Supper. The first line of the hymn was "O
great and righteous God" (O höchster und gerechter Gott").[37]
Stanzas one to eleven were to be sung by the children and
the final four stanzas by the entire congregation. In the vein
of Pietism, the hymn was melodramatic, the children asking
their parents to sob and cry that God give them the power to
remain faithful and swear with them, with heart and voice, to

serve their Savior faithfully.   In the final stanzas the entire
congregation swore greater faithfulness to the Savior.

Another supplement was A Spiritual Song concerning
the Divine Essence and its Attributes.   The hymn was "O
Gott, du Tiefe sonder Grund, " a hymn of adoration declaring
the majestic essence and attributes of God. [38]

Since the enlarged catechism was to be used also in
schools it further contained The Golden A B C for Children,
The Seven Penitential Psalms, and the Multiplication Table.
The A B C was introduced with the admonition: A disciple
of the Lord Jesus devotes himself (herself) to be "Attentive
to the Word of Christ."   Christian virtues or characteristics
were set forth in alphabetic order with Bible references added
for each one.

MARBURGER GESANG-BUCH (1757-1799)

This hymn book included the text of Luther's Small
Catechism to assist the faithful in their home devotions and
in the instruction of their children.   It was one of the many
different hymn books brought to this country by the German
immigrants and used by both Lutherans and Reformed, particularly in Pennsylvania, though not limited to that area.
The Union of Churches in South Carolina prescribed it in its
constitution of 1788 for both confessions. [39]

The Marburg Hymnal had originally appeared in 1549
as a small collection of 80 hymns.   Over the years it grew,
so that by the time the Pennsylvania Lutherans reprinted it,
it had developed to some 649 psalm phrases and hymns.
During this period of growth it was strongly influenced by
Pietism.

The hymn book seems to be the one most frequently
used by Mühlenberg who utilized it as a devotional book as
he ministered to the sick and the dying. [40]   Because the
Dutch Lutherans in New York were accustomed to singing the
rhymed psalms in the manner of the Reformed, Mühlenberg
complained of the difficulty in choosing good Lutheran hymns
when he preached in their midst.   Under such circumstances
he took great pains to teach them one from the Marburg Hymnal. [41]

The Marburg Hymnal was printed in Germantown by

Christoph Saur.   The full title was,

> The Complete Marburg Hymnal, For the Practice
> of Godliness, in 649 Christian and Richly Comfort-
> ing Psalms and Hymns by Dr. Martin Luther and
> other Godly Teachers.   Germantown: Christoph
> Saur, 1757. [42]

The following issues appeared over the years,

> Germantown: Christoph Saur, 1759.
>
> Germantown: Christoph Saur, 1762.
>
> Germantown: Christoph Saur, 1770.
>
> Germantown: Christoph Saur, 1774.   4th edition.
>
> Germantown: Christoph Saur, 1777.   5th and en-
> larged edition.
>
> Philadelphia: Carl Cist, 1799.   New edition, care-
> fully purged of printing errors.

In Pennsylvania it was eventually supplanted by the Ministerium hymnal of 1786.

The section containing the catechism presented the Luther text in such a way that the Five Chief Parts and their
subdivisions were linked into a whole through questions and
answers.   The catechism became a convenient means for
parents to assist their children in preparing for confirmation
and their first communion.

The introduction began with a direct question, "Are
you a Christian?" and the answer, "Yes, Sir." "How do
you know this?" "Because I have been baptized in the name
of Jesus Christ and know and believe the Christian doctrine."
The introduction continued with the question, "What is the
Christian doctrine?" and the answer, "The one set forth and
comprehended in the writings of Moses, the prophets, and the
apostles." With that the catechism launched into Luther's
text with the question, "How many Chief Parts are there in
the Christian doctrine?" These then were listed, followed
by the question, "What common purpose do all these serve?"
and the answer, "That we recognize, first who we are and
how we stand before our Lord God; thereupon who our Lord
God is and how we may be reconciled and united with him."

There is a warm and personal approach throughout the

catechism. Additional questions to Luther's text were kept
minimal, usually only one to a commandment to help summarize or affirm the meaning of Luther. Similarly a question was added to each of the three articles and some twelve
to summarize the Creed. A similar pattern continued for
the other Chief Parts. The text, however, does not indicate
that the linking questions were added and were not originally
a part of Luther's catechism.

Luther's Confession of Sins was given at the end of
the Lord's Supper. The catechism included the Christian
Questions and Answers and the Table of Duties, but omitted
Luther's prayers.

DER KLEINE DARMSTÄDTISCHE CATECHISMUS
1759 AND 1763

Among the Palatinates and other Germans who had
come to Pennsylvania there were a considerable number who
emigrated from the vicinity of Darmstadt, in Hesse-Cassel.
A goodly number of these had settled in Germantown. Mühlenberg spoke highly of them saying, "there are many members from the province of Darmstadt who must have had good
instruction in their youth. "43 His Journals indicate that he
had frequent contacts with the Darmstadt Consistory. 44

The State church of Hesse-Cassel included Reformed,
Lutheran, and Union churches. The Lutheran congregations
used the Darmstädtische Catechismus as prescribed in the
Hessische Kirchenordnung of 1724. However, the use of this
catechism was not restricted to the Lutheran congregations.
Because of its popularity among some of the pastors, its
unofficial use was permitted in some of the Reformed churches
in the Cassel Consistory as well. 45

Whether it was due to nostalgia or because of some
dissatisfaction with the Brunnholtz catechisms, which by this
time had appeared in at least four editions, the Darmstädtische Catechismus was reprinted in Germantown in 1759,
and again in 1763, on the Chr. Saur press. The full title
was,

The Small Darmstadt Catechism of Dr. Martin Luther, Together with Questions for Those especially
who, according to Christian Practice, are to be
Confirmed and thereupon Partake of Their First
Communion. Germantown: Chr. Saur, 1759.46

The Darmstädtische Catechismus is especially interesting because it contained only Luther's Small Catechism,
including even his introduction. None of the orders of salvation, so popular among the Pietists, were incorporated.
This may provide a clue why the catechism was published.

The Luther text was the same as the one in the Marburg hymn book with the addition of Bible passages to support the material, usually only one for each answer.

Luther's Confession of Sins was made even more
meaningful through a modified form of role playing.   The
roles were those of a student, a servant or maid, and a
husband or wife, followed by a more general or common
confession.   These were succeeded by the absolution of sins.

The catechism did include Luther's prayers which had
been omitted in the Marburg Hymnal.   After the Christian
Questions and Answers it concluded with Paul Eber's hymn
for a blessed end, "Lord Jesus Christ, true Man and God,"[47]
and prayers for the sick and dying.

HENRICH MILLER REVISION (1765-1776?)

As early as 1765, another major revision of the
Brunnholtz catechism was printed in Philadelphia by Henrich
Miller, a Moravian.   In that year an advertisement appeared
in his paper, the Philadelphische Staatsbote,[48] dated Dec. 2,
giving substantially the same title as a later edition in 1770,
of which a copy is available.[49]   Mühlenberg referred to this
printing when he reported that he had a visit from Mr. Heinrich Mueller "who wants to print our local Catechism before
the stamp-tax is imposed."[50]   It must have appeared shortly
thereafter for Mühlenberg purchased 100 copies from Peter
Mueller on August 4 for the Yorktown congregation.[51]

Judging from the nature and spacing of the advertisements it appears that another edition was printed in 1767,
when the Philadelphische Staatsbote again announced the catechism on Sept. 21.[52]   No copies with these dates have been
found by the writer.   All the known editions of this series
were printed by Miller.   Who was responsible for the revision is not known.   The previously enlarged edition continued to be printed alongside of this revision for some time.
However, the Miller version eventually became one of the
two sources for the 1785 official catechism of the Pennsylvania Ministerium.

The Small Catechism of the Blessed Dr. Martin
Luther, together with the Usual Morning-, Table-,
and Evening Prayers. To which are added the
Orders of Salvation, in a Hymn, in Short Statements, in Questions and Answers, in a Table, as
also the Württemberg Brief Children's Examination,
the Confirmation, Confession, Communion Prayers
and Hymns; and the Unaltered Augsburg Confession.
To which are Appended for the Youth the Golden
A-B-C. Philadelphia. 1765. 53

Philadelphia: Henrich Miller, 1767.

7th edition. Philadelphia: Henrich Miller, 1770.

8th edition. Philadelphia: Henrich Miller, 1774.

Philadelphia: Henrich Miller, 1776.   ?

More concrete data concerning the contents of these
catechisms come from the 1770 edition. From this copy we
see that the revision was primarily in the form of omissions
and additions rather than in textual changes. In Luther's
text the Bible references were omitted after the paragraphs
dealing with the Chief Parts. Other omissions in the Miller
edition from that of the Brunnholtz edition were: III. The
Holy Scriptures Summarized Briefly in the Form of a Hymn
and two parts of Supplement IV.; 2. Treasures of Salvation;
and 7. A Spiritual Song concerning the Divine Essence.

Two major additions were made in the new revision.
The first was the inclusion of the first 21 articles of the Unaltered Augsburg Confession (pp. 105-119). The other addition was the inclusion of the formula described as A Short
Examination through Questions and Answers which are to be
taken up with the Children in Public Worship before the Rite
of Confirmation, taken for the most part from the Württemberg Catechism, Children's Instruction and Communicants
Booklet (pp. 67-104). 54 This major addition replaced the
Renewal of the Baptismal Covenant and the Formulas for the
Confession of Sins. The Miller edition of 1765, was apparently the first American catechism to include the Württemberg
Formula for Confirmation. Because the formula was later
included in the official catechism of the Ministerium, it war-
rants special attention.

The first part, as the title implies, contained a series
of questions and answers to be asked of the children at the
time of their confirmation. In the section dealing with Holy
Baptism, the ambiguity concerning the precise meaning of the

baptismal covenant, found in most of Pietism, was perpetuated, namely whether this covenant was unilateral, one of
grace, made alone by God with the child at the time of his
baptism and independent of the child, or whether it was a
bilateral covenant, i. e., a two-party agreement, one made
by both God and the child, or whether it was a covenant by
God and simply a vow made by the child through his sponsors in response to God's grace.   The confusion comes to
the fore in the emphasis given to the renewal of the baptismal covenant by the child at the time of his confirmation and
whenever thereafter he prepared himself for the Lord's Supper.   In the baptismal covenant, according to the formula in
the catechism, God promised the child to be his gracious
God and Father (p. 69), while the child in turn, presumably
through his sponsors, had renounced the devil and all his
works, binding himself to serve God and the Lord Jesus
throughout his life. [55]   Furthermore, the confirmand now
promised to renew his baptismal covenant daily, especially
when he communed.   In short, the promise that the confirmand
made at confirmation and presumably made at his baptism,
was not referred to simply as a vow or a promise in response
to God's gracious covenant, but treated as though it were his
part of the baptismal covenant.   In so doing the young Christian could readily lose sight of the fact that God's covenant
with him was one entirely of grace and therefore not condi-
tioned on his or any one else's promise.   It was enduring
throughout his life and was not in need of a renewal. [56]   Interestingly enough, the enduring quality of God's covenant was
indeed correctly expressed in the prayer suggested before
Holy Communion: "O thou Friend of my soul, Lord Jesus,
who has since my holy baptism betrothed thyself with me for
all eternity...." (p. 94).

On the other hand, the renunciation of the devil on the
part of the confirmand was correctly stated in contrast to many
later renditions.   The formula recognized clearly that the renunciation at confirmation was not an initial one, as it had
been at Baptism, but rather a repetition of the initial one.
The question stated this clearly: "Do you again renounce the
devil and all his works and ways?" Similarly the vow of
faithfulness was not regarded as an initial one, but one which
the confirmand knowingly had made many times prior to his
confirmation (p. 81).

Included in this section were a number of prayers
suggested for various steps in the confirmation rite and for
participation in the Lord's Supper.

This edition was again reprinted in 1774, as the 8th
edition. Presumably it was the same as the 7th, though no
copy of it has as yet been found. It was the 8th edition
which later was officially designated by the Ministerium as
one of the two sources for its official catechism of 1785.

KUNTZE'S REVISION (1781)

It is evident that there was considerable dissatisfaction with the traditional catechisms currently in use in many
of the Lutheran congregations. The appearance of Miller's
revision seemed not to have quieted the criticism in some
quarters. As early as 1778, Mühlenberg made references
to a revision that was being prepared by his son-in-law, John
C. Kuntze (1744-1807), pastor at that time in Philadelphia. [57]

Even when the enlarged Brunnholtz catechism and the
Miller version continued to be printed in Philadelphia, Germantown, and Lancaster, Kuntze pressed toward the publication of his revision, submitting on occasion a copy to Mühlenberg for criticism and additional suggestions. [58] Finally,
in June 1781 the new publication appeared from the press of
the Philadelphia printers Steiner and Cist, who had recently
purchased the printing establishment of Henrich Miller,

> The Catechism of the Blessed Dr. Martin Luther,
> Together with the usual Morning- Table- and Even-
> ing Prayers. To which is Added a further Instruc-
> tion in the Christian Doctrine for the more Ad-
> vanced and the Confirmands. Philadelphia: Steiner
> and Cist, 1781. [59]

One of the major additions in the new catechism was
Kuntze's Analysis of the Catechism. This was a detailed
outline, with appropriate Bible references, of the Five Chief
Parts of Luther's catechism prepared particularly for advanced children and confirmands. The outline, as so often
was the case by those influenced by Pietism, was again struc-
tured as though Luther had intended his catechism to be an
order of salvation. Thus Kuntze treated the Ten Commandments as the Law element that was to prepare children for
the Gospel, to be found in the Second Chief Part. This was,
of course, not Luther's purpose, for the Small Catechism
was not intended to present Law and Gospel in opposition to
one another nor were they to follow one another time-wise.

In a similar vein of Pietism, Kuntze continued to ex-

plain the Sabbath in the Third Commandment as though it
were a New Testament Sabbath, rather than Luther's more
free interpretation which did not place the emphasis on a
particular day of the week but on honoring God's Word re-
gardless of the day.

The doctrine of God appeared in the First Article of
the Creed, i.e., statements concerning the Trinity, the divine attributes and the works of God. Luther had not treated
these details but had concretized the Trinity in the three articles. He taught this fact through God's relationship and
action toward his people.

Prayer continued to be presented as a means of grace,
i.e., as the true power for finding and continuing on the way
of salvation. The Second Petition of the Lord's Prayer was
taught exclusively as a mission prayer, namely that the Gospel be spread among the nations.

The influence of Pietism was further evidenced by the
stress on the individual or the personal value of the Lord's
Prayer. No mention was made of the sacrament's power and
use for strengthening the fellowship of believers. There was
no reference to the confession of sins as such, though it was
probably implied as a preparation for the Lord's Supper without specifically being stated.

Mühlenberg was involved as a consultant in the preparation of the Analysis. As early as Sept. 18, 1778, he
wrote, "Today I finished copying Pastor K comments on part
five of Luther's catechism."[60] He frequently made use of
the Analysis even before it was published when he addressed
young pastors. Thus he recorded on Jan. 17, 1781, "Did
some writing on Pastor K explanation of the five chief parts
on Luther's catechism in order to present a manuscript copy
of it to one of our young preachers elevated to office here."[61]
Again on March 15, he recorded, "I wrote a few lines to
Pastor Buschkirch and sent him my manuscript of the explanations of the five chief parts of Luther's Catechism, composed by Pastor Kuntze."[62]

Apparently the Analysis was well received by the pastors for it was later included by direction of the Ministerium
in its catechism.

Much in the same vein as the Analysis was Kuntze's
poetic rendition called, The Catechism in Verse. In this

rendition Kuntze concentrated on the basic questions in Luther's catechism and less on his explanations, particularly
with the first three chief parts.   The sacraments of Baptism
and the Lord's Supper were warmly personalized, much more
than was usually the case.   When Mühlenberg saw the new
catechism for the first time in print, he was very pleased
with this rendition, "because I have long wanted to see this
done."[63]

In a somewhat more venturesome moment Kuntze revised the popular Hymn of Faith and gave it its original title
The Order of Salvation in Verses.   He made a number of
changes in the hymn clarifying particularly the references to
the sacraments.   The original, as noted above, had been
taken from Starcke.   When it was first embodied in the catechism of 1749, Ziegenhagen's rendition was used.   At the
time Mühlenberg was still not satisfied with it.   He felt that
the changes had not gone far enough.   When he read Kuntze's
version the first time he was pleased because he felt that
Kuntze had improved the poetry and had made a number of
expressions clearer.   Furthermore, he had emphasized it as
an order of salvation and that was to Mühlenberg's liking.[64]

It should not be surprising that in spite of Mühlenberg's enthusiasm for Kuntze's version, the older form, long
memorized by pastor and people alike, was later retained in
the official catechism.

Another major change by Kuntze was his omission of
Starcke's Order of Salvation as a Short Table.   He replaced
this with a more detailed one of his own.   Whether the sub-
stitution was suggested by a similarly long one by Starcke is
uncertain.[65]   There was very little similarity between the
two beyond the general subject matter.

Kuntze's Table, as the title would suggest, was a series of logical and detailed divisions of the Christian doctrine.
It is difficult to imagine how this rendition could have been
effective with children and even with most adults.   It lacked
warmth and was very impersonal.   It might have been more
suitable for students of theology than for the average layper-
son.   It is not surprising that it was not retained in later
editions of the catechism.

The Table listed the means of grace as being, 1) Prayer,
Luke 11:13; 2) The Word of God, James 1:8--a.   The Law,
Rom. 3:20 and b.   The Gospel, Rom. 10:7; and 3) The Sacra-
ments.

Under the Lord's Supper, the Table gave a clear presentation of the sacramental presence of our Lord. The article of faith on the church was not treated.

A major addition to Kuntze's catechism was the inclusion of Johann A. Freylinghausen's Order of Salvation. [66]
This order had previously appeared in an American print in
1776, also from the press of Steiner and Cist, from which
Kuntze probably had taken it. [67]

In the usual manner of orders of salvation, Freylinghausen set forth in a series of questions and answers the
Christian faith, beginning with a doctrinal statement on the
Holy Trinity and the creation, continuing with the fall of
mankind, and the redemption won by Jesus Christ as revealed
in the Gospel. Emphasis was placed particularly on the penitent life of the Christian through the aid of the Holy Spirit
who supported that life through the sacraments. Freylinghausen's order avoided many of the usually abstract concepts
and supported his statements by interspersing his text with
numerous Bible references. This order proved very popular
and was embodied in the official catechism. It found its way
into the English catechism as early as 1802. [68]

Another addition to Kuntze's version was A List of the
Most Important Key Passages of Holy Writ by which the Chief
Articles of Faith, Set Forth in a Convenient Order, are Established. He probably adopted this list from the booklet
containing Freylinghausen's order, since it was included in
the booklet according to the extended title. [69] This list was
included also in the 1785 catechism of the Ministerium.

Besides the additions mentioned, Kuntze's catechism
revision omitted a number of parts from the earlier editions.
In general where this revision differed from the past it favored the changes made in the Miller version. It retained
most of the Württemberg Formula for Confirmation found in
the Miller version. However, it differed from this version
by omitting The Augsburg Confession. This omission does
not indicate confessional laxity on the part of Kuntze for his
stand in this regard was unequivocal. It probably reflected
the opinion that it was not suitable to the level of the catechumens for whom the book was intended.

The revision omitted all but one of the hymns found in
both the Miller version and the enlarged Brunnholtz edition.
It retained the confirmation hymn, "O höchster and gerechter

Gott." It inserted, however, two of its own, "Meine Seele!
ermuntere dich" and "O Gottes Lamm, mein Element." It
retained from the earlier editions the Seven Penitential Psalms
and the Golden A, B, C.

Mühlenberg evidently had some misgivings as to how
well the new version would be received by the pastors and
congregations and whether its introduction might not bring
about more confusion. After its publication, Mühlenberg noted
in his Journal,

> Perhaps it would have been advantageous to have
> recommended to all the members of the ministerial
> conference that they introduce the new edition in an
> orderly fashion into their schools and the instruc-
> tion of confirmation, in view of the fact that at
> first it could cause some confusion if some should
> say, "We will hold to the old edition"; and others,
> "We shall adopt the new." The printer, too, could
> probably suffer some loss if some members were
> to have the old edition reprinted. The new edition
> pleases me very much, and in the future it can
> serve as a symbolic treasure to the good and bless-
> ing of our Evangelical Lutheran congregations, if
> it is recommended by all the united laborers in
> their respective congregations. [70]

His concerns were evidently well founded. Kuntze's
revision never became the official catechism of the Ministerium although it played a significant role in the formulation of
the official catechism of 1785 since it was one of the two
renditions used as a basis.

A second printing of this catechism appeared in 1782.

Chapter III

THE CATECHISM OF THE PENNSYLVANIA
MINISTERIUM, 1785-1857

Mühlenberg's concern that several different catechisms
independently published might add to the confusion among the
United Congregations was shared by many others.   This concern surfaced at the 1782 meeting of the Ministerium.   There
steps were taken to prepare an official catechism which would
permit no changes "except with the approval of the Synod."[1]
In implementing this decision it was resolved that in the next
edition the catechism printed by Henrich Miller in 1774,
should be taken as a basis.   The Synod particularly designated the sections from the following pages to be printed
without change and that the rest be dropped: pp. 1-64 [The
Small Catechism of Luther, The Orders of Salvation: The
Hymn of Faith, in Short Sentences, in Questions and Answers,
and in a Short Table]; pp. 69-89 [The Württemberg Formula
of Confirmation]; p. 94 [The Children's Confession of Sins];
pp. 123-144 [two "Awakening" Hymns: "Mein Heiland nimmt
die Sünder an" and "Wer ist wohl wie du?," Confirmation
Hymn: "O höchster und Gerechter Gott," The Golden A, B,
C and the Penitential Psalm].[2]

Furthermore, Kuntze's catechism of 1781 referred to
as the Steiner edition, was to serve as the second source
for the proposed catechism.   From this catechism pp. 35-47
[The Analysis of the Catechism] should be taken after some
slight changes had been made.[3]   The changes later made by
the committee for the most part affected only the Bible references.   Here there were a limited number of omissions,
additions and substitutions.   A few minor changes and additions to the text were also made for the sake of clarification.

The Ministerium further resolved that "all quotations
from the Catechism in The Württemberg Formula of Confirmation be altered to conform with this Catechism."[4]

Finally it was "Resolved, that this Catechism be generally introduced, and, as far as possible remain unchanged."[5]

The following year, 1783, the Ministerium resolved that "the Catechism shall be printed as decided last year. Mr. [John C.] Kunze undertook to attend this."[6] No mention was made who else might have served on the committee to produce the proposed catechism.

Not until early in 1785 did the new catechism appear in print. On Feb. 7, Mühlenberg noted that a German printery had been established in nearby Germantown by Leibert and Billmeyer. "They have printed," he wrote, "our Lutheran catechism, which had hitherto been used in our United Congregations, and have offered it for sale."[7] The full title of the new publication was,

> The Small Catechism of the Blessed Dr. Martin Luther, together with the Usual Morning- Table- and Evening Prayers. To which are added the Orders of Salvation in a Hymn, in short Statements, In Questions and Answers, in a Table: as also An Analysis of the Catechism: The Württemberg Brief Children's Examination, the Confirmation, and Confession; and several Hymns, Freylinghausen's Order of Salvation, the Golden A, B, C, for Children, and the Seven Penitential Psalms. For use of Young and Old. 1st ed. Germantown: Leibert and Billmeyer, 1785.[8]

The new catechism appeared as authorized, though the committee apparently took the liberty of making some additions on its own. It added from Kuntze's catechism Freylinghausen's Order of Salvation, the List of Most Important Key Passages, and the hymn, "O Gottes Lamm, Mein Element." From the Miller catechism of 1774 it further added A Short Explanation of the Ten Commandments in Verses. Apparently on its own, the committee added the hymn, found in neither of the appointed catechisms, "Steh, armes Kind, wo eilst du hin?"

The text of Luther's Small Catechism continued to follow the popular version as it had evolved over the centuries. It included the following additions and changes that had found their way into the catechism. It omitted Luther's preface to the catechism and added the enumerations for each of the

parts, as they were originally set forth in the Nürnberger
Kinderbüchlein of 1531.   It included as part of the First
Commandment the introductory words, "I am the Lord your
God," first found in the Nürnberger Kinderpredigten of 1533.
From the same source came the addition of "strong" [starker]
to the words of the Conclusion, "I the Lord, your God, am
a strong, jealous God."   The Second Commandment included
the threat of Ex. 20:7b, "for the Lord will not hold him
guiltless that taketh his name in vain," as one finds it in the
Nürnberg catechism prints of 1531 and 1558.   Furthermore
it included the doxology of the Lord's Prayer, also first
found in the Nürnberg print of 1558.

A form of the Office of the Keys was inserted after
the Lord's Supper consisting of three Bible passages: Luke
10:16; Matt. 16:19; and John 20:22.23.   This was the same
as found in the enlarged Brunnholtz catechism of 1752.9   The
better known rendition of the Office of the Keys by Osiander
and Sleupner from the Nürnberger Kinderpredigten was not
used.   It further included the Christian Questions and Answers
by Johannes Lange of Erfurt, which were usually attributed to
Luther but not found in any of the catechism editions prior to
Luther's death.   Only the first three questions and answers
of Luther's Confession were retained.   Thus it omitted the
Brief Form of Confession.

The Table of Duties included two sections not originally found in Luther's text but traditionally included, What
Hearers owe their Pastors and Teachers and Duties of Subjects.   The hymn stanza added to each of Luther's prayers
were likewise not a part of the original text of the Small Catechism.

Thus the catechism of the Pennsylvania Ministerium,
like so many others before and after its time, did not cor-
respond with the text found in any of the editions prepared
under Luther's supervision nor with the text found in the
Book of Concord.

By including Kuntze's Analysis of the Catechism, the
new catechism further encouraged the use of Luther's catechism as a summary, or as a systematic compendium of
Christian doctrine rather than for its intended purpose which
was to teach young Christians the meaning and use of the
Gospel as a source of power for the new life in Christ.   The
inclusion of the orders of salvation tended further to encourage the use of Luther's catechism as simply another order.

This too did not conform with his purpose in writing the catechism. Yet this was not unique to this catechism since neither much of Lutheran Orthodoxy nor of Pietism had in the past grasped Luther's intended purpose.

The authorized catechism continued to serve to a large extent as a series of texts rather than as a single exposition of the Christian doctrine. Thus it served as a resource for pastors and teachers who were ministering in a variety of circumstances and at different levels of religious maturity.

This newly adopted catechism continued to be the official German text of the Ministerium for some 72 years, until it was replaced by a revision in 1857.[10] While it no doubt was by far the most commonly used text, it did not, as we shall see, keep individuals from producing supplementary texts and even substitute catechisms of their own.

During the long period in which it served as the official catechism it was printed by some 25 different printers in more than 70 editions. In the earlier period, from 1785 to 1826, Leibert and Billmeyer of Germantown and their successors apparently regarded themselves as the "official" printers. With one minor exception, no changes were made in the text in the 16 printings of this firm, even though the printer numbered them as 11 different editions. A minor change in Freylinghausen's Order of Salvation occurred already in the second edition of 1786. Leibert and Billmeyer's stance as the official printer was apparently disregarded by Carl Cist of Philadelphia, who produced five prints between 1786 and 1805.

In later years three printers produced a considerable number of prints, especially George W. Mentz of Philadelphia and his successors. This firm produced at least 15 prints between 1811 and 1847, one without a publishing date. During the later period Heinrich Ludwig of New York also produced four prints between 1837 and 1848. At least another 19 printers, mostly in Pennsylvania, with a few in Ohio and Maryland, produced some 25 different prints of this catechism. Apparently individual pastors, congregations or smaller conferences continued to take the initiative, as the need arose, to have the catechism printed, usually at a nearby printery.

Since the supervision by the Ministerium was minimal, it is rather surprising that changes over the years were so

few in number and for the most part minor.   Perhaps one of
the more interesting variations were the three variants found
in Freylinghausen's Order of Salvation.   The first edition of
the 1785 catechism followed the text in Kuntze's catechism.
Only three other prints adhered to this pattern.   As early as
the second edition of 1786, by Leibert and Billmeyer, a new
pattern appeared which placed a greater emphasis on the subjective element of repentance, i. e. the new life in Christ.   A
paragraph was added which had the individual Christian "feel"
[verspüren] the power of atonement.   In general this pattern
was more congenial to Pietism.   At least 46 different prints
followed this pattern.

In 1791, Carl Cist's edition led the way with a third
pattern that again emphasized the atonement, putting less
stress on the subjective, however.   At least eleven other
editions followed this pattern.

Because the catechism was used also in schools where
other subjects were taught, all the earlier catechisms continued to include the multiplication table.   By about 1828,
this did not seem to be important any more and the multiplication table was dropped from the text in many of the prints.
The editions after 1830, were frequently embellished with a
picture of Luther as a frontispiece.

Heinrich Ludwig, beginning probably with the 1844
print, added an appendix to the text which included the Augsburg Confession and several hymns. [11]   This addition reflected
the growing confessional consciousness which was being felt
in the Lutheran Church in America during that decade.

Jacob Schnee of Lebanon, Pa., took the liberty of
changing the order of several sections and inserted a variant
Golden A, B, C.   Perhaps the most significant changes were
made in the edition by Heinrich C. Neinstedt of Gettysburg,
who referred to himself as the printer for the theological
seminary.   His 1828 print omitted a number of portions from
the text.   He omitted the Württemberg Formula of Confirmation, except the confession of sins, The List of Most Important Key Passages, Freylinghausen's Order of Salvation,
Golden A, B, C, and the multiplication table.

An interesting sidelight to the use of this catechism
outside the Pennsylvania Ministerium was the reaction of the
Missouri Synod in 1850.   The use of the Ludwig edition of
the catechism was considered by a committee of the Synod

during its fourth meeting in 1850. The committee that had
studied the catechism advised against its use because the
text of Luther's catechism omitted the traditional form of
the Office of the Keys, customarily found in Luther's catechism. [12] Furthermore, it had omitted several sentences in
the Morning and Evening prayers and made some additions
to the Table Prayers. The Ludwig edition had also made
some changes in the Württemberg Kinder Examen. The written report did not further identify the changes. [13]

The committee's insistence on the continued use of the
traditional form of the Office of the Keys, because it was
customarily found in the Small Catechism, did not take into
consideration that it was actually not a part of the Luther
text. In fact it was not even written by him.

Which sentences were said to have been omitted in the
prayers is difficult to establish since the text in the Ministerium catechism was identical with the Book of Concord, and
even that followed in later editions of Missouri's catechisms. [14]

The Table Prayers of the Pennsylvania catechism did
make some minor additions, but they in no way detracted
from the Luther text. Spurious, to be sure, but no more
so than the Office of the Keys attributed to Luther.

Prompted by the report of its catechism committee,
the Missouri Synod in convention adopted the resolution, "Because the lack of a Lutheran catechism with a brief explanation is clearly evident, be it therefore resolved that the older
Darmstadt edition of Luther's Small Catechism, be published
at the cost of the publishing house treasury." This resolution, for reasons not known, was never put into action. [15]

The wide use of the Pennsylvania catechism and the
frequent printings give evidence that a large number of Lutherans, at least among the Germans, were affected little
either by Rationalism or by the New Measures that scorched
American Lutheranism after the Revolution and well into the
first half of the 19th century. When the Ministerium in 1792
failed to include a confessional standard for its clergy and
congregations, a large number of them nevertheless continued
to use the Small Catechism as included in its catechism,
thereby retaining some confessional consciousness within its
midst.

While other German catechisms did appear during this

period, only a few showed the influence of the current tendencies. Some in fact served as a reaction to the threat
against confessional Lutheranism and were even more confessional than the Ministerium catechism. The story of the
English catechism in the United States is quite different, as
will be shown later.

The following reprints of the 1785 copy up to 1850,
have been located:

> Germantaun: Leibert und Billmeyer, 1786. 2nd
> ed.
>
> Philadelphia: Carl Cist, 1786.
>
> Philadelphia und Lancaster: n.p., 1787. 1st ed.
>
> Germantaun: Michael Billmeyer, 1789. 3rd ed.
>
> Germantaun: Michael Billmeyer, 1790. 3rd ed.
>
> Philadelphia: Carl Cist, 1791.
>
> Chestnut Hill, [Pa.]: Samuel Saur, 1792.
>
> Germantaun: Michael Billmeyer, 1793. 4th ed.
>
> Philadelphia: Carl Cist, 1793.
>
> Germantaun: Michael Billmeyer, 1795. 4th ed.
>
> Philadelphia: Carl Cist, 1795.
>
> Philadelphia: Henrich Schweitzer, 1798.
>
> Germantaun: Michael Billmeyer, 1800. 5th ed.
>
> Philadelphia: Henrich Schweitzer, 1800.
>
> Germantaun: Michael Billmeyer, 1801. 5th ed.
>
> Philadelphia: Henrich Schweitzer, 1802.
>
> Germantaun: Michael Billmeyer, 1802. 6th ed.
>
> Germantaun: Michael Billmeyer, 1803. 7th ed.
>
> Philadelphia: Henrich Schweitzer, 1804.
>
> Germantaun: Michael Billmeyer, 1804. 8th ed.
>
> Ephrata, [Pa.]: J and R Johnston, 1805.
>
> Philadelphia: Carl Cist, 1805.
>
> Germantaun: Michael Billmeyer, 1807. 9th ed.
>
> Libanon, [Pa.]: Jacob Schnee, 1808. New ed.

Carlisle, [Pa.]:   F. Sanno, 1808.

Germantaun: Michael Billmeyer, 1809.   9th ed.

Philadelphia: Jacob Meyer, 1810.

Philadelphia: George W. Mentz, 1811.[16]

Philadelphia: Jacob Meyer, 1812.

Philadelphia: G. und D. Billmeyer, 1814.   10th ed.

Philadelphia: Jacob Meyer, 1814.

Philadelphia: G. und D. Billmeyer, 1815.   10th ed.

Baltimore: William Warner, 1815.   1st ed.

Chambersburg, [Pa.]:   Johann Herschberger, 1815. 1st ed.

Philadelphia: George W. Mentz, 1817.

Hagerstaun, [Md.]:   Gruber and May, 1819.

Baltimore: Schäffer und Mund, 1819.

Lancaster: n.p., 1820.

Canton, O.:   Jacob Sala, 1822.

Philadelphia: George W. Mentz, 1825.

Lancaster: Johann Bär, 1825.

Germantaun: M. Billmeyer, 1826.   11th ed.

Philadelphia: Conrad Zentler, 1828.

Lancaster: H. W. Villee, 1828.

Gettysburg: Heinrich C. Neinstedt, 1828.

Lancaster: Johann Bär, 1828.

Reading: G. A. Sage, 1829.

Harrisburg: Jacob Baab, 1831.

Philadelphia: G. W. Mentz und Sohn, 1833.

Philadelphia: G. W. Mentz und Sohn, 1836.

New York: Heinrich Ludwig, 1837.

Philadelphia: G. W. Mentz und Sohn, 1837.

Philadelphia: G. W. Mentz und Sohn, 1838.

Allentaun: A. und W. Blumer, 1839.

Lancaster: Johann Bär, 1839.

Philadelphia: G. W. Mentz und Sohn, 1839.

Philadelphia: G. W. Mentz und Sohn, 1841.

Philadelphia: Mentz und Rovoudt, 1843.

Philadelphia: Mentz und Rovoudt, 1844.

New York: Heinrich Ludwig, 1844.

New York: Heinrich Ludwig, 1845.

Philadelphia: Mentz und Rovoudt, 1845.

Philadelphia: Mentz und Rovoudt, 1846.

Philadelphia: Mentz und Rovoudt, 1847.

New York: Heinrich Ludwig, 1848.

Sumnytown, [Pa.]: Enos Benner, 1849.

Allentown: Blumer, Busch, and Leisenring, 1850.

Germantaun: C. Saur, n. d.

Pittsburgh: Robert Ferguson und Co., n. d.   1st
ed.

Philadelphia: Wm. G. Mentz, n. d.

Easton: Heinrich und Wilhelm Hütter, n. d.   1st
ed.

Baltimore: J. T. Hanzsche, n. d.[17]

Chapter IV

INDEPENDENT GERMAN CATECHISMS,
1786-1804

German catechisms and companion volumes to Luther's catechism continued to appear in print even though the Ministerium had published an official catechism by which it had hoped to bring about a degree of uniformity. The independent catechisms appearing during next decade or so, varied greatly in their confessional witness. Some were influenced by the early inroads of German Rationalism while others adhered more closely to the traditional Lutheran witness to the Gospel.

CATECHISM OF VALERIUS TSCHERNING (1786)

The first of the independent catechisms was a reprint of Valerius Tscherning's bulky catechism which had originally appeared in Heilbronn, Germany. Apparently there was some dissatisfaction with the format of the Ministerium's catechism. Instead of a catechism in the form of a source book containing a variety of expositions and orders of salvation, there must have been some who felt a need for a single but a more extensive explanation of Luther's Small Catechism. Some of the Lutherans who hailed from Württemberg, and perhaps those especially who came from Heilbronn, must have remembered the catechism of a former pastor there, Valerius Tscherning, published in 1755. Here was a catechism with which they had become familiar in their youth and no doubt some still used it privately in their homes. At any rate in 1786, the year after the publication of the Ministerium's catechism, there appeared an American reprint of this catechism.

> Valerius Tscherning. Catechism, or Brief Instruction for a Salutary Feeding of Souls, Explained and Confirmed with Evidence from Holy Scripture. Philadelphia: E. Ludw. Baisch, 1786.[1]

The Tscherning catechism, like the Darmstädtische
Catechismus which had preceded it, limited itself to a single
explanation of Luther's catechism, containing none of the
other materials customarily found in the catechisms in use
in America. Following the simple text of Luther, which was
expanded to Six Chief Parts to include the last two questions
of the traditional Office of the Keys and the Confession of
Sins after Baptism, Tscherning began his explanation of it.
The exposition was much broader, however, than Luther had
intended his catechism to be. Before Tscherning actually
unfolded his exposition he felt constrained to introduce the
material with five subsections, covering some 30 pages, on
Religion, God, the Marks of a Christian, Scripture, and the
Catechism. When he finally got to the First Chief Part, he
again paused to introduce it with some 103 far-extending
questions on the Law. Thus while the catechism purported
to be an exposition of Luther's catechism it was in fact a
systematic treatise on theology. Again, after addressing
himself to the Ten Commandments, he concluded that part
with two appendices, one on the Fulfillment of the Law and
another on the Correct Use of the Law. The Creed was introduced with a minimal number of questions, but the other
Chief Parts did not fare as well. The explanation of the
Lord's Prayer was preceded by a lengthy section on prayer
in general. Baptism afforded another opportunity for an extensive introduction plus an appendix on a baptism of fire
and of the cross, as well as a baptism for the dead. The
Lord's Supper was similarly treated. In his treatment of
this sacrament he spoke of three types of communion or
fellowship, between the elements and Christ's body and blood,
between the communicant and Jesus Christ, and the fellowship of all the communicants. The catechism concluded with
Christian Confirmation Questions in a brief appendix.

It is highly unlikely that this catechism was widely
used, for no further references to it have been found. It is
not listed in the existing bibliographies.

VELTHUSEN'S CATECHISM SERIES
PREPARED IN GERMANY FOR THE
CAROLINAS, 1787-1788

As stated earlier, Adolph Nüssmann had come to North
Carolina in 1773, upon the recommendation of the Hanover
Consistory. The year before his arrival, a delegation of two
laymen had been sent by some of the Lutherans in North

Carolina to seek a pastor and some financial aid.   The delegates were Christopher Rentelmann from Organ Church,
Rowan Co. and Christopher Layrle from St. John's Church,
Mecklenburg, now Cabarrus Co.[2]   On their way to Hanover
they stopped off in London.   Here John Caspar Velthusen,
who at the time was one of the two court preachers at the
Chapel of St. James, became deeply interested in the plight
of the German Lutherans in North Carolina and enlisted the
aid of the British king.   He in turn proclaimed a drive for
the purpose of collecting money for books and urged the Hanover Consistory to secure candidates to minister to the Lutherans in North Carolina.[3]   In time two men were enlisted.
One was Nüssmann and the other Gottfried Arend, a teacher.
Both agreed to serve in America and were sent by order of
King George III.

        Nüssmann entered his new ministry with an interest-
ing background.   He had been a member of the Franciscan
Order, though even as a Catholic preacher he had gained the
reputation of being "no strict papist."   After his change to
Lutheranism he studied at Göttingen and at the Teachers
Seminary in Hanover.[4]

        During his study of philosophy at Göttingen, Nüssmann
came under the influence of the Wolffian system that sought
to make philosophy and Christianity compatible to one another.
Chr. von Wolff of Halle (1679-1754), espoused the philosophy
that by use of logical methods of proof the essential truths
of Christianity, as he viewed them, could be proven and made
acceptable so that inevitably revelation and faith made way
for a natural theology.   While Nüssmann did not go the entire way that Wolff was ready to go, he was affected considerably by him.

        Soon after Nüssmann came to North Carolina, the
Revolutionary War broke out which cut off all American contacts with London and Hanover.   During this time Velthusen
accepted a professorship at the University of Helmstedt.
Finally, after an interval of more than ten years of forced
silence, contacts between Velthusen and Nüssmann were again
resumed in 1786.   In a letter of May 11, Nüssmann made a
strong plea for additional manpower and books.   In a graphic
manner he described the conditions of the Lutheran Church
where he was ministering.

        For the want of instructors and school teachers it
        has become completely degenerate, and must, if

> help does not come soon, revert completely to a
> state of heathenism.   Thousands of homes with nu-
> merous children know still less of it and the next
> generation will be veritable heathen.   There are no
> teachers there capable of instruction; and those
> which are there destroy more than they build up. [5]

The difficult conditions under which Nüssmann labored
prompted him further to make a request that had far-reaching
consequences.

> One more anxiety I have, which I must disclose.
> No greater vexation has amazed me than the vari-
> ous kinds of catechisms that are floating about here
> in this country.   God knows how anxious I am to
> educate thoroughly the youth of this place, especially
> those of the age for religious instruction.   The need
> is obvious, and much more urgent than in Germany.
> Poorly instructed children are at once led astray
> when they come in contact with unbelievers or with
> those of false beliefs.   In this country there ought
> to be a catechism which would stand up under the
> severest test, that might serve as a safe guide for
> the children, and one that would furthermore re-
> flect credit and honor wherever it was seen.   The
> most respected people of all congregations offer the
> same complaint; for the evil is obvious to all. [6]

He then continued,

> If you now wish to render a genuinely true service
> to our local youth as well as to the entire Evangel-
> ical Church of this section please formulate for us
> an entirely different catechism, have the same
> printed and send it to us.   In my humble judgment
> the arrangement might be as follows:
>   Part I: An introduction to the Christian doctrine,
> which would recount in story form the history of
> the Old Testament, the life-work of Jesus Christ
> and the more important events of the Christian
> Church, somewhat like Seiler's Catechism, [7] which
> was printed in Bayreuth in 1780, and which later
> accidentally came into my hands.
>   Part II: The fundamental truths of Christianity;
> perhaps according to the pedagogical methods of
> Mr. Jacobi, who is also very popular in your coun-
> try: however, without questions, which are not very

practical, and are furthermore exposed to the ridicule of the sectarians.

Part III: Moral teachings, repentance, faith, gratitude and duty, likewise according to Mr. Jacobi's method. The moral teachings should be paramount, should constitute the greater part, and should seem very obvious and pronounced. This would convince our sectarians that we are seriously concerned about a real Christianity.

The ten commandments might be related with some explanations in their proper place in the history of the Old Testament. Still you know all this better than I can tell you. Nevertheless I wanted in a measure at least to express my thoughts [on this matter]. But you may arrange this as it seems best to you. Since you are a Professor of Dogmatics and Ethics, and at the same time train students in the teaching of the catechism, this undertaking would fit well with your regular work, even though you should in the end have to compose an entirely new catechism; and to bring the love and religion of Jesus into the wilderness will certainly furnish you with inspiration. [8]

Nüssmann's letter prompted quick action on the part of Velthusen. He not only looked about for additional men to serve as missionaries but he also formed a mission society among the faculty members for the express purpose of helping the German Lutherans, especially by collecting books, and what was more urgent, for preparing suitable textbooks for the children.

Since Velthusen had already given some thought to the preparation of a catechism for the local Catechetical Institute and for the weekly instruction of the class being prepared for confirmation, he combined Nüssmann's request with his own needs. [9]

Keeping in mind Nüssmann's request that the text for the children contain only a few explanatory notes and consist primarily of quotable Bible passages and provide a "complete code of morals,"[10] Velthusen designed a set of five texts built around a single outline, namely three catechisms of varying degrees of difficulty, a question book for parents and teachers, and a list of Bible passages arranged topically.

The outline for the texts is significant, not only for its

contents and omissions, but for the obvious tendencies that it reflects. The outline comprised 22 "doctrines":

1. The existence of God.
2. The kindness, wisdom and might of God.
3. The holiness, truth and eternal justice of God.
4. The eternal changelessness, holiness, omnipresence, etc. of God.
5. The divine providence and care of God.
6. The immortality of the soul.
7. The higher revelation of God in the Holy Scriptures.
8. The commandments of God.
9. The angels.
10. The sin of mankind and its dire consequences.
11. The resolve of God to pardon mankind.
12. The adoration of Father, Son and Holy Ghost.
13. Redemption of mankind through the Son of God.
14. Repentance and faith.
15. Sanctification.
16. Death and eternity.
17. Obligations toward the Law of God.
18. Duties toward God.
19. Duties toward ourselves.
20. Duties toward our fellowmen.
21. Duties toward those close to us.
22. Baptism and the Lord's Supper.

Among the several textbooks published by the mission society, the following five by Velthusen are of special interest. Each of them was published in 1787, the year of Mühlenberg's death.

J. C. Velthusen's First Catechism with the Five Chief Parts. Leipzig, Siegfried Lebrecht Crusius, 1787.[11]

This was a 24-page booklet intended for small children prior to their going to school and was an extract of the larger catechism with a selected number of Bible passages. Appended to the booklet were the Five Chief Parts of Luther's catechism, but without his explanations. Five prayers were appended (thanksgiving, morning, school, table, and an evening prayer), none of which referred to the forgiveness of sins except the last one.

J. C. Velthusen's Second Catechism with Questions

> and with the Five Chief Parts and Luther's Explana-
> tions.   Leipzig: Siegfried Lebrecht Crusius, 1787.[12]

This was a 62-page booklet intended for children in
early years of school and beginning confirmation instruction.
It consisted of the doctrinal statements of the outline above,
interspersed with questions and answers in parentheses and
Bible passages.   It contained Luther's catechism with explanation.   Starred explanations of Luther's text were given as
footnotes.   Thus for example, the word "sacrament," was
explained to mean a religious rite wherein we solemnly pledged
ourselves to faith and obedience or faithfulness to God (p. 58).

> Helmstedt Catechism or Christian Religious Instruc-
> tion under the Guidance of Holy Scripture.   Leipzig:
> Siegfried Lebrecht Crusius, [1787].[13]

A second edition, identical in every way except for a
two-page introduction, was called the North Carolina Catechism (Nordcarolinischer Katechismus) and was printed the
following year, 1788.   The change in the title, according to
the introduction, was done in deference to Nüssmann.   Neither
edition included Luther's Small Catechism.

The Helmstedt and the North Carolina catechisms indicate clearly some of the rationalistic influences of the times.
While the catechisms still posited the Trinity, the eternal
Godhead of Christ, the virgin birth, and Jesus' resurrection,
they did not hesitate to make use of human reason to support
some of the articles of faith in a misguided effort to undergird the Scriptures.

Some of the following emphases will point up the general tendency of the two catechisms.   As an introduction to
the study of the Christian religion, the catechisms "proved"
the existence of God from the creation about us.   From there
they went to Scripture for a clearer knowledge of God.   Much
was made in the Question Book, to be explained later, of the
truth of natural religion and that of revealed religion.   In
fact, the first six doctrines of the outline were said to deal
with natural religion.[14]

Much was made of the immortality of the soul on the
basis of reason.   Similarly it was argued, that death could
not be the end of man's existence, especially for Christians.[15]
The soul therefore was immortal and had within it the poten-
tial of ever becoming better and more perfect which in the

Christian occurred when the body died and the soul went to
the Heavenly Father (p. 29).

Through Jesus' death and resurrection men were now
able to live the life acceptable to God.   The emphasis was
not on man being justified by grace but on his ability now to
live the desirable life before God.   Jesus became man in order to mediate mankind's forgiveness of sins (p. 18).

> He who would have a part in the redemption of Jesus
> Christ must recognize his most secret error and
> vice with sincere remorse and loathing.   At the
> same time, he must humbly recognize his deserved
> punishment before God.   The deeper the impression
> makes on his mind, while at the same time remem-
> bering the crucifixion of the Son of God, the more
> will his evil desire to repeat the wicked matter, be
> disarmed [p. 67].

According to the catechisms, "God does not promise
his grace in his word to anyone who does not have the earnest
desire to better himself" (p. 72).   Thus the emphasis was
placed on the Christian's desire to avoid sin and to improve
himself and so make himself fit for the gracious reward
[Gnadenlohn] (p. 76).   The Holy Spirit's task in all this was
to help and encourage us to fight evil and to do good works
(p. 74).

As the outline indicated, the Law became primarily a
guide to morality.   Thus a heavy emphasis was placed on
ethics or the duties of the Christian (17 through 21).

In the light of this, the sacraments were not means
of grace, as understood in the Lutheran Confessions, but
their purpose was to impress on Christians their obligation
to live virtuous lives and avoid every form of sin and vice
(p. 141). 16

> Question Book for Parents and Teachers or a Guide
> for Questions and Discussions concerning the Cate-
> chism with Consideration for the Differences in
> Abilities and Age of the Children, prepared by Jo-
> hann Caspar Velthusen.   Leipzig: Siegfried Lebrecht
> Crusius, 1787. 17

This was a 200-page book and, as the title indicated,
offered helps and hints to teachers and parents in teaching the

catechism. It contained also further theological explanations
to help teach the material to fit the lives of the children. It
suggested further questions at several levels of maturity (for
the ordinary child, the more gifted, and for the few youths
of extraordinary ability). Sometimes questions were suggested
for children with special problems, e.g. p. 137. The concern for individual differences among children was a strong
reaction to the prevalent practice of rote learning.

A second edition of the Question Book appeared in 1790,
which was considerably enlarged. 18

> J. C. Velthusen's Index of Bible Passages for the
> Catechism. Leipzig: Siegfried Lebrecht Crusius,
> 1787. 19

This was a 24-page booklet to help pastors and teachers by giving them a quick overview of the Bible passages
used in the catechism and so assist them in hearing memory
work. The passages were grouped according to the doctrinal
statements of the outline.

One of the suggestions to the teachers and parents in
the Question Book is of special interest. It suggested that
when going through the catechism with the children for the
first time, they should skip doctrines 7 through 14 and continue with 16 through 21 (dealing with the duties of Christians),
choosing only such topics which the children could understand
and apply to themselves. After that they should take up 8
through 15 and then continue with 22, dealing with the sacraments. They may finally close with 7, which dealt with
Scripture (p. 111). Thus the moralism of the catechism was
further highlighted.

These five books were in use in Helmstedt for some
time and were, according to the preface in the North Carolina
edition, well received in America. Specifically, Velthusen
there mentioned its use in Charleston, S.C. (St. John's),
where John Christopher Faber (1764-1818) ministered to a
Lutheran congregation made up not only of Lutherans, but
also Reformed and Roman Catholics, who according to Faber,
lived and worshiped together in peace. 20

The reports of the Helmstedt mission society indicated
that copies of these five texts were regularly sent to North
Carolina over a number of years. No record of any opposition to the texts has been found. This is especially strange

in view of Velthusen's sermon delivered in 1788, when he
ordained Carl August G. Storch for service in North Carolina. In the sermon he elicited the vow that Storch would
not preach and disseminate any doctrine "other than the pure
Evangelical [Lutheran] doctrine, such as are taken from the
Word of God and proclaimed among the followers of the Augsburg Confession here in Germany."[21] Obviously the Lutheran
pastors sent by the Hanover Consistory to the Carolinas saw
no conflict between the Lutheran Confessions and the catechisms that had been prepared for them. Even G. D. Bernheim and Geo. H. Cox make no comments concerning the
theological direction of the texts. Bernheim made references
to them but, judging from some of his allusions, it is very
probable that he personally had not seen them.[22] How widely
and how long the Velthusen catechisms were in use in North
Carolina is not known.

    As stated earlier, the Marburg Hymnal served both
Lutherans and Reformed congregations in South Carolina and
it is quite probable that its catechism was used by the Lutherans. There is no reference to the Velthusen catechisms
in the Constitution of the Union of Churches in South Carolina.

G. HENRY ERNST MÜHLENBERG,
ABRISS DER CHRISTLICHEN LEHRE,
1796 AND THEREAFTER

    In 1796 or earlier, G. Henry Ernst Muhlenberg (1753-
1815), the youngest son of the patriarch, while pastor at Lancaster, Pa., prepared a four-page tract titled, Epitome of
the Christian Doctrine for the Evangelical Youth.[23] Later
editions, all undated, one before G. H. E. Mühlenberg's death
and at least three afterward have the revised title, Epitome
of Instruction in the Christian Doctrine for the Evangelical
Youth.[24] These editions were used not only by Mühlenberg
but also by his successor Christian F. Endress (1775-1827).
After Mühlenberg's death editions were printed also for John
C. Baker (Becker) and S. Trumbauer and probably by others
in the Lancaster area.[25] Schmucker believes that the English
translation was prepared by Endress.[26]

    According to Schmucker, the text of the Abriss, or
Epitome, remained unaltered in later editions,

        but some citations of proof passages and hymns,
        and some initial capitals referring to sentences in

the Explanations, were added, both by the author,
and by those who used it after him in successive
editions.   How much earlier than 1796 it was prepared and the Abriss printed, we have not been
able to ascertain.   An account of his mode of instruction given in a letter to his father, April 2,
1785, Lancaster Memor. Vol. p. 67, shows that it
was then already much like that followed in this
Catechism, but does not seem to imply the use as
yet of an Abriss.[27]

The Abriss was a brief outline of 24 statements or
theses, some in the form of definitions, with Bible references
for proof and some references to hymns.   Apparently it was
to be memorized by the children.   The pastor or teacher used
with it an explanation and application, also prepared by Mühlenberg.   The exact title is not known.[28]   The English translation printed considerably later, in 1857, indicates its long
continued use.   It bore the title, A Companion to the Catechism, or A Course of Instruction in the Christian Religion.
The book contained the Abriss and an explanation and application of it.[29]   The latter consisted of 319 questions, the
answers to which are found either in the Abriss, the Bible
references or in Luther's catechism.   The Abriss and the
Companion followed the order of Luther's text, except that
the Ten Commandments were treated after the First Article
of the Creed.

The Abriss placed heavy emphasis on the Christian
life with a strong moralistic overtone.   Consequently the
clear Gospel message was somewhat muted by its emphasis
on man's obedience to God.   The only reference to the sacraments was their listing among the commands that "a true
believer will and should use all diligence to keep" (p. 21).

The explanation of the epitome found in A Companion
to the Catechism gave the pastor the opportunity to shift the
emphasis of the sacraments into a more correct perspective
by referring directly to Luther's text on Baptism and the
Lord's Supper.[30]

With this distortion of the meaning of the sacraments,
it was natural that both the Abriss and the Companion limited
the sanctifying power of the Holy Spirit to the preaching of
the Word of God.[31]

The earlier translation of the Abriss by Endress was

in general similar to that of F. A. Mühlenberg, though for
some unknown reason, Endress did omit Jesus' "sitting at
the right hand of God."[32]   There were some minor changes
also in the Bible and hymn references.   Endress did add a
free translation of Starcke's Hymn of Faith, as it had been
revised by Ziegenhagen.   Unfortunately Endress further weakened the sanctifying work of the Spirit in this hymn, leaving
further room for his Arminian tendencies.

GOEHRING'S ORDER OF SALVATION, 1798

In 1798, Jacob Goehring (1755-1807), [33] while pastor
at York, Pa. (1782-1807), issued his own order of salvation
to be used with his confirmands.   Goehring was regarded as
an outstanding preacher and was held in high esteem by his
colleagues, including Mühlenberg, who wrote in 1785 that he
had "a reputation of being orthodox in Evangelical Lutheran
doctrine, exemplary in life and conversation and uncommonly
diligent in studio theologico."[34]   His parsonage was described
as being a training center for pastors.   He had as many as
22 students in the course of his pastorate.[35]

The title of Goehring's order was,

The Socalled Order of Salvation, in Questions and
Answers, for Use by the Tutored.   York: Salomon,
Mäyer, 1798.[36]

The order was a series of 117 questions and answers, without Bible references, presumably to be memorized by the
children.   The questions served as an outline or summary of
what was to be learned in preparation for confirmation.   Like
most outlines the material lacked warmth.   The order con-
stantly divided and subdivided the articles of faith into logical
parts.   There were, for example, four states of man, four
parts to the state of grace, three offices of Christ, three
kingdoms of Christ, five steps in His humiliation and five in
His exaltation, four offices of the Holy Spirit and six gracious
acts of the Spirit.

The order began with the question, "Is the Christian
doctrine a divine or a human doctrine?"   Answer: "A divine
doctrine."   How many parts comprise the Christian doctrine?"
Answer: "Two parts.   The first part deals with God.   The
second with people."   Thereupon the order continued under
these parts.   The order was frequently very sparse in treat-

ing important parts of the Christian doctrine. Thus the word
"sacrament" was explained to mean in German an oath or an
obligation, after which the sacraments were simply mentioned
with no further attention given them. The church, too, was
simply mentioned. A distinctive Lutheran witness was seriously absent throughout the order.

The personal warmth for which Goehring was noted
was obviously not reflected in the order. The methodology
reflected in the order would certainly help lay the ground-
work in time for those who felt that confirmation should be
replaced by New Measures, or revivals. We must assume
that Goehring's lively presentation of the material compen-
sated somewhat for the cold systematic arrangement of the
order.

It is listed here among Luther's catechisms because
presumably it was intended by Goehring to be used alongside
of the Luther text, though we have no firm evidence that this
was normally the case.

THE MORAVIAN EDITIONS OF LUTHER'S CATECHISM, 1802 AND 1818

The Moravians had published the first 21 articles of
the Augsburg Confession without further explanations as early
as 1775.[37] In 1802, they printed Luther's Small Catechism,
also without explanation.

> The Small Catechism of Dr. Martin Luther. Bar-
> by: Conrad Schilling, 1802.[38]

With some minor exceptions the text was the same as
traditionally found among the Lutherans in America. Some
of the variations were in fact closer to the official text in
the Book of Concord than were the catechisms in use among
the Lutherans. It omitted, for example, the doxology in the
Lord's Prayer and the two paragraphs under the Table of
Duties, What Hearers Owe to Their Pastors and Of Subjects
which were later additions. The prayers at the end of the
catechism were limited to those found in the official text.
Lutherans frequently added a few traditional prayers or hymn
stanzas which were not written by Luther but were well known
among the Lutherans. The Moravian edition further omitted
the Office of the Keys but it did include the Christian Questions and Answers, wrongly ascribed to Luther. However,

the edition omitted the Confession of Sins that Luther did write.

Another print of this catechism appeared in 1818, printed by Conrad Zentler of Philadelphia.

LOCHMAN'S GERMAN CATECHISMS (1804-1821)

In 1804, John George Lochman (1773-1826), while pastor in Lebanon, Pa. (1794-1815), [39] prepared a German catechism for the children of his parish called,

> A Brief Summary of Christian Doctrine together with a Short History of the Church of the Old and New Testaments. Lancaster: Johann Albrecht, 1804. [40]

Lochman prepared this book in the form of statements which the children were to memorize. In it he advised parents and teachers, as they explained the material, to look up the Bible references with the children. Similarly the children were to sing the hymn stanzas. One hoped, Lochman said, this would help the children better to understand the Bible, the catechism and the sermons.

While the catechism made no reference to Luther's catechism, it may be assumed that Lochman had the Ministerium's catechism in mind, which did contain the Luther text. Neither the form nor the order of the material suggested a relationship with the Small Catechism.

The first edition, according to Schmucker, was printed in 700 copies. [41] In the subsequent editions the title was changed to The Chief Contents of the Christian Doctrine.... [42]

The catechism began with a brief introduction concerning religion in general. This was followed by two major parts: Concerning the Articles of Faith and The Christian Duties for the Christian in his Life. Part I began with statements on angels, man, Jesus Christ, the Holy Spirit, the means of grace, baptism (with an appendix on confirmation), the Lord's Supper, the order of salvation, prayer, and finally closing with a section on death, resurrection, judgment and eternal life. Part II began with a brief reference to the Ten Commandments, followed by sections on the duties toward

God, self and the neighbor.   Under the latter section the
Table of Duties was worked in.   An appendix referred to
one's duties toward animals.   Later editions subsumed this
under one's neighbor.   The final section dealt with means
for the improvement of one's moral life.   Slightly more than
a third of the catechism was thus devoted to moral theology.
The catechism closed with a 19-page history of the church
in the Old and New Testaments.   The latter part brought
the history up to date.

While the catechism reflected some influence from
European Rationalism by its emphasis on moral theology, it
did not deny any of the major tenets of Christian theology
even though its Gospel witness was dulled somewhat.

Besides the change in title, subsequent editions continued to make minor changes in the text.   Some of the statements were modified and the less relevant ones were omitted.
Occasionally the divisions were improved.   The number of
Bible references was cut back and the hymn stanzas were
frequently changed or omitted.   At the end of the catechism
text three full hymns, addressed to children, were added.
While minor changes were made in each of the revisions,
the fifth and final edition limited the changes to orthography.

The subsequent editions were,

The Chief Contents of the Christian Doctrine, together with a brief History of the Church.   Libanon: 1808.   2nd rev. ed. [43]

Philadelphia: Jacob Schnee, 1810.   3rd rev. ed.

Libanon: Joseph Schnee, 1813.   4th rev. ed.

Reading: Heinrich B. Sage, 1821.   5th rev. ed.

Chapter V

EARLY ENGLISH CATECHISMS,
1749-1811

The publication of English Luther catechisms in America had a very slow start and its history was quite different from that of the German catechisms. At first the latter had served to replace the wide variety of catechisms from the different state churches in Germany and with that they found their place on the American scene. As we have seen, over 40 German editions made their appearance during the 50 years after the first American print was published in 1749 under Lutheran sponsorship. They were needed to serve the estimated 122,000 Lutherans who were predominantly German and whose number was growing daily with the tide of immigration.[1]

In the face of such numbers the need for English Luther catechisms did not seem to be so urgent. The possible loss of the younger generation to the English-speaking denominations did not appear to be a serious threat. More seemed to be gained in the long run by holding on to the German than could possibly be won by surrendering to a language that most believed was unsuited to express the Lutheran faith. A few Lutherans of Swedish and Dutch descent from their own experiences did read the future correctly and they were instrumental in preparing the first catechisms. But there was no follow-up. It was not until near the turn of the century that the demand for English catechisms was heeded, first in the New York area and then for the cities of the mid-Atlantic states.

CATECHISM OF BRUNNHOLTZ AND KOCH (1749)

In 1749, the same year that the first German catechism was published in America by Lutherans, the first English translation of Luther's Small Catechism also appeared in print. Peter Brunnholtz, having become pastor in Philadelphia, was soon faced with the task of instructing the children of the Dutch, and especially Swedish Lutherans who were concerned that their English-speaking children would defect from the Lutheran Church. One of these was Henry Schleydorn, a Dutch merchant. Another was Peter Koch (Kok or Kock), a prominent Swedish merchant and a loyal supporter of Mühlenberg from the start. Koch was an officer of the Gloria Dei congregation and had been instrumental in allowing the Germans, after they first organized, to worship in the Swedish church. He had been one of the leaders in urging a union between the Swedish and the German Lutherans in 1744. [2]

Reporting to the authorities in Halle and to Ziegenhagen, Peter Brunnholtz wrote in a letter, April 11, 1749,

> I have instructed Mr. Schleydorn's son in English and confirmed him.... This summer I am preparing Mr. Koch's children in the same language, for which purpose Mr. Koch and I have caused to be printed Luther's Catechism translated into English, of which I transmit two copies. [3]

Schmucker concluded from this that Brunnholtz was assisted in the task by Koch and together they secured the publication of the catechism. [4]

It was probably printed by Benjamin Franklin, since his office printed the German catechism early in the same year.

> [Luther's Small Catechism, tr. by Peter Brunnholtz and Peter Koch. Philadelphia: Benjamin Franklin, 1749.]

No known copy of this catechism has been found and no further details are available. Whether the catechism contained only the Luther text or whether the Hymn of Faith or another order of salvation was included cannot be determined.

CATECHISM BY CARL M. DE WRANGEL (1761)

After years of neglect, the Swedish Lutherans in Philadelphia and vicinity finally began to make a greater effort in ministering to their English-speaking adherents. This began with the appointment of Dr. Carl Magnus de Wrangel (1727-

1786) as provost of all the Swedish Lutheran Churches in America in 1758. [5]   Among his many endeavors he started an English school in Wicaco (Philadelphia).   Under these circumstances de Wrangel soon saw the need for an English catechism.   Already in September 1760 he had urged the necessity of publishing a new edition of Luther's catechism in an improved translation for those who understood little or no Swedish or German. [6]   Acting on his own suggestion he revised the earlier translation which was then printed by Henrich Miller in 1761.   Included in the catechism was a translation of Starcke's Order of Salvation in a Short Table, which he used to great advantage in his congregation. [7]   A report of the new publication was made to the Preachers Conference of the United Swedish and German Ministerium in June 1762. [8]

The new translation was used in both the Swedish and German congregations.   On July 31, 1761, Mühlenberg wrote, "Visited the German printer Mr. Heinrich Mueller in the evening and paid £4 for several dozen copies of the English edition of Luther's Small Catechism." [9]   He recorded a similar purchase at a later time for the Yorktown congregation. [10]

On January 12, 1768, Henrich Miller advertised in his Der Wochentliche Pennsylvanische Staatsbote that he had available copies of The Rudiments of the Lutheran Catechism with an Abridgment of the Principles of Religion.   Similar notices appeared frequently in his newspaper during 1768, 1769 and the early part of 1770.   Presumably Miller was referring to de Wrangel's edition.   If this was the case we have a clue to the title since no other English translation is known to have existed at this time.   It may suggest, too, where Kuntze got the title for his 1785 catechism, which was strikingly similar.

With these data we may reconstruct the title as follows:

[The Rudiments of the Lutheran Catechism with an Abridgment of the Principles of the Christian Religion.   Tr. by Carl Magnus de Wrangel.   Philadelphia: Henrich Miller, 1761.]

Wrangel's catechism may well have been reprinted several times, for as late as 1780, Mühlenberg used an English catechism, very likely de Wrangel's, with a 19-year-old girl for instruction in the preparation of her baptism. [11]   No copy of the catechism is known to exist.

KUNTZE'S CATECHISM (1785)

John C. Kuntze left Philadelphia in 1784, to accept a
call to the parish in New York. He arrived in August soon
after the ratification of the treaty that established the American independence.[12] It wasn't long after his arrival that he
recognized the need to reintroduce the English services which
his father-in-law Mühlenberg had begun in 1751, but which
subsequently had been discontinued. Kuntze valiantly attempted
to preach in English himself but soon gave it up as too difficult.[13] He did, however, continue to instruct the children in
English and for this he prepared his own catechism with the
title,

> The Rudiments of the Shorter Catechism of Dr.
> Martin Luther. Appointed for the Instruction of
> Children and Young People. Published in English,
> Chiefly for the Use of those of the Lutheran Con-
> gregations in America. To which is Annexed, An
> Abridgment of the Principles of the Evangelical Re-
> ligion. Philadelphia: M. Steiner, 1785.

As soon as the first copies came from the printer,
Kuntze sent six copies to Mühlenberg,[14] who shared three of
them with J. Andreas Krug, a pastor in Frederick (Friedrichs-
stadt), Md.[15]

The new catechism was not, as sometimes stated, a
translation of Luther's catechism,[16] but as the title seemed
to imply, simply the elements of Luther's catechism. This
English rendition did not include Luther's explanation of the
Chief Parts. For the most part Kuntze merely reproduced
the Scripture citations in Luther's text according to the King
James version. Thus the Ten Commandments were a re-
statement of Exodus 20:1-7. The Lord's Prayer was taken
directly from Matt. 6:9b-13. The sections on Baptism and
the Lord's Prayer merely rendered the Bible passages which
Luther had quoted. The Creed was simply the rendition of
the Apostles' Creed without further explanation, though divided
into the three articles of faith. The Confession of Sins was
omitted. Therefore, nothing in the catechism was distinctly
from Luther except the general outline of the contents.

Kuntze's catechism contained also an order of salvation of some three and a half pages, An Abridgment of the
Principles of the Evangelical Religion. Whether this was
original with Kuntze or an adaptation of an earlier order can-

not be determined.   The similarity of the title might suggest
that Kuntze took it from de Wrangel's catechism.   The order
was a very sparse presentation in outline form, with Bible
references for each of the points made.   The abridgment
bore some similarity to the Order of Salvation in a Table by
Starcke which had been reprinted in earlier German catechisms.   However, the parallelism may be due to the similarity of the subject matter and the form that was followed,
rather than because of a direct relationship between the two.

The order had a strange term taken directly from the
Latin, for what was usually called Christ's state of humiliation, namely "exinanition." As was done in other orders of
salvation, prayer was listed as a means of grace, together
with "Using the Word of God (Law and Gospel)" and the sacraments (pp. 13-14).

Kuntze's catechism was not widely used and in 1795,
he replaced it with another translation which was more faithful to Luther's text.

KUNTZE-STREBECK CATECHISM (1795)

John C. Kuntze's second attempt to prepare a much
needed English translation of the catechism fared better than
the first.   This time he was assisted by George Strebeck for
whom the English language was no obstacle.[17] Strebeck had
been brought up as a Lutheran in Baltimore but had become
a Methodist itinerant preacher.   Because of his desire to
serve the Lutheran Church he was called to New York in
1794, as an assistant pastor.   Soon thereafter he passed his
examination and was ordained by the New York Ministerium
in 1796.[18]

"Catechism"--Appendix to A Hymn and Prayer-Book
for the Use of the Lutheran Churches as use the
English Language.   Collected by John C. Kunze.
New York: Hurtin and Comardinger, 1795.

As noted in the title, Kuntze's catechism was appended
to a hymn and prayer book, the first English hymnal for Lutherans in America.   The book contained some 239 hymns
which Kuntze had collected.   In addition it included the first
English translation of the Pennsylvania Agenda of 1786.   The
catechism section comprised pages 88 through 150 and comprised seven parts.

The special significance of this catechism is in the
fact that it became the basis in 1804, of the catechism authorized by the New York Ministerium, the first official English catechism in America.

The minutes of the New York Ministerium in 1803,
suggest that the Kuntze-Strebeck catechism had also been
printed separately in at least one other edition.[19]

1. Luther's Catechism

The most important part of the catechism was the new
translation of Luther's catechism (pp. 88-100). Unlike Kuntze's
attempt in 1785, it included Luther's full explanation. The
merit of the new translation may be seen, as Schmucker
pointed out, in the fact that "fully half of the text has attained
the shape which it has retained ever since."[20] The second
article of the Creed is probably the best example of this.
Nevertheless some of the wording sounds strange to the modern ear. In the second commandment the translation has
"incantate," for "use witchcraft" or "zaubern" (p. 88). Baptism is referred to as "a graceful water of life" and "the
love of regeneration in the Holy Ghost." The latter was corrected to read in an 1802 catechism as "laver of regeneration," which was undoubtedly what Strebeck had in mind.

There was one striking change in the Luther text.
Each of the explanations of the commandments inverted Luther's order of, "We should fear and love God" to read, "We
should so love and fear God."

The catechism omitted the paragraph in the Lord's
Supper that dealt with the benefits of such eating and drinking. In view of the content this seems to have been done
inadvertently. It was restored in the New York Ministerium
edition, on which publication committee both Kuntze and Strebeck served.

The Office of the Keys and Confession of Sins were
not a separate part but followed the Lord's Supper. This
section concluded with Questions and Answers for Those who
would Prepare themselves to go the Sacrament. Surprisingly,
Kuntze omitted the word "true" in the question, "Dost thou
believe that the true body and blood of Christ are in the sacrament?", thus setting a pattern for later translations. The
basic Luther text was the same as that of the Pennsylvania

catechism, using the same rendition of the Office of the Keys but omitting the Table of Duties. [21]

2. Fundamental Questions

Luther's catechism was followed by Fundamental Questions (pp. 100-106). These appear to have been original with Kuntze. They have not as yet been found in any of the earlier German catechisms nor in any of the later editions. They were included in the New York Ministerium catechism of 1804. As Schmucker has suggested, they seem to have been intended as a resume "of what had been learned from the catechism and its Scripture references."[22]

Written with the pattern of an order of salvation in mind, the questions and answers followed in logical sequence. This was prompted no doubt by the criticism of those who were being influenced by the encroaching Deism of the day. The order began with a very general question, "How many religions are in the world?" and then narrowed to the Christian and the Lutheran religion. From there the questions proceeded, as did some of the other orders, with God, creation, the Fall, the consequences, the redemption of Jesus Christ, the Holy Ghost, the means of grace, Scripture (O. and N. T.), Law, Gospel, the sacraments, heaven, resurrection, and judgment.

Unfortunately the Lutheran thrust became somewhat fuzzy as the questions broke up the several articles of faith. Room was left for synergism and there was an alarming mixture of Law and Gospel. The following questions and answers point this up:

> Q. 57: What must we do in order to receive faith from the Holy Ghost?
> A. Desire it and pray for it.

> Q. 70: What is the law?
> A. The will of God, concerning those things we ought to do.

> Q. 71: What is the gospel?
> A. The will of God, concerning those things we ought to believe.

> Q. 72: What does save us, the law or the gospel?
> A. The gospel.

Q. 75: Ought we learn the law, although it represents the wrath of God?
A. Yes, because it leads to the knowledge of
sin.

Q. 76: Why is the knowledge of sin necessary for
our salvation?
A. Because it leads us to repentance, the first
part of conversion.

The pietistic idea that man does something in baptism
was still present:

Q. 87: What are we doing in Baptism?
A. We make a covenant with God and God with
us.

3.   Order of Salvation in Systematical Connection

This section (pp. 106-110) is the same as the Order
of Salvation in a Table, taken from Starcke, found in the
earliest German catechisms and retained in the catechism of
the Pennsylvania Ministerium.   As mentioned previously this
order had already been translated by de Wrangel for his 1761
catechism.   Whether Kuntze-Strebeck took over this translation or worked over a new one is not known.   At any rate,
one major change is contained in this version of Starcke's
order, and that an unfortunate one.   As noted earlier, Brunnholtz had adopted a changed text in his 1752 edition that had
left room for synergism.[23]   The translation now took this
change one step farther, allowing for some cooperation of the
natural man for his obtaining salvation.   The change now read,

The remaining strength of our free will, which we
have by nature, is not adequate to salvation. 1 Cor.
2:14. Such, however, as apply it well, will be led
to the means. Acts 10, Eph. 5:14 [p. 108].

Subsequent English translations of this order followed
the lead, so that the change became a part of the English
catechetical literature for some time.

4.   The Christian Duties

This section (pp. 110-113) too may have been added by

Kuntze to meet a criticism of the day that Christianity was
more concerned with dogma than it was with life itself. The
list of duties much like Velthusen's catechism, was arranged
as follows,

> Duties towards God and our Lord Jesus Christ
> Duties toward Ourselves
> Duties toward Others.

The similarity to Velthusen's rendition may be seen
throughout the material though Kuntze did not hesitate to re-
arrange the data or to substitute other Bible references as
he saw fit. With some modifications, he combined Velthusen's duties "to those living close to us," under the latter
part of "Toward others."

5.   A Short Account of the Christian Religion

This (pp. 113-134) was not simply a historical sketch
of the Christian Church but a theological defense of the Christian religion against detractors of the time. This may be
seen from the opening paragraph.

> We daily see things rise, which were not before,
> and we ourselves were not a few years hence.
> This leads us to a supposition, that there is an
> author of all things, who always was and whose be-
> ing is necessary. In contemplating the affairs of
> this world, we discover footsteps of his government
> and in the order of things, the change of seasons,
> the motion of heavenly bodies, the provision for
> wants and necessities, his omnipotence, wisdom
> and benevolence are discoverable. This being we
> call God.

From this argument for the existence of God, he found
a purpose for life and the thought of another and never-ceasing
life after the present one. "The Christians are people, who
claim a certainty in the knowledge of these things from historical accounts." This led him to give his historical account
of mankind from the Fall to the founding of the church. This
was followed by an account of the Christian religion, what life
in the church means, baptism, worship, and sacrifice (the
Lord's Supper), order and discipline.

The account was hardly suitable for children and probably not for most adults.   It was evidently intended to furnish arguments in behalf of the Christian religion against encroaching Deism.

6.   A Short Account of the Lutheran Church

This (pp. 134-143) was a more historical account than the previous section but it too attempted to explain some of the past animosities between Christians, including the "two protestant Churches."   But the reader was assured "that such times are past," which should bring great joy.   The present great need "which likewise ought not to be concealed" is that the evangelical church "stands highly in need of a new and energetic revival and it is doubtful in many cases whether the present union of the two Churches, which however every true Christian will wish to be indissoluble, is to be derived from enlightenment notions or worldly interest, from brotherly love or from indifference."

7.   The Seven Penitential Psalms

The final section comprised The Seven Penitential Psalms (pp. 144-150).

THE "ENDRESS" CATECHISM (1802)

Dr. Martin Luther's Catechism for Children and Young People.   Philadelphia: Henry Sweitzer, 1802.

This rendition of Luther's Small Catechism was a revision of the Kuntze-Strebeck catechism but was much more free in its rendition than the original warranted.   This is evident especially in the Creed and more particularly in the Second Article where the translator omitted the last two clauses of Luther after "live with him in his kingdom."   In an effort to keep away from Luther's repetitive but simple, "What is that?" in the explanation of the Ten Commandments, the translator varied the question, but in a less simple way, with such questions as, "What is the import of this commandment?", "What is the signification of" the commandment?, and the instruction, "Explain this commandment."

Furthermore the translator did not hesitate to make additions if he felt they were needed.   Each of the Five Chief

Parts of Luther's catechism was introduced with one or more
transitional questions.

At the end of the section on Baptism, he also added
four questions and answers to help distinguish between adult
and infant baptism.   They were no doubt added to ward off
the criticisms of the Baptists who actively spoke out against
infant baptism and who were regarded a serious threat to
English speaking Lutherans.   A similar concern was reflected
in a number of catechisms of this period.

Q. 1: What do we receive in Baptism?
A.   The Holy Ghost--wherefore it is regeneration
to such as do not and such as cannot resist his
operation therein.

Q. 2: Who are those who do not resist the Holy
Ghost in Baptism?
A.   Such adults as are sincere and upright of heart
therein.

Q. 3: Who are those who cannot make this resistance?
A.   Infants--wherefore we infer the propriety of
infant Baptism from this argument.

Q. 4: From what do you further prove the propriety of infant baptism?
A.   1.   From the institution of baptism in the
Christian Church; of which children were the proper
subjects, see Collos. ii. 11, 12.
        2.   From their right of Church membership.
Our Lord declares, Mark x. 14, that "Of such is
the kingdom of God"; wherefore, if they are proper
members of the Church, they are proper subjects
for all her ordinances of which they are capable.

In connection with the Lord's Supper the translator
dropped the word "true" in the answer to the question, "What
is the Sacrament of the Lord's Supper?"   Hence he had Luther simply say, "It is the body and blood of our Lord Jesus
Christ."   This omission was welcomed by those of the Reformed tradition who denied the sacramental presence.   The
omission was perpetuated in the catechisms of the New York
Ministerium, Philip F. Mayer, the General Synod, as well
as others.

In general this catechism bore no major resemblance

to the later New York Ministerium catechism of 1804, though
it is evident that the Ministerium's committee had its Luther
text before them and at times were influenced by the translation.

The catechism did not include the Office of the Keys,
the Confession of Sins, the Christian Questions and Answers,
nor the Table of Duties.

The second part of this catechism contained a translation of Freylinghausen's Order of Salvation from the Pennsylvania catechism, without identifying it as such.   The title
simply stated, "Additional Questions setting forth the true
Way to Salvation."   This was the earliest English translation
of the Freylinghausen order.   The translation followed the
text pattern of the earliest editions of the Pennsylvania catechism which was somewhat less Pietistic than the two later
patterns.   As with Luther's text, the editor took some liber-
ties with the material and frequently used different Bible references than Freylinghausen did.

The third part of the catechism contained the Seven
Penitential Psalms.   These were followed by a 37-page section titled, "Hymns and Prayers for the Use of Schools."

The name of the editor was not given in the catechism.
Schmucker has suggested that Christian F. Endress was the
author also of this catechism, as well as the translator of
G. H. E. Mühlenberg's Abriss, described earlier.[24]   Endress
had been engaged as an English teacher and some time principal of the large parish school of Zion and St. Michael's in
Philadelphia until 1801.[25]   As such he was both capable and
interested in preparing a catechism for children and young
people.

NEW YORK MINISTERIUM CATECHISM (1804)

Though two English translations of Luther's catechism
had been printed in recent years, the pastors in the New York
area apparently experienced considerable difficulty in procur-
ing copies.   Furthermore, the textual variations were a source
of irritation for both parents and congregations associated with
the Ministerium since English was an accepted medium of instruction and worship.   Consequently it was resolved at a
meeting of the Ministerium, October 10, 1803, that a committee be elected "to prepare and issue a new edition of Luther's
catechism in the English language which may be generally ac-

cepted." John C. Kuntze, Frederick H. Quitman, and George
Strebeck were requested to undertake this assignment. The
synodical treasury was to bear the cost and receive the profit
of the publication.[26]

At the next meeting, September 1804, the committee
reported that the catechism was not ready for review and
publication because Strebeck had withdrawn from the Ministerium and had joined the Episcopal Church and had published
a catechism of his own for his congregation.[27]

Later during the meeting it was again resolved that the
English catechism be revised by the Ministerium and "that
Messieurs Frederick H. Quitman and Philip F. Mayer, be a
committee to prepare it for the press and procure its publication" and, "that this Catechism be exclusively introduced
into all our churches for the instruction of those who make
use of the English language."[28]

Young Mayer's membership on this committee was
somewhat unusual and was no doubt due to Kuntze's influence,
whose place he took. Mayer was only 23 at the time. He
had been ordained the previous year, October 10, 1803, and
was now, on Kuntze's recommendation, at his first charge
at Loonenburgh (Athens), N.Y.[29] His initiation into this task
proved to be a valuable experience for such a time when he
would prepare English catechisms of his own.

With the committee's revision completed, the catechism was printed at Hudson, N.Y., which was across the
river from where Mayer was pastor. Apparently the final
details of seeing the catechism through the press was Mayer's
responsibility. This was the first catechism officially authorized by the New York Ministerium.

> Dr. Martin Luther's Catechism. Translated from
> the German. A New Edition of the Evangelical Lu-
> theran Church in the State of New York. Hudson:
> Henry Croswell, 1804.

The new catechism was in fact a revision of the Kuntze-
Strebeck catechism of 1795. How much the original committee
had finished before Strebeck left is not known though the time
element suggests that most of the work was likely completed.
Nevertheless it does appear that Quitman's influence left its
mark on the latter section. Already at this time Quitman's
confessional witness was murky. Nicum suggests that Kuntze's

presence on the committee as author of the 1795 catechism
and as Senior of the Ministerium prevented Quitman from
becoming more outspoken in his non-Lutheran views.   Nicum
senses Kuntze's concern, for at the 1806 meeting shortly before his death, he expressed his dissatisfaction with the non-
confessional spirit that was permeating the Ministerium. [30]

In general the new catechism followed the Luther text
of Kuntze-Strebeck with some variations, most of them of
minor import.   In the Second Commandment the awkward
"incantate" (for zaubern) became "or use it as a charm."
In a number of instances it is clear that the committee consulted also the 1802 catechism.   This was evident particularly with the omission of "true" in the definition of the
Lord's Supper. [31]

If Mayer's later catechism of 1806 may be used as a
guide his influence on the committee is clear.   Several of
the linguistic changes in the 1804 edition were accepted by
Mayer's catechism.

The remaining sections of the authorized catechism
were the same as the Kuntze-Strebeck edition except the accounts of the Christian religion and of the Lutheran Church,
the prayers and the hymns, which were omitted.   The new
catechism concluded with the Seven Penitential Psalms.

The most significant changes in the text of the authorized catechism were in Kuntze's Fundamental Questions.   In
addition to a number of minor linguistic changes and the addition of several questions, the most serious revision was
the omission of Question 94, which asked, "Is the body and
blood of Jesus Christ really present in the Lord's Supper?"
and its answer, "Yes, because there is a communion."   In
view of future events this omission undoubtedly reflected
Quitman's influence.

Ironically, what was no doubt a printer's error, Question 102 was made to read, "What will be the final state of
those, who live ungodly and with [sic] faith?"   To which the
answer was given, "They shall be consigned to eternal damnation with soul and body."   While Quitman did, at least later,
deny that unbelievers were consigned to eternal damnation,
one can hardly attribute this wording to him.   If there were
later printings of this edition, this error may have been corrected. [32]   Pastor A. T. Braun, who in 1811 reprinted large
portions of this catechism, including the Fundamental Questions, did have a corrected version of this question. [33]

The translation of Starcke's order of salvation from
Kuntze-Strebeck was quite generally adopted except for an
additional listing under the means of grace as part c.: "The
confession and the office of the Keys of the Kingdom of Heav-
en, considered as connected with the use of the Lord's Supper and as a preparation for worthily receiving it.   Matt.
xvi, 19.   Luke x, 16.   John xx, 22.23."

No changes were made among the Christian Duties except the addition, "Duties toward animals" and the fact that
all Bible references were printed as a convenience to the
learners.

Apparently the new catechism as authorized by the
Ministerium was at first well received by many.   After two
years only 362 copies remained unsold out of a printing that
probably did not exceed a thousand. [34]   However, the authorized catechism did not keep others from publishing their own
as the Ministerium had hoped.

ENDRESS' ENGLISH PENNSYLVANIA CATECHISM (1805)

Not until 1805, did an English translation of a major
portion of the Pennsylvania Ministerium catechism appear on
the scene.   The overwhelming use of the German in Pennsylvania did not create a demand for an English version.   Only
as individual congregations faced up to the need of English
were catechisms prepared.   The translation of 1805 was prepared by Christian Endress, then pastor at Easton, who produced it for the use of his congregation and "those annexed
to it."   While his name did not appear in the catechism, a
misprint prompted him to append a note to it as a preface,
which gives a clue that he was the author. [35]

> The Shorter Catechism by Dr. Martin Luther, with
> The customary Family Prayers.   To which is added
> The Order of Salvation in Nine Short Sections and
> by Questions and Answers, etc.   Easton: Jacob
> Weygandt & Co., 1805.

Endress' catechism included the following sections of
the Pennsylvania catechism: Luther's Small Catechism with
all the additions, the Order of Salvation in Nine Short Sentences, the order "In short and simple Questions and Answers" and the hymn, "Steh armes Kind."

There was little resemblance between this catechism and that of the 1802 edition, whose translation has been attributed to Endress. This may be explained by the fact that here he was trying to reproduce faithfully major portions of the Pennsylvania catechism for his congregation. A few differences, however, should be noted. Endress again tried to vary Luther's repeated, "Was ist das?," from a literal, "What is that?" of the 1795 edition to such variations as, "What is enjoined upon us in...?" "What is required of us...?" or "What is intended by this commandment?" to mention a few. Admittedly these variations were somewhat smoother than his more stilted questions in the 1802 edition.

Following the lead of the previous English translations, the Third Commandment was changed to conform to Exodus 20, "Remember the Sabbath Day to keep it holy."[36]

The NOTA, attributing the Questions and Answers for those Desiring Commune to Luther, was omitted. Some changes were made in the Table of Duties. The section on "Wives" was shortened to a simple quotation from Eph. 5, 22, thus omitting the quotation from 1 Pet. 3, 6. The paragraph on "Christians in General" was omitted entirely, together with the two-line rhyme usually found at the close of the Table of Duties.

The prayers and the Order of Salvation in Nine Sections were substantially the same in the Pennsylvania catechism. However, the order containing the series of Short and Simple Questions and Answers was reduced by nine questions without substantially changing the meaning.

PHILIP F. MAYER'S CATECHISM (1806-1814)

The origin of this English catechism stemmed from a heated controversy when an effort was made to introduce an English service in the mother church in Philadelphia, St. Michael's-Zion. While the problem was not new, the turn of the century had brought with it a growing desire for English by some and a consequent insistence by others that German remain the sole medium of worship.

The question at this point was not whether to eliminate German but whether an English service might be added and whether the instruction of the catechumens might be in English for those who preferred it.

Unlike New York, where the problem had more or less been decided earlier, [37] the Pennsylvania Lutherans were more tenacious in holding on to the German. This was largely due to the fact that there were many more Germans in Pennsylvania, especially in the rural areas where they had congregated in large numbers so that the need for English did not appear as great.

When the demand for English was made, as for example in Philadelphia, it was at first usually a request simply for an additional service in English. Such a request was often countered with the observation that this was not necessary since everyone could or should learn German and this would eliminate the need for English.

The strong desire on the part of the pastors and congregations to maintain the German language had prompted the Pennsylvania Ministerium to change its name, with the acceptance of a revised constitution in 1792, to "The German Evangelical Lutheran Congregations in Pennsylvania and the Adjacent States." [38]

The reason for or against the use of English varied with the individuals or the locale. In many instances there were in fact a combination of reasons. Those holding for the introduction of the English language usually argued that English was needed to preserve the youth for the Lutheran witness. They pointed to the serious losses, either to the Episcopalians and the Presbyterians, or what was more serious, losses to the church as a whole. They saw the trend to Americanize as a reality and a necessity to be met by the introduction of English so that Lutheranism would survive the change.

There were, of course, some who did not regard the change over to the Episcopalians or the Presbyterians as a threat to Lutheranism. As far as they were concerned the doctrinal differences were minimal. In fact some even referred to them as English Lutherans.

Some of those who insisted on the sole use of the German language among Lutherans regarded this to be necessary for the survival of Lutheranism. They argued that the English language was too weak to reflect the true spirit of Lutheranism. They further argued that the German hymns, liturgy and the devotional literature could not communicate as well in translation.

Still others regarded the English people as too shallow, frivolous and less pious than the Germans. Consequently they feared that these traits would soon become characteristic of English-speaking Lutherans. Thus they were appalled at the losses suffered by the Swedish Lutherans in Philadelphia and along the Delaware River to the English-speaking churches.

Perhaps equally as strong as the fear that confessional Lutheranism would be weakened was the concern by others that it would mean a loss of their German heritage and culture. Hence the strong desire to retain the German language brought the Lutherans more closely together with the German Reformed and the Moravians. The language bond was stronger than the confessional heritage. German-speaking Reformed might be preferred to English-speaking Lutherans. The Rev. J. H. C. Helmuth, pastor at St. Michael's Church, vehemently opposed the introduction of English in his congregation while at the same time was intimate with the German Moravians in the area. Thus his opposition to English cannot be attributed exclusively to a desire to remain confessional. In fact it has been said that Helmuth's aversion to explicit theological definitions stemmed from his close contacts with the Moravians.[39] Some of the strongest opposition to the introduction of English naturally came from the union churches in rural Pennsylvania.

Such were the differences that finally came to a boiling point by 1803 in St. Michael's-Zion congregations in Philadelphia. Led by General Peter Mühlenberg,[40] president of the association that governed the two congregations, the English party asked that English services be introduced and that a pastor be called to minister in English. The congregation voted the request down.[41]

This did not bring an end to the matter. The problem was brought to the Ministerium, where Helmuth was president. Here the English party lost again. In fact the petition triggered a resolution to supplement the constitution saying that the Ministerium must remain a German-speaking body and that no regulation may be adopted which would introduce another language in the meeting. Delegates of English-speaking congregations could join after an examination but they, too, would have to speak in German in addressing the synod.

This was by no means the end of the dispute. In fact it grew sharply. The matter was again brought to a vote on January 6, 1806, when some 1400 votes were cast by the association of the two congregations. The German party won by some 130 votes.[42]

As a result the English party withdrew to form a separate congregation which was named St. John's. In time they called Philip F. Mayer from Loonenburgh, N.Y., who accepted. He retained his membership in the New York Ministerium throughout his life.

Soon after taking charge of St. John's in October, Mayer proposed to the board of officers that they publish an English catechism. He saw this as one of several ways to minister to the congregation, especially to the youth, without a major loss. The committee of the board gave a favorable report and in November 1806, the new catechism was printed.[43]

Mayer vigorously pursued the instruction of the children in the new catechism on Sunday afternoons, some two to three hundred in number, so that by Maundy Thursday, 1807, he confirmed 139.[44] Small wonder that the first edition of 1,000 copies sold out in a very short time, necessitating a second printing in 1807.

> [Dr. Martin Luther's Catechism. Translated from the German. Philadelphia: John Geyer, 1806.]
>
> Philadelphia: John Geyer, 1807.
>
> Philadelphia: Conrad Zentler, 1814.

No copy of the 1806 edition has been located. The title page was taken from the 1807 edition.[45]

The catechism contained five sections:

1. Dr. Luther's catechism (pp. 3-15), without the Office of the Keys and the Confession. It was largely based on the New York Ministerium catechism, on which committee Mayer had served, except in a few minor instances. Mayer also varied Luther's "What is that?", to introduce the explanations to the Ten Commandments, as had already been done in the 1802 catechism. In some instances Mayer went on his own, though he did retain the awkward, "What is the signification of this commandment?"

2. Questions and Answers for those who would Prepare Themselves to receive the Lord's Supper (pp. 16-19). These were the same as translated by Kuntze-Strebeck in 1795, with only a few minor linguistic changes.

3. Starcke's Order of Salvation in a Short Table,

called here The Order of Salvation In Systematical Connection
(pp. 19-25). This was substantially the same as the translation by Kuntze-Strebeck and the New York catechism, including the faulty addition found in all previous English translations relative to man's free will in his natural state. However, Mayer did change the previous translation by omitting
the reference to the Office of the Keys and confession as belonging to the sacrament.

4. The Christian Duties (pp. 25-29). This section
retained the Bible passages without the traditional headings.

5. Prayers and hymns for the use of children (pp.
30-34). This section included prayers and three hymns suitable for private and home devotions.

Mayer's Notes on the Order of Salvation

The obvious fact that the text used by an instructor to
teach the youth may not accurately reflect what was actually
taught is illustrated by the dictated notes that Mayer used in
teaching Starcke's Order of Salvation, section 3, of his own
catechism. A set of such notes, dated 1808, has been found
with his 1807 catechism.[46] They posit a theological viewpoint not always in harmony with his own catechism. The
notes are in the form of dictated questions and answers built
on the order and its Bible references.

Mayer's elaborations frequently reflected the current
effort to use rational arguments in support of Scripture. Thus
to the request, "Please to state [sic] some principle [sic] arguments which prove the immortality of the soul," the student
was to say, "The high powers and faculties of the human soul.
2. The imperfect distribution of rewards and punishment in
this life. 3. The expectations and desires which god [sic]
has implanted in the human soul. 4. Our great abhorance
[sic] of annihilation; the universal concent [sic] of mankind."

More "proofs" are set forth in behalf of the truth of
Christianity with such arguments as "the miracles of Christ,
his prophecies, the divine [sic] purity of his character, the
intrinsic excellency of his Religion." Again, "proofs" are
later offered for infant baptism: the nature of the Institution,
Christian Prudence, the Acts of the Apostles, and the first
history of the Christian Church.

The instruction, "Prove why Christ's state was a state

of Humiliation," brought the response, "In order to suffer
and thereby to give us a more perfect model of virtue,"
though elsewhere Christ's redemptive work came through
clearly.   Included in Christ's humiliation was his descent
into hell, though the order itself had listed it under Christ's
state of exaltation.

After stating that we were made partakers of Christ's
redemption by being called into the church, the question was
asked, "Does this infer that all those which have not been
called within the pale of the Church, shall not be saved?";
the answer was, "No," and then explained that they will be
judged, "By the light of nature," but this was not to under-
value our own "privileges."

While Starcke's order called "taking up the cross and
prayer" auxiliary means of grace, Mayer placed them on a
par with the word and sacraments.   To the question, "How
does prayer become to us a means of grace?" the answer
was, "It exercises us in Christian graces and virtues, and
thereby renders us proper objects of divine [sic] favour."

After defining a sacrament with "It is an outward and
visible sign and pledge of spiritual grace ordained by Christ
himself," baptism was described correctly as the sacrament
"by which we are emissiated [sic, for "initiated"?] into the
Christian Church."   Luther was cited in connection with it.

The value of the Lord's Supper was weakened with the
description, "It is that Sacrament in which we profess our
continuance in the Christian Church."   Though Luther's catechism was quoted, the emphasis throughout was placed on
what the communicant was doing by participating in the sacrament.

Mayer's notes present an interesting sidelight.   They
clearly indicate how much liberty even a man like Mayer
could take with the text the children had before them.

REPRINTS OF MAYER'S CATECHISM (1811 AND 1819)

Apparently at least two unauthorized reprints were
made of Mayer's catechism, one in Frederick, Md., in 1811,
and another in Hagerstown, Md., in 1819.   Who sponsored
these reprints is not known.   Apparently an English catechism was needed in these places and someone printed it on
his own.

Fredericks-town: Matthias Bargis and Son, 1811[47]

This edition had only two minor changes.   It added
three questions to Questions and Answers for those Preparing for the Lord's Supper after the question, "Is it thy hope
to be saved?"

> What are the constituents of a well founded hope?
> True repentance and faith.
>
> What do you understand by repentance?
> A total change of the heart and mind.
>
> What is faith?
> It is the substance of things hoped for, and the
> evidence of things not seen.

In Starcke's Table several Bible references under the
nature of God were added.

Hagers-town: Gruber and May, 1819[48]

This reprint retained the three questions mentioned
above but made additional changes by restructuring Starcke's
Order of Salvation from its table form to a series of questions and answers without thereby changing the contents.   In
fact, it was more readable than the original structure had
been.

The sponsor of this reprint explained parenthetically
the meaning of "hell" in the Second Article of the Creed as
being "the place of the departed spirits" and repeated this
when speaking of Christ's state of exaltation.

The fifth section of the catechism was entirely revised.
He omitted all the prayers and hymns and substituted ten
hymns of his own.   He further enlarged the number of Bible
passages which served as the Table of Duties by adding 17
passages, though all could not be regarded as "duties," e.g.
Matt. 3:17; John 1:29; and 1 John 2:12.

JOHN SCHMUCKER'S CATECHISM, C. 1804

> John George Schmucker, "Catechism for the Use of
> those who prepare for Confirmation," MS, 26pp.

This catechism, though not a published edition, was used over a long period of time by John G. Schmucker during his ministry. It was apparently used by him while both at Hagerstown (1795-1809) and at York (1809-1836). He customarily dictated the material to his catechumens or permitted them to make a copy from one of his manuscript copies.[49]

The catechism comprised a series of 240 questions and answers based largely on Starcke's Order of Salvation as a Short Table, probably from the New York catechism.[50] He further augmented the material from Starcke's Longer Table or a work based on it.[51]

The questions were probably used along side of Luther's catechism or were a complement to be used toward the close of confirmation instruction. Though B. M. Schmucker described it as thoroughly evangelical and distinctly Lutheran in doctrine, this seems to have been somewhat euphoric.[52] The catechism retained both the strength and the weakness of Starcke's Table, though J. Schmucker added a few weaknesses of his own. In speaking of natural religion he cited as one of its values that "it may induce us to receive Christianity" (Q. 6), thus giving room for men to play a part in being moved to accept the Gospel.

As was frequently the case, Schmucker described the religion of the Old Testament as the knowledge and worship of God according to the laws of Moses (Q. 10), ruling out the Gospel element in the Old Testament.

In view of later controversies among Lutherans in America, his position on God's election is of some interest. After stating God has elected fallen man, he asked the question,

113   Who has God thus elected?
        The fallen race of Adam.

114   Why then are not all blessed with the Gospel?
        Those who are not, have not yet the necessary knowledge preparatory to a saving reception of it.

115   Why then are not all those saved, who live and die under the Gospel sound?
        Because only such can enjoy eternal felicity, who repent and die in the faith of our Lord Jesus Christ.

116   Why do the rest remain impenitent unbelievers?
Because, as free agents, they reject the
proffered grace of God, by which they might
be saved.

117   Has God predestinated any to be reprobated by
an absolute decree?
No not one, those who remain impenitent,
will not come to Christ that they might have
life.

118   Who then has God elected to eternal life?
Not persons, but characters; such as maintain a lively faith, in gospel obedience, unto
death.

Schmucker included also prayer, but not the cross, as
a means of grace.   Infant baptism was taught according to
the Lutheran witness and, in the tradition of the day, confirmation was required of children who had been baptized in
their infancy in order to renew their baptismal vow.   In the
Lord's Supper, Christ made us partakers of his body and
blood as he promised, "with all the benefits of his sacrifice,
as surely as I partake of the consecrated bread and wine"
(Q. 204).

THE "BARDSTOWN" CATECHISM (1811)

Doctor Martin Luther's Shorter Catechism.   Mostly
translated from the German.   Bardstown: William
Bard, 1811.

This was apparently an original translation of Luther's
catechism and of some related material prepared by an unknown translator and published anonymously.   Even though we
may assume the publication place to be the Bardstown (or
Beardstown) in Kentucky, we still have no further clue since
no Lutheran congregation seems to have been established
there in 1811.[53]

The 48-page catechism contained the Five Chief Parts
and the Table of Duties of Luther's catechism, as well as
Starcke's Order of Salvation in Short and Simple Questions
and Answers, Questions and Answers for the Youth Preparing
themselves to receive the Lord's Supper, a rite of confirmation, together with prayers and hymns for the use of children
and others.

The new rendition of the Small Catechism bore no resemblance to earlier English translations. It was not as
smooth and was often marred by awkwardness. The First
Commandment read, "I AM the Lord thy God, thou shalt
have no other gods but me." The Second Commandment
struggled with the German "zaubern" and came up with the
admonition to avoid "conjuration." The translator gave a
clear Lutheran witness of the sacramental presence in the
Lord's Supper, not only with the translation, "It is the real
body and blood of our Lord Jesus Christ" but with the added
footnote, "The Lutheran Church believeth a real presence
and sacramental union, but abhorreth professedly transsub-
stantiation, consubstantiation, impaniaton [sic], and such other
like errors" (p. 12). 54

The relationship of the duties of Subjects or Common
Citizens to the government was explained in an annotation:

> To Christians, who live under a republican form of
> government, it must not appear offensive, that our
> Lord and his Apostles occasionally admonished peo-
> ple to submit themselves to the authority of kings,
> etc. It must be observed that they did not inter-
> fere with politics at all, but left them in every
> country as they found them, and solicited their fol-
> lowers to submission and obedience towards their
> lawful rulers. Had they have preached the Gospel
> in a country like ours, their admonition would have
> been the same. Their object was not the reforma-
> tion of politics, but their grand and most important
> object was the eternal salvation of souls [pp. 14f.].

The translation of Starcke's Order of Salvation appeared
also in a new translation, though somewhat reduced in size.
Instead of 165 questions there were only 116. In general the
omissions dealt with details of secondary importance keeping
in mind the purpose of the order. Otherwise it shared in the
weaknesses that the original order had manifested.

The examination in 64 questions for those preparing
themselves to receive the Lord's Supper was an extensive
overview of the Christian doctrine. It was followed by a
brief rite for confirmation. The final section contained family prayers and several morning and evening hymns.

Chapter VI

ENGLISH CATECHISMS DURING A PERIOD
OF CRISIS, 1811-1816

The elements within the New York Ministerium who
were influenced by the climate of Rationalism grew in bold-
ness after the death of John C. Kuntze in 1807. Up to now
the effect of Rationalism on the catechism texts had been
minimal, limited on occasion to an inordinate stress on morals, bordering at times on a moral theology. The same tendency surfaced also among Lutherans in other states, notably
in the Carolinas with the use of Velthusen's catechisms. But
with Kuntze's death, the time seemed ripe to accommodate
the changes brought about by Deism, especially with the
English-speaking membership who had broader contacts among
the general populace.

Already in 1809, the New York Ministerium appointed
a committee to prepare a new English catechism "that would
meet the needs of the oncoming generation and introduce the
same in the congregation." The committee was composed of
Pres. Fried. H. Quitman, Fried. W. Geissenhainer Sr., August Wackerhagen, and Ralph Willeston.[1]

The resolution might have sounded innocent enough
were it not for the fact that only five years earlier the Ministerium had authorized its first English catechism, patterned
after an earlier catechism by Kuntze. Furthermore the appointed committee was apparently strongly inclined toward
Rationalism. Both Quitman and Wackerhagen were known
for their liberal views. Willeston defected to the Episcopalians the year after he was appointed. Quitman had already
left some traces of his views in the 1804 catechism where
he weakened the Lutheran witness to the sacramental presence
of our Lord in the Supper.

The Ministerium did not convene in 1810, due to the
illness of a number of its members but at the 1811 meeting,
Wackerhagen presented a draft of the proposed catechism

which was referred to Fried. Mayer and P. W. Domeier for
review. No report was ever made by the examining committee and the entire matter was lost from the official minutes.[2]

BRAUN'S CATECHISM (1811-1812)

Meanwhile, Anthony T. Braun, pastor at Gilead Church,
Brunswick, N.Y., reprinted a major portion of the 1804 Ministerium catechism at his own expense under the title,

> Dr. Martin Luther's Shorter Catechism. Translated
> from the German. Troy [N.Y.]: R. Schermerhorn,
> 1811.

The catechism made its appearance prior to the 1811
meeting and this enabled the synod to purchase 500 copies
directly from Braun, one half of the total number of copies
printed.[3] Evidently Braun, known for his loyalty to a Lutheran witness, had given a sizeable group the opportunity to
voice their opposition to a trend that was gaining power in
their midst.[4]

Braun's edition was the same as the 1804 print except
that he omitted the Order of Salvation in Systematical Connection and the Penitential Psalms. He did, however, add his
own 16-page section on Private and Family Prayers. He introduced it with a brief treatise on the importance of family
worship, to which he appended his name. In addition, there
was a final section of hymns.

Interestingly enough, someone else also reprinted the
1804 catechism the following year.

> Dr. Martin Luther's Shorter Catechism. Translated
> from the German. Boston: Lincoln & Edmunds, 1812.

The catechism was identical to Braun's edition except
that it included Bible references under the various parts of the
catechism and omitted Braun's section on Prayers and Hymns.

There was no further identity of the person responsible for having it printed. There was no Lutheran congregation in or near Boston at the time.[5] However, the copy located by the writer had been in use in Waldoborough, Maine
(then still a part of Massachusetts) and had been deposited in
the local museum.[6] That leads to the likelihood that the catechism may have been authorized by Johann Wm. Starman,

a licentiate member of the New York Ministerium, who had
accepted a call to Waldoborough in 1811.[7]

QUITMAN'S "EVANGELICAL CATECHISM" (1814)

But in spite of the resistance of men like Braun, Quitman and his party's spirits were not dampened for long. Because of the war, there was no synod in 1812. The catechism
matter came to the fore again in 1813. The synod again resolved to publish an English catechism and set up the following specifications: 1) The Ten Commandments were to come
after the Creed; 2) the Office of the Keys was to be "ex-
punged"; 3) the Chief Parts of Luther's catechism without his
explanations were to be included; and 4) Quitman was asked
to write the preface and comment on the changes made.
There is no record of the names of the committee appointed.[8]

Due to the war, the 1814 synod could not be held,
nevertheless late in 1814 a catechism by Quitman appeared
in print bearing the statement on the frontispiece, "With the
consent and approbation of the Synod." When and how this
approval was given remains a mystery. The 1813 meeting
had merely asked him to write a preface for the proposed
catechism. Whether he was on the committee or whether
he was the committee, was not stated in the minutes. In
his preface to the catechism, dated November 1, 1814, Quitman stated, "I have voluntarily undertaken the task of preparing the work, which in its present form, is offered to
your serious consideration." On the surface this seemed to
imply that he had acted on his own or in behalf of the committee. Certainly no approval of the catechism could have
been given in 1814, since the synod had not met. It is possible, though highly unlikely, that the synod had given its approval of the catechism prior to it having been written. If
so, the minutes do not indicate this.

Whatever the case may be, there is no doubt that
Quitman claimed to have had the approval of the Ministerium.
His catechism appeared under the title,

> Evangelical Catechism: or a Short Exposition of
> the Principal Doctrines and Precepts of the Chris-
> tian Religion, For the Use of the Churches belong-
> ing to the Evangelical Lutheran Synod of the State
> of New York. To which are added I. A scriptural
> advice to the young. II. Sir M [atthew] Hale's
> character of a true Christian. III. An address to

those who wish to be confirmed. IV. A sketch of
the history of Religion. V. A collection of prayers
for parents and children. Hudson: William E. Norman, 1814.

The catechism section proper contained the following
parts: The Apostolic Creed, the Ten Commandments, Prayer,
Sacraments, and the Final Destiny of Man or Future State of
Existence.

The contents of the catechism were unmistakably non-
Lutheran and were deeply influenced by the prevailing Rationalism in Germany which was affecting American Protestantism,
including American Lutherans, especially its English-speaking
members. It contained no trace of Luther's catechism.

The catechism fairly bristled in its appeal to human
reason and experience, especially concerning the nature and
being of God. In the opening section of the Creed, under the
First Article, there was a lengthy discussion about God but
there was no reference to the Trinity. Nor was there a reference to the Trinity elsewhere in the catechism. Though
Jesus Christ was referred to as the only begotten son of God
(e.g., Q. 1, p. 29) and much was said about his divine authority and divine mission, these were merely matters of
titles. To Question 17 (p. 34), "Why is Jesus styled, the
only begotten son of God?", we find the answer: "As well
on account of his exalted dignity and pre-eminence above all
created beings, as on account of the great love, which his
heavenly Father has manifested for him."

The next question asked was, "Why is Jesus emphati-
cally called our Lord?" to which the answer was, "Because
on account of his obedience to his father, and his great suf-
ferings for the benefit of mankind, God has committed to him
the government of his church, so that we are obliged to acknowledge him as our king, lawgiver and judge."

Equally interesting and devastating was Q. 33 (p. 38),
"Which are the reasons assigned in holy writ for the suffer-
ings and death of Jesus?" The answer was, "It is stated in
the gospel, that Christ suffered and died, that he might seal
the doctrine, which he had preached with his blood."

The doctrine of justification by grace through faith was
denied. In fact the meaning of faith "as represented in holy
Writ, as the condition of man's acceptance with God" was
carefully explained in A. 23 (p. 47), "An impressive sense

of the glorious perfections of God, and his relation to men, as their creator, preserver, governor and judge, and a corresponding pious disposition, arising from it." To the outright question, "What is faith in Christ?" the catechism answered, "A firm belief in the divine authority of Jesus, and of his doctrine and promises, expressed by a sincere zeal to cherish christian sentiments and dispositions, and to cultivate christian graces. Rom. 8,9." (pp. 47f.)

The "reward that God has graciously promised to the true believers in Christ" is "justification, or the assurance of pardon of sin and of everlasting salvation" (Q. 29, p. 48). Earlier it had been stated that the blessings of God so graciously offered through Jesus Christ are designed, "For all without distinction, that are willing to receive and to improve them" (Q. 33, p. 40).

The Ten Commandments were set forth "in conformity to the other Protestant Churches and of an express resolution of the Synod" (Preface). They were taken from the Protestant Episcopal Prayer-Book, [9] and explained much the same way.

The sacraments received minimal attention and were not regarded as means of grace. Water, it was said, was prescribed in Baptism,

> To signify, that in the same manner, as water cleanses our bodies; so we find in communion with Christ, in all that he has effected for the good of mankind, and is still operating by his spirit and doctrine, whatever is necessary to purify our souls, whatever can afford us comfort and ease, and render us perfectly happy. (Q. 5, p. 109)

According to the catechism, when Christians take the initiative to be received into the Christian Church by Baptism, "They engage to purify themselves from all uncleanness of the flesh and the spirit, and to accomplish their sanctification in the fear of the Lord" (Q. 6, p. 110).

Emphasis was placed on infant baptism because of the moral tendency it induced. "Parents that offer their children for baptism, manifest a religious sense highly beneficial to their family and offspring, whilst children, that are early made sensible of their allegiance to Christ will be induced to become acquainted with their Lord and benefactor" (Q. 12, p. 111).

The purpose of the Lord's Supper was primarily to be a memorial (Q. 19, p. 113). This expression implied,

> That in that solemn ordinance, we ought to direct our whole attention to our Saviour, and to what he has done, and suffered for our sake, meditating on his holy doctrine, his blameless and beneficent life, his magnanimous sufferings, and meritorious death. (Q. 20, p. 113)

The worthy communicant derived profit from this sacrament,

> He thereby strengthens his attachment to his Lord and Saviour, and his affection to his fellow-men; excites himself to new resolutions of holiness; increases his inclination and sense of his duty to promote the cause of Christ; sets a good example to those around; and renews his impressions of the saving and comfortable doctrine of the death, and resurrection of Christ. (Q. 24, p. 114)

The supplements to the catechism strongly reinforced the moral theology that permeated the main section. The instruction before the rite of confirmation stressed its importance and declared them eligible to commune. "The subsequent celebration of the Lord's Supper renders this act still more impressive. By partaking of this sacrament you declare your allegiance to Christ, and avow to the world, that you wish to be considered as friends of Jesus, and members of his household" (p. 145).

Quitman's catechism has earned for him the designation as being a rational supranaturalist, for he did not overtly reject Scriptures as a revelation from God. Instead he employed human reason and used it to interpret and support it. He maintained that revelation and reason were in harmony with one another. Thus at the outset of his catechism he stated that the grounds of rational belief are "Either natural perception and experience; or the authority of competent witnesses; or finally, unquestionable arguments of reason" (p. 6). With that working principle he undermined every major tenet of faith historically held by the Christian Church.

The Sketch of The History of Religion had an interesting section on the Lutheran Church which betrayed Quitman's view of Luther and the Lutheran Confessions.

The Lutheran or rather Evangelical Church has gen-

erally distinguished itself by faithful adherence to
that fundamental principle of the reformation, according to which: not human authority, but the
scriptures only ought to be considered as the standard of the christian in matters of faith.   Animated
by this spirit, the friends of Luther ventured even
in his life time to differ from him, in some doctrinal points.   And as the great reformer was silent to these improvements by his friends; it appears as well from this circumstance, as from
many expressions, contained in the works, which
were published by him in the later part of his life,
that he approved of these emendations.   Thus the
dogmas of the entire moral incapacity of man, and
of the absolute or unconditional divine decrees,
which most of the reformers had imbibed in the
school of Augustine bishop of Hippo in Africa, were
very early discarded from the list of the creed of
the Lutherans, and the more rational and scriptural
doctrines of free agency and universal grace substituted in their place. [pp. 174f.]

Among those who thus freed the Lutheran Church were,
according to Quitman, men like Baumgarten, Semler, and
Seiler.   The list further contained leading German theologians
whose rationalistic tendencies were well known.   As Jacobs
summarized it in speaking of the men named, "There can be
no mistaking the type of theology which such a catechism represented."10

The saddest part of all this is that the New York Ministerium never officially repudiated Quitman's catechism after
its appearance.   But even that judgment must be placed in
its proper setting.   The New York Ministerium of that time
was a small group of men when it met in convention.   In
1806, only six pastors out of about 14 were present.   Only
six congregations out of 44 were represented by delegates.
Small wonder that it did not convene in 1810 because of the
illness of some of its members.   In 1813, in the midst of
the war, there were only five present out of 11 and only 12
congregations were represented out of a total of 47.   In 1815,
the year following the appearance of the catechism, 16 out
of 20 pastors were present but only seven congregations out
of 51 congregations were represented by a delegate.11

With such small groups before him, it is easy to understand how a man like Quitman could dominate the synod.
Physically he was a man of admirable build.   He was a per-

suasive speaker who spoke fluently in English, German and
Dutch. His academic record was impressive. He had been
a student of the liberal theologian Johann S. Semler at the
University in Halle. Just recently he was awarded the D. D.
from Harvard. He was not a man against whom the average
pastor would care to take issue, especially when we realize
that the 1815 synod was held in Quitman's own parish.

As was frequently the case in the early history of Lutheran synods, Quitman was interrelated to three of the synod's pastors. The brothers Philip and Friedrich Mayer were
his stepsons and Wackerhagen, secretary of the Ministerium,
and who was later to succeed Quitman to the presidency, was
his son-in-law, having married a sister of the Mayer brothers. [12]

But opposition Quitman did have, the silent kind, that
has not usually been considered by eager critics of the Ministerium. The catechism simply did not sell, even though
the proceeds were to flow into the Ministerium's treasury
and Quitman was ready to underwrite each edition in an
amount of 50 dollars. Ten years later the printer had to
remind the Ministerium that he still had over 200 copies on
hand and asked that the synod take them over. In a letter
to Wackerhagen, dated September 14, 1824, the printer wrote,
"I had every reason to expect that the books would not remain unsold so many years." The synod, however, took no
action in the matter. [13]

The silent treatment came also from the Pennsylvania
Ministerium. In 1816, the New York Ministerium's representatives who were appointed to attend the Pennsylvania meeting
in Philadelphia, were instructed to give copies of the Quitman
catechism to that synod. [14] This was dutifully done but no
action was taken other than a "hearty thanks" for the gift. [15]

PHILIP F. MAYER'S "INSTRUCTION IN THE
PRINCIPLES AND DUTIES OF THE
CHRISTIAN RELIGION" (1816-1846)

A more vocal protest against Quitman's catechism came
from his son-in-law, Philip F. Mayer of Philadelphia, who
only a little more than a year later came out with a new catechism of his own featuring Luther's Small Catechism. [16] It
bore the title,

Instruction in the Principles and Duties of the Chris-

<u>tian Religion for Children and Youth</u>.   Philadelphia:
Daniel Braeutigam, 1816.

As related earlier, Mayer had already published a
translation of Luther's catechism in 1806, which had been
reprinted in 1811, and which was to appear again in 1819.
We know, too, that Mayer and Quitman had been working together in preparing the final copy of the New York Ministerium catechism of 1804.   Past experience made Mayer a most
likely candidate to make Luther available again in English, if
he had the will thus to repudiate the president of the synod
who was also his stepfather.   For this responsibility Mayer
was ready.

His rendition of Luther's catechism, while largely
based on his 1806 edition, showed a number of variations,
most of which were improvements.   In fact B. M. Schmucker
observed that nine tenths of the translation still remained in
his time (1886) as the accepted version.[17]

Mayer did retain the weakened version of the Lord's
Supper, "It is the body and blood of our Lord Jesus Christ."
He further weakened the opening words of the explanation to
the Third Article to read, "I believe that I cannot, merely
[sic] by my own reason or natural power, believe...."   On
the other hand, he caught Luther's meaning in the Third
Commandment by speaking of not despising "the preaching of
his gospel" rather than the "preaching of his word."

Mayer omitted Luther's Confession of Sins and the Table of Duties as well as the two selections erroneously attributed to Luther, The Office of the Keys and the Christian
Questions and Answers.   The latter had been in his 1806 edition.

The new catechism did not fare so well in the selection of the materials that were further included.   The first
of these was a Scripture Catechism of the Principles of the
Christian Religion Laid Down in the Words of the Bible (pp.
19-52).   Whether Mayer composed this selection or adapted
it from elsewhere has not been determined.   It seems unlikely that the format would appeal to children since the direct Bible quotations given as answers did not usually mesh
clearly with the questions asked.   In many instances the
teacher would have to explain the Bible passages to show how
they might fit the questions asked.   Thus a clear and crisp
statement of our justification alone by grace through faith in
the Redeemer cannot be found, though this article of faith is

nowhere explicitly denied. Because of the ambiguity built
into the format, some room was left for man's cooperation
in effecting his salvation. Thus

> 97 Q. But will the free gift of eternal life be be-
> stowed upon any who do not strive to be-
> come qualified for it?
>
> A. Be not deceived, God is not mocked. What-
> soever a man soweth, that shall he also
> reap. He that soweth to his flesh, shall
> of his flesh reap corruption. But he, that
> soweth to the Spirit, shall of the Spirit
> reap life everlasting. Gal. vi, 7.8.9.
> [p. 49]

Similarly the format gives minimal treatment to the "outward
rites to be used," i.e. the sacraments. The three answers
for Baptism and the five concerning the Lord's Supper leave
much to be desired, especially since prayer is included as
another "means," which "we must use for preserving our
Christian principles and growing in Christian virtues" (Q. 87,
p. 45).

The second addition was The Christian Character and
Duties Expressed in the Words of Scripture (pp. 53-70). In
the absence of a clear statement on justification this section
could readily be understood as a treatise on moral theology
concerning the Christian life, particularly the duty of piety
and those of a personal and social nature.

Next followed a brief section on The Christian's Comforts and Hopes Expressed in the Words of Scripture (pp. 71-
75). Included is a one-page subsection on the Christian's
assurance of the forgiveness of sins (p. 73) from which one
may gather the doctrine of justification.

The fourth section is A Historical Catechism for Children and Youth (pp. 77-96) by Isaac Watts (1674-1748), the
non-conformist English divine, noted hymn writer and pastor
in London. On the opening page Mayer said that he made a
number of changes in this catechism, omitting a few questions
and answers, altering some expressions, and adding a small
number of articles. The catechism reviewed the historical
events in Scripture in the form of questions and answers. It
was refreshingly simple and direct even though some of the
items may have been too brief, due largely to the format.

Section five was titled, Elements of Religion and Morality for Younger Children (pp. 97-103). Mayer stated in the opening note that this was "first published in New England, with the initials only of the editors' names." It again set forth duties without noting the need for a Gospel motivation. Thus it comes through primarily as law and a form of moral theology.

The final section contained a number of prayers, morning and evening and at meals (pp. 104-108).

All in all, it must be said that while Mayer repudiated Quitman's coarse Rationalism, he was not as forthright with a Lutheran witness as one might have hoped. The blending of Pietism and Rationalism that had produced an undue emphasis on moral theology at the expense of the Gospel had taken its toll even with a man such as Mayer. The Lutheran Confessions, with the exception of the Small Catechism were becoming a secondary matter. Yet the bright side was that Luther's catechism continued to be available both in English and in German for a large number of Lutheran congregations. Mayer's catechisms alone appeared in a total of six editions, several sponsored by the Tract and Book Society of Mayer's congregation in Philadelphia:

Philadelphia: Daniel Braeutigam, 1821.

Philadelphia: Daniel Braeutigam, 1828.

Philadelphia: Printed for the Tract and Book Society of the Evangelical Lutheran Church of St. John, 1834.

Philadelphia: Printed for the Missionary, Tract and Book Society, of the Evangelical Lutheran Congregation of St. John's Church, 1839.

Philadelphia: Printed for the Tract and Book Society, of the Evangelical Church of St. John, 1846.

Chapter VII

FRONTIER CATECHISMS BY PAUL HENKEL,
1809-1816

Undoubtedly one of the major contributions for the study and furtherance of Lutheran catechisms in America was made by Paul Henkel (1754-1825), the most versatile frontier missionary of his day. Besides being a pioneer missionary he was an organizer of synods,[1] author of books and tracts, hymnologist,[2] and founder of the Henkel Press in New Market, Va. His ancestors had come to America in 1717, and had settled in Pennsylvania under the leadership of the Rev. Anthony Jacob Henkel (1663-1728), sometimes called Gerhard.[3]

Paul was the fourth generation Henkel in America.[4] While still a layman he preached his first sermon in 1781.[5] Under the tutelage of the Rev. John Andrew Krug (1732-1796), pastor at Frederickstown, Md. (1771-1796) and the Rev. Christian Streit (1749-1812), pastor in Winchester, Va. (1785-1812), he was licensed to preach by the Pennsylvania Ministerium in 1783.[6] His ordination was authorized in 1792.[7]

Henkel's early ministry was centered in the Shenandoah Valley in Virginia. He made his first trip back to his home state North Carolina in 1785, and from 1800-1805, he made Rowan County the center of his operation, whereupon he returned to New Market, Va.[8] He was appointed traveling missionary in 1806.[9] His territory at various times was Ohio, Kentucky, Tennessee, North Carolina, as well as Virginia.

Conditions on the frontier were primitive not only economically but above all else spiritually. For the most part the bitter struggle for existence had crowded out any spiritual meaning to life for most settlers. Consequently there was frequently strong resistance against any effort on the part of

missionaries to gain their interest.   To be sure, a few struggled to remain faithful and eagerly baptized their children,
confirmed their youth, and earnestly attended public worship
when this was possible.   It was for these especially that Paul
Henkel prepared his catechisms though he strongly hoped the
Gospel might again revive the faith of others if they read
them.   He often brought catechisms along on his trips or
when the supply was depleted, promised to supply them on
a future visit or send them through someone going that way.[10]

GERMAN LUTHERAN CATECHISMS (1809-1811)

Although the catechism of the Pennsylvania Ministerium
had wide circulation and by 1809 had appeared in over 25
editions and printings, Henkel did not regard it suitable for
frontier distribution and use.   Henkel considered it too com-
plex to be useful.   He needed a simple exposition of Luther's
Small Catechism for the average German rather than a number of orders of salvation and doctrinal tables.   Besides, it
was too costly for the average family.   Nor was he satisfied
with Lochmann's Chief Contents of the Christian Doctrine,
since his primary concern was to distribute the text of Luther in as simple a form as possible.

Finding none of the available catechisms suitable for
his purpose he prepared one himself.   It appeared under the
title,

> The Small Catechism of the Bl. Dr. Martin Luther,
> in which the Five Chief Parts are analyzed and set
> forth in short Questions so that the Contents may
> be Learned more easily and be better Understood.
> Together with other Questions.   As well as edify-
> ing Morning-, Table-, and Evening Prayers and
> Songs and whatever else is necessary.   New Mar-
> ket, Schenandoah County (Virg.):   Ambrose Henkel,
> 1809. [11]

While Luther's catechism had originally been written
for the simple folk, Henkel felt that even this might prove
too difficult for the average frontier parent who did not have
recourse to regular instruction and weekly worship.   Henkel's
concern for simplicity is already stated in the extended title
of the catechism.   His preface makes it even clearer.

To all who are concerned or affected.

Dear Friends!

With this edition, Luther's Small Catechism is given
into your hands so that your children will more
likely learn it and be able to understand it more
easily than usual.   Experience will teach that sufficiently in the case of children that learn from it.

Here you will find the five Chief Parts broken
up and set forth in additional questions so that the
answers to almost all questions are shorter and the
children will find them easier to learn.   However,
nothing in the individual Chief Parts has been
changed.

That we have added a supplement to each of the
Chief Parts comprising a series of short and simple questions, was done to give the children a
deeper insight into the matter, as one does in the
instruction with other questions.

The dearth of German school instruction and catechisms will be acknowledged by every right think-
ing person who will recognize too how important it
is that one proceeds to do something about it in this
manner so that the youth will learn from God's
Word.

New Market, July 11, 1809.

Henkel's primary concern was to provide a catechism
for the parents' use, but he was not unmindful that it should
serve a useful purpose when read during public worship and
assigned to the children for memorization.   The special conference of pastors in Virginia had resolved the previous year
that in the event a pastor was absent, the congregation should
appoint by vote a suitable layman who would read a sermon,
a portion of Scripture or some other pertinent book, and a
prayer, and "to assign a section of the catechism to be memorized for the following Sunday."[12]

Henkel's concern for simplicity was evident on every
page.   To keep the Luther text brief and uncluttered, he
omitted the Bible references that were customarily added by
editors.   While most Lutherans have regarded the text simple enough, except perhaps the long explanations to each of
the three articles of the Creed, Henkel broke up even the answers to the Ten Commandments and the petitions of the
Lord's Prayer.   With the exception of the First and the Sixth
Commandments, he divided the explanations into two questions,

one for the negative or the prohibition, and one for the posi-
tive, or the command. The explanations for the articles of
the Creed were divided into four or more questions. As
might be expected Henkel's divisions often interrupted Luther's flow of thought and weakened the explanations.

At the end of the Chief Parts and in the case of the
Creed, at the end of each of the three articles, he inserted
the supplements referred to in the preface. The brief supplements were to help amplify in a simple way the meaning
of the text and served as thought bridges between the Chief
Parts. For instance, under the article on creation he not
only detailed the creation account himself, but included man's
fall into sin, thus preparing the learner for the next article
which dealt with redemption.

Henkel's problem with frontier Christians who denied
infant baptism was reflected in the emphasis he placed on
baptizing children. One approach was to show the parallels
between circumcision of the Old Testament and baptism in the
New Testament. In baptism children have covenanted themselves to learn and keep God's commandments. God thereby
promised them power and endurance through His Spirit to
walk in His ways. True faith, Henkel said, was attained
through sincere prayer, reading and study of the Holy Scriptures, hearing preaching and the faithful use of the Lord's
Supper. The ongoing power of baptism was not mentioned.

Henkel's reference to prayer as a means of grace had
been a frequent addition in Lutheran circles of that time.
Nor was the equation of the Gospel with the Scriptures unique
to Henkel. [13]

Henkel's catechism closed with the Confession of Sins,
the Christian Questions and Answers and Luther's Table of
Duties.

The final portion of the book contained a few hymns
and prayers, a form for private confession, and the Office
of the Keys. None of the hymns were taken from the Pennsylvania catechism though his form for private confession
was the same.

Continued experience with the 1809 catechism soon
convinced Henkel of the need to expand his catechism and include several traditional parts. Therefore, early in 1811,
he issued a revised catechism, doubled in size, from 66 pages

to 129.   It bore the same title but gave no indication on the title page that it was a second edition or that it was revised.

New Market, Schenandoah County (Virg.): Ambrosius Henkel and Co., 1811.[14]

Instead of having a supplement to each of the Chief Parts of the catechism, Henkel now combined and enlarged them all into a single exposition and inserted the supplement after the Luther text.   A major expansion of the explanation was made in reference to baptism, indicating again how this article of faith was under question among many of the people with whom he dealt.   In addition to his stress on the parallelism between circumcision and baptism, he emphasized the regenerative power of the sacrament.   Apparently he had met with criticism on this point by those who pointed to Jesus' baptism, who obviously had needed no regeneration.   Consequently Henkel elaborated on the distinction between John's baptism which Jesus received and the baptism which he later instituted for the church.   In addition to the changes in his own rendition, Henkel added from the Pennsylvania catechism the traditional Order of Salvation in Questions and Answers.

To make his catechism more serviceable as a text to be used in church, Henkel added also a form for the confirmation of children in the presence of the congregation.   The form seems to have been original with Henkel for it is not found in the Pennsylvania Agenda of 1786, still in use at the time, nor in any of the catechisms extant.   The four questions asked of the children are of interest.

1.   Do you in the presence of this congregation renounce the devil and all his works and being?
Answer: Yes, we renounce.

2.   Do you acknowledge that you believe from your heart all that you were taught in your catechism to be in accord with the Word of God?
Answer: Yes, we believe.

3.   Do you intend diligently to live according to it; to be obedient to the order of the Christian church and thereby renew your baptismal covenant?
Answer: Yes.

4.   Do you intend to remain faithful to the pure

doctrine of the Christian church even unto
death?
Answer: Yes. [pp. 96f.]

Henkel did not follow the Pennsylvania Agenda which
pledged the catechumens to the doctrine of the Evangelical
Lutheran Church.

The rite was further emphasized by the addition of
three confirmation hymns, one taken from the Pennsylvania
catechism and two others that appeared for the first time in
a catechism. These two were placed at the end of the book.
Three other hymns from the Pennsylvania catechism were
inserted by Henkel.

The Seven Penitential Psalms that most catechisms
included were also added, no doubt reflecting the traditional
preference of those who still remembered "how it was in the
past."

THE CHRISTIAN CATECHISM (1811-1816)

Henkel had frequently expressed the fear that English
would drive out the German language among the Lutherans
and with it bring about a loss of their confessional heritage.[15]
Yet he was enough of a realist to accept that the change was
inevitable. He therefore produced on the one hand German
religious books of all kinds (A B C books, tracts and hymnals, besides catechisms) to maintain the German as long as
possible, and on the other hand produced and printed English
books, tracts, and hymnals to meet the changing needs where
this had already occurred. For this reason, too, he planned
a catechism that would be faithful to the Lutheran witness of
the Gospel but would not appear too denominational in its approach lest he turn away such who were unchurched but still
had some latent loyalty to a long neglected denomination or,
who in the course of their life, had acquired a prejudice
against Lutheranism without any direct experience with it.
Desirous therefore of witnessing the Gospel under all circumstances that the frontier might bring with it, he prepared an
English catechism to which he gave the tempered title,

The Christian Catechism, composed for the Instruction of Youth in the Knowledge of the Christian Religion, Together with Morning and Evening Hymns,
Prayers, etc. 2nd ed. New Market: Ambrose
Henkel and Co., 1811.

In writing this catechism Henkel faced a double task, first to minimize the denominational thrust without denying the essential Lutheran witness and secondly, to do this in English, a language in which he was not as fluent as he might have wished. He was not entirely successful in either case, though we must admire him for his valiant attempt.

The Christian Catechism appeared early in 1811, perhaps in April. No copy of the first edition has as yet been found. A second edition appeared with the date 1811 on the title page and April 1, on the frontispiece. Since the Henkel Press sometimes used the plates of an earlier edition without changing the dateline, it is difficult to establish whether the second edition actually appeared in 1811, or whether it appeared later, but still retained the 1811 date.[16]

We do have a 30-page extract of the catechism, which appears from the preface to have been taken from the first edition. In fact it may have been the first edition. It bore the title,

> The First Chief Head of the Christian Catechism, for the Instruction of Youth in the Knowledge of the Christian Religion, Together with Morning and Evening Hymns and Prayers. New Market: Ambrose Henkel & Comp., 1811.

If the item above was not the first edition but merely an extract of it, we may still assume that the first two editions were basically the same. The Christian Catechism before us contained the following parts: The Chief Heads of the Christian Doctrine (pp. 5-27); A short and simple Explanation of the Five Chief Heads of the Christian Doctrine (pp. 27-79); Order of Salvation in short Questions and Answers (pp. 79-101); Of the Power of the Church [The Office of the Keys] (pp. 102-103); A short explanation of sundry Feasts, Festivals and Sundays retained in the Christian Church (pp. 104-114); Of Confirmation (pp. 114-117); The Confession of Sins (p. 117); Hymns [and Prayers] (pp. 118-139); A Table of Duties (pp. 139-140).

In his preface Henkel had written,

> You find here the form and plan of Luthers Shorter Catechism; yet not in all points; neither is what you find here a correct translation of said Catechism; yet containing the same doctrine.

While using much of his German Luther catechism as a guide in the way he presented his material in English, he did make some unfortunate concessions in his desire to be non-denominational. As he said, the catechism did not follow Luther's text "in all points." This was especially true of the Ten Commandments where he followed the Reformed division, making two commandments into one. Here it was evident that Henkel's limited theological insights did not caution him against using the Old Testament wording, for he failed to reflect the New Testament revisions that liberated Christians from the ceremonial and cultural restrictions of the old covenant.

Yet his changes in the Luther text for the explanation of the Third (his Fourth) Commandment were striking for their good news/bad news quality that one finds in a single sentence. Accordingly his explanation to this commandment taught us "not to neglect or despise the preaching of God's gospel-word, especially on the sabbath day." His rendition of Luther's "Word" as "gospel-word" was excellent while the emphasis "on the sabbath-day" was regrettable (p. 9).

On Baptism he changed the answer to Luther's question, "What does Baptism give or profit?" from "It works forgiveness of sin" to "Baptism with faith brings the pardon of sin," thus weakening it considerably (p. 22).[17]

On the Lord's Supper he changed Luther's rendition from "true body and blood" to read "It is the body and blood of our Lord Jesus Christ," leaving room for either a spiritual or a sacramental presence.

The translation of the Luther text which seems to have been original with Henkel was not as smooth as Kuntze-Strebeck's was and was often quite awkward, as the caption already indicated. For Luther's "Hauptstücke," he had the literal "Chief Heads," rather than the more accurate "Chief Parts." His occasional improvisations of the text were not always fortunate either.

The questions in the Short and simple Explanation of the Five Chief Heads were frequently taken from Henkel's own Luther catechism though expanded considerably. Here again his explanation of the Ten Commandments reflected a Reformed tradition to which he probably was not sensitized due to his own somewhat Pietistic leanings. He lost much of the evangelical freedom that Luther reflected in his expo-

sition of the Third Commandment as one notes from the questions and answers (Q. 41 through 53).   Henkel assumed that
the restrictions of the seventh day had for the most part been
transferred to the first day of the week.   In this he reflected
what earlier catechisms also had said.   According to Henkel,
besides worshiping at home and at church, only works of necessity and of mercy were permitted.   All other works on
the sabbath day were forbidden by God according to the law
of Moses.

While many of the earlier catechisms had glossed over
the article of faith on the church, Henkel gave a beautiful description of it.   After a statement that we are to believe in
a holy catholic church, he came through with a clear Lutheran
witness.

> 182.   Whereof doth that church consist?   That
> church consists of all true christians, in all
> places and at all times, throughout the whole
> world.   Acts 10:35.

> 183.   Why is it called the christian church?   Be-
> cause Jesus Christ instituted that church,
> and every regular member thereof is bap-
> tised in his name.

> 184.   Why is it called a holy church?   Because,
> all true believing members of the christian
> church are cleansed from sin and made holy.
> John 1:7.

> 185.   By what means is it that such are made holy?
> They have the word of God to teach and di-
> rect them, and the holy sacraments to
> strengthen their faith; and to assure them of
> the pardon of their sins [p. 54].

As might be expected the sections on the sacraments
were somewhat weakened in order to attract a wider reader-
ship.   However, Henkel made no concessions concerning infant baptism.   The same elaborate arguments on the parallelism of circumcision and baptism and the differences between
John's baptism which Jesus received and the baptism which
our Lord instituted, were repeated.   He did omit the specific
question on the mode of baptism which he had in his German
catechism, but he still insisted that the amount of water used
had nothing to do with the validity of baptism.   Henkel called

baptism a seal of God's covenant which by implication made
even children members of the Christian church. Strangely
enough, however, there was no clear and concise statement
on the regenerating power of baptism in his explanation.

A sacramental presence of Christ's body and blood
was not stated explicitly but seemed only to be implied in
the section on the Lord's Supper. Nevertheless he had a
Lutheran emphasis on the benefits of the sacrament. There
was an interesting footnote showing a pastoral concern at the
end of this section. It dealt with the question whether those
who were "not fully converted to God" and partook of the
sacrament, brought everlasting damnation on their souls because of what Paul said in 1 Cor. 11:29. Henkel pointed
out that the word "damnation" meant "judgment" and that
this judgment for the Corinthians in their situation was "bodily sickness and weakness, plagues and death" (pp. 74-78).

The Order of Salvation, like that of the German Luther
catechism, was that by Christoph Starcke, so popular in many
of the early catechisms of the time. The translation was "by
another hand" according to later editions of his catechism but
not otherwise identified. [18] It was much more faithful to the
original text than the translation which had previously appeared in 1805, in the Shorter Catechism, attributed to Christian Endress, pastor of Easton, Pa. [19] Yet the version in
Henkel's catechism did not forego editorializing if the translator thought it necessary.

As was frequently the case at the time, the translator
felt constrained to use the King James "thee's and thou's"
when referring to the young readers of the catechism. This
is probably more disturbing to modern readers than it was
in Henkel's day when it was thought that the language of religious matters should be more dignified than that of the mar-
ketplace.

Whether Henkel chose this longer order of salvation,
which in many ways was quite satisfactory, because it treated
the sacraments sparsely, particularly the Lord's Supper, may
be questionable even though it was consistent with the broader
purpose he had in mind in distributing his catechism.

Of the Power of the Church was the familiar Office of
the Keys without further explanation. However, he did not
follow the traditional wording but made some changes to accommodate the three Bible passages cited in place of the tra-

ditional text.   These were found in the Pennsylvania catechism.   Interestingly, Henkel detached it completely from
Luther's text and so was far ahead of later publishers.

The Short explanation of Sundry Feasts was an unusual
contribution to the catechism.   Was it composed because frontier people had lost all sense of a church year?   How was it
received by those who traditionally regarded such observances
as "Catholic"?   Or did Henkel sense a need for fellowship on
special days and sought to give them Christian meanings?
Whatever the reason, it was a significant addition.   Henkel
limited the days chiefly to major festivals and seasons, though
he included such somewhat uncommon festivals as Shrove
Tuesday and the several Epiphany Sundays.   Worthy of note
was his explanation of New Year's Day as a festival.   As the
New Year festival took note of the beginning of the common
year, so the circumcision of our Lord marked the day when
he began the work of our Redemption.

Of Confirmation was both an explanation of confirmation and how the rite was to be performed, including the vows
the catechumens were to make.   It was thus an expansion of
what he had included in the German Luther text.   As one
might expect from the tenor of the time, confirmation was
regarded as the office "by which persons are received as
full Members of the Christian Church and consecrated there-
to," implying in fact that baptism had not bestowed such membership.   Henkel, like most others, did not see therein a
contradiction of his own insistence that baptism already had
made one a member of the Christian Church as he had so
clearly stated earlier.[20]   Considering Henkel's purpose for
this catechism it was but natural that his confirmation rite
retained the bland pledge to remain true to the doctrine of
the Christian Church as found also in his German Luther Catechism.

The Confession of Sin was the same found in earlier
catechisms and used also by Henkel in his earlier catechism.

The section on hymns and prayers contained hymns to
be sung before and after catechism instruction, at confirmation, at the confession of sin, before, during and after Holy
Communion, together with morning and evening hymns.   The
prayers were primarily for home devotions, morning, evening
and at meals.

The Table of Duties was taken from Luther with some

additions. For Rulers and Magistrates, Henkel inserted Ex.
23:6-8 and Deut. 1:17 and transferred Rom. 13:1 to the next
paragraph on Subjects. He also added two new categories,
Of Aged Men, Titus 2:2, and Of Aged Women, Titus 2:3.4.

The First Chief Head, published the same year and
referred to above, was simply a reprint of the Ten Commandments. More than half of its contents consisted of
hymns and prayers suitable for home and school devotions.
This may imply that it was in fact the first edition which
Henkel enlarged during the next few months.

It is but natural that Henkel's irenic spirit and his
somewhat nondenominational approach would be criticized by
later church historians.[21] Considering, however, the conditions which Henkel met day after day during his frontier ministry, the spiritual ignorance, apathy and sometimes hostility,
circumstances difficult for us to understand, one should admire Henkel for his vision and persistence. Most missionaries of his day relied on camp meetings to bring about con-
versions. Instead, Henkel relied on the Gospel witness
through instruction. And while his Christian Catechism had
its shortcomings, its general content was Lutheran in spite
of a few soft spots. It was unaffected by the encroaching
Deism of the older regions. His vision regarding the use of
the English language among Lutherans and his readiness to
tackle the problem, places him well ahead of some of his
later critics who tended to cradle their orthodoxy in a German manger.

There is no question as to the reception given Henkel's
catechism. He made numerous references to the various
uses he put his catechism. Some he gave away but most of
them were sold. Henkel recorded with some satisfaction
"that it seems this [English catechism] has found a wider reception than all other writings."[22] Other pastors found them
useful also within their parishes. Gottlieb Schober [Shober]
eagerly received a considerable portion of the books from
Henkel "as he had a large number of half-English families in
his charge."[23] Early printings were soon exhausted and
eventually it went into at least five editions.

Third edition. New Market: Ambrose Henkel and
Co., 1813.

The title page for this edition was the same as the
second. The basic material was essentially the same also,

except for a few minor editorial changes. One of these stated that The Order of Salvation was translated "by another hand" (p. 96). This edition retained the April 1, 1811, date for the preface.

The major addition, interestingly enough, was in the Short Explanation of Sundry Feast. Here details were added for the season of Lent. The Sunday before Lent was given the alternate designation of Shrove Sunday together with a brief explanation. The five Sundays in Lent were each named and described. Maundy Thursday was added to the church year listing and also explained. Some additional notes were included for Easter and the Sundays after Easter until Pentecost. Strangest of all, considering the circumstances, was the addition of a number of Saints' days, including two for the Virgin Mary, as well as Michaelmas and Allsaints-day.

Additional prayers and hymns were included to serve for devotions at school or at catechising.

> Fourth Edition, enlarged and improved. New Market: S. Henkel's Printing Office, 1816.

A comparison of the title page with earlier editions indicates the addition ... also, an Explanation of Sundry Feasts, Festivals and Sundays, etc. This edition was registered with the clerk of the District of Virginia on January 9, 1816, giving the Henkel Press propriety rights to the book. The frontispiece still retained the April 1, 1811, date of the earlier editions. This edition had some major typographical changes and a number of reference corrections. While most of the editorial changes were of minor significance, two at least bear mentioning, both in connection with Baptism in the Luther text. Concerning the benefits of Baptism the text was strengthened to read, "Baptism brings the pardon of sin" instead of "Baptism with faith brings the pardon of sin" (p. 16). Similarly Henkel strengthened the description of Baptism to read "a gracious water of life and laver of regeneration in the holy Ghost" (p. 16). The earlier editions had merely "laver of regeneration."

The catechism was further enriched to include the three ecumenical creeds (pp. 106-110). The book concluded with a brief supplement giving the reader a short account to show what time a number of feasts and festivals were instituted "and ordained in the christian church, by order of Synods, etc." (p. 110).

Der Kleine

Catechismus

Des seel. Herrn

D. Martin Luthers,

Nebst

Den gewöhnlichen Morgen = Tisch = und
Abend = Gebätern.

Wobey

Zum Gebrauch der erwachsenen Jugend
hinzugefüget:

Die

Ordnung des Heyls

In einem Lied bekant unter dem Namen

Das Glaubens = Lied

Und

In kurtzen einfältigen Fragen und
Antworten

In Schulen und bey der Kinder =
Lehr nützlich zu gebrauchen

Die zweyte Auflag

Philadelphia,
Druckts und verlegts Benjamin Fräncklin,
und Johann Böhm, 1749.

Brunnholtz's Catechism, 1749.

(Universitätsbibliothek, Göttingen, West Germany)

THE
RUDIMENTS
OF THE
SHORTER
CATECHISM
OF
Dr. *MARTIN LUTHER.*

APPOINTED

For the Inſtruction of CHILDREN
and YOUNG PEOPLE.

Publiſhed in *ENGLISH,*

Chiefly for the USE of thoſe of the
LUTHERAN CONGREGATIONS
in *America.*

To which is annexed,

An ABRIDGMENT of the PRINCIPLES

OF THE

EVANGELICAL RELIGION.

PHILADELPHIA:
Printed by M. STEINER, in *Race-ſtreet,* near *Third-
ſtreet.* 1785.

Kuntze's English Catechism of 1785.

(Lutheran Theological Seminary, Philadelphia, Pa.)

Nordcarolinischer
Katechismus,

oder

Christlicher

Religionsunterricht

nach Anleitung
der heiligen Schrift,

entworfen

von

Johann Caspar Velthusen,

Doct. und ordentlichem Lehrer der Theologie, erstem
Prediger in Helmstädt u. Generalsuperintend,
auch Abte des Klosters Marienthal.

Zweyte Auflage.

Leipzig,
bey Siegfried Lebrecht Crusius,
auch zu haben
in Helmstädt im Fürstl. Waisenhause. 1788.
(kostet ungeb. 5 ggr., geb. 6 ggr.)

Velthusen's <u>North Carolina Catechism</u>, 1788.

(Lutheran Theological Seminary, Gettysburg, Pa.)

Die sogenannte

Heils=Ordnung,

in

Frag' und Antworten,

zum Gebrauch

der

Informanten.

By Rev. J. Goering

* * *

* *

*

York: Gedruckt bey Salomon Mayer.
1 7 9 8.

Johann Goehring's Order of Salvation, 1798.

(Lutheran Theological Seminary, Gettysburg, Pa.)

THE SHORTER
CATECHISM

BY

D. MARTIN LUTHER,

WITH

THE CUSTOMARY FAMILY PRAYERS.

TO WHICH IS ADDED

' THE ORDER OF SALVATION
IN NINE SHORT SECTIONS AND BY QUESTION
AND ANSWER, &c.

৶৶৶৶৶৶৶৶৶৶৶৶৶৶

TRANSLATED FROM THE GERMAN.

৶৶৶৶৶৶৶৶৶৶৶৶৶৶

EASTON:
Printed by JACOB WEYGANDT & Co. 1805.

Endress' English Pennsylvania Catechism, 1805.

(Presbyterian Historical Society)

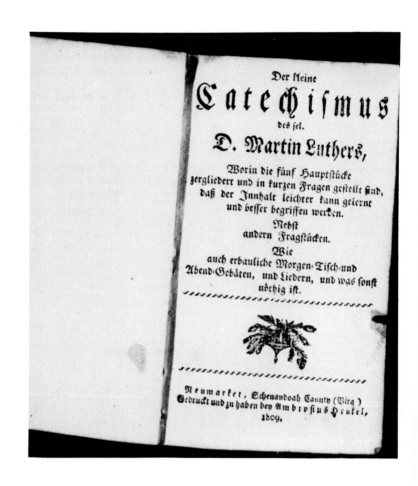

Der kleine

Catechismus

des sel.

D. Martin Luthers,

Worin die fünf Hauptstücke
zergliedert und in kurzen Fragen gestellt sind,
daß der Innhalt leichter kann gelernt
und besser begriffen werden.

Nebst
andern Fragstücken.

Wie
auch erbauliche Morgen-Tisch-und
Abend-Gebäten, und Liedern, und was sonst
nöthig ist.

Neumarket, Schenandoah Caunty (Virg)
Gedruckt und zu haben bey Ambrosius Henkel,
1809.

Paul Henkel's German Catechism, 1809.

(Virginia State Library, Richmond, Va.)

DOCTOR MARTIN LUTHER'S
SHORTER
CATECHISM,

TREATING

1. OF THE TEN COMMANDMENTS,
2. OF THE APOSTLES' CREED,
3. OF THE LORD'S PRAYER,
4. OF THE SACRAMENT OF BAPTISM,
5. OF THE SACRAMENT OF THE LORD'S SUPPER.

TO WHICH IS ADDED,

1. A TABLE OF DUTIES,
2. AN ORDER OF SALVATION IN SHORT QUESTIONS AND ANSWERS,
3. QUESTIONS & ANSWERS FOR YOUTH WHO ARE PREPARING THEMSELVES TO RECEIVE THE LORD'S SUPPER,
4. PRAYERS AND HYMNS FOR THE USE OF CHILDREN, &c.

MOSTLY TRANSLATED FROM THE GERMAN.

BARDSTOWN,

PRINTED BY WILLIAM BARD.

1811.

"Bardstown" Catechism, 1811.

(Presbyterian Historical Society)

EVANGELICAL

CATECHISM:

OR

A SHORT EXPOSITION

OF THE PRINCIPAL

DOCTRINES AND PRECEPTS OF THE CHRISTIAN RELIGION,

For the Use of the Churches belonging to the

EVANGELICAL LUTHERAN SYNOD OF THE STATE OF NEW-YORK.

TO WHICH ARE ADDED:

I. A scriptural advice to the young. II. Sir M. HALE's character of a true Christian. III. An address to those who wish to be confirmed. IV. A sketch of the history of Religion. V. A collection of prayers for parents and children.

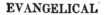

By FREDERICK HENRY QUITMAN, D. D.

President of the Synod, and Minister of the Gospel in Rhinebeck.

With consent and approbation of the Synod.

HUDSON:

PUBLISHED BY WILLIAM E. NORMAN.

1814.

Quitman's Evangelical Catechism, 1814.

(Author's copy)

INSTRUCTION

IN THE

PRINCIPLES AND DUTIES

OF THE

CHRISTIAN RELIGION,

FOR

CHILDREN AND YOUTH:

CONTAINING

1. Dr. Martin Luther's Short Catechism, translated from the German.
2. A Scripture Catechism.
3. The Christian Character and Duties, and the Christian's Comforts and Hopes, expressed in the words of Scripture.
4. A Historical Catechism.
5. The Elements of Religion and Morality, for younger Children.
6. To which are added a few Prayers.

PHILADELPHIA:

PRINTED FOR DANIEL BRÆUTIGAM,
No. 194, North Second Street.

Conrad Zentler, Printer.

1821.

Ph. Fr. Mayer's Instruction, 1821.

(Lutheran Theological Seminary, Gettysburg, Pa.)

PRINCIPLES

OF THE

Christian Religion,

IN QUESTIONS AND ANSWERS,

DESIGNED

FOR THE INSTRUCTION OF YOUTH

IN

Evangelical Churches.

By

George Lochman, D.D.

HARRISBURG:

Printed by John S. Wiestling.

....

1822.

Lochman's <u>Principles</u>, 1822.

(Lutheran Theological Seminary, Gettysburg, Pa.)

THE

LUTHERAN

CATECHISM;

OR,

AN EXPOSITION OF THE FUNDAMENTAL DOCTRINES OF

CHRISTIANITY,

AS CONTAINED

IN THE SHORTER CATECHISM,

OF

Dr. Martin Luther.

———◦◦◦———

CANAJOHARIE:

PRINTED BY H. HOOGHKERK,

1827.

The "Canajoharie" Catechism, 1827.

(Lutheran Theological Seminary, Gettysburg, Pa.)

DOCT. MARTIN LUTHER'S

SMALLER

CATECHISM,

TRANSLATED FROM THE GERMAN;

WITH PRELIMINARY OBSERVATIONS BY THE TRANS-
LATOR. REVISED AND PUBLISHED BY ORDER
OF THE EVANGELICAL LUTHERAN
TENNESSEE SYNOD.

TO WHICH ARE ADDED SUNDRY

HYMNS AND PRAYERS.

———

NEW-MARKET:

PRINTED IN SOLOMON HENKEL'S OFFICE.
1828.

David Henkel's Catechism, 1828.

(Lutheran Theological Seminary, Gettysburg, Pa.)

THE SMALLER

CATECHISM,

OF

DR. M. LUTHER.

TRANSLATED FROM THE GERMAN.

PUBLISHED BY ORDER OF THE GENERAL SYNOD OF THE
EVANGELICAL LUTHERAN CHURCH IN
THE UNITED STATES.

FREDERICK, Md.

PRINTED AND PUBLISHED BY CHARLES NAGLE

1826.

General Synod Catechism, 1826.

(Lutheran Theological Southern Seminary, Columbia, S. C.)

Catechismus der

Chriſtlichen Lehre,

in Fragen und Antworten.

Gehorche Jeſu Lehre,
So wird die Jugend rein,
Dein Alter Glück und Ehre,
Dein Ende ſelig ſeyn.

Von
G. F. J. Jäger, Lutheriſchem Prediger in
Berks Caunty, Pennſylvanien.

Kutztaun,
Gedruckt bey Hawrecht und Wink.
1833.

G. F. J. Jäger's Catechism, 1833.

(Lutheran Theological Seminary, Philadelphia, Pa.)

Dr. Martin Luthers
Kleiner
Catechismus

Auf Churfl. Durchl. zu Sachsen
Gnädigsten Befehl,

Vom Ministerio z. H. Kreuz in Dresden
durch Frag und Antwort erläutert, auch mit
angeführten Sprüchen Heil. Schrift bekräftiget,
und nach vorhergegangener

Des Kirchen = Raths und Ober = Con-
sistorii, auch beider Theol. Facultäten in
Leipzig und Wittenberg

CENSUR und APPROBATION,

In Kirchen und Schulen zum allgemei-
nen Gebrauche eingeführet und von
Druckfehlern geläutert.

* * * * * * * * * * *

Mit Königl. Sächs. allergnädigstem
Special-Privilegio.

Buffalo,
Gedruckt in der Druckerei v. G. Zahm,
1845.

Dresden Cross Catechism, 1845.

(Concordia Historical Institute, St. Louis, Mo.)

DR. MARTIN LUTHER'S

SMALLER CATECHISM;

TO WHICH IS ADDED,

THE ORDER OF SALVATION

AND

AN ANALYSIS OF THE CATECHISM,

WITH OTHER MATTERS RELATING TO CONFIRMATION.

TRANSLATED FROM THE GERMAN, SOME OF WHICH HAVE NEVER BEFORE
APPEARED IN THE ENGLISH LANGUAGE.

TO WHICH IS ADDED

THE AUGSBURGH CONFESSION,

CAREFULLY TRANSLATED FROM THE GERMAN.

NEW YORK:

PUBLISHED BY HENRY LUDWIG, PRINTER,
Nos. 70 & 72 Vesey-Street.

AND FOR SALE BY WM. RADDE, 322 BROADWAY.

AND THE PRINCIPAL BOOKSELLERS THROUGHOUT THE UNION.

———

1 8 4 7.

Henry Ludwig's Catechism, 1847.

(Author's copy)

> Fifth Edition, from the fourth enlarged edition, New
> Market, Va.: S. Henkel's Printing Office, 1816.

Though the edition before us bore the date 1816, it
carried a resolution from the minutes of the "German and
English Lutheran Church, in N.C." which began the third
Sunday of October, 1817.

> It is the duty of every preacher, to instruct all the
> children from 12 years old and upwards in the cat-
> echism.--The small catechism of Doctor Martin Lu-
> ther in the German Language; and the Christian Cat-
> echism, (edited by the Rev. Paul Henkel, and printed
> in New Market) in the English Language are to be
> used for such instruction.

While the original date for the 5th edition may have
been 1816, it is obvious that the date in subsequent printings
remained unchanged even when an 1817 reference was inserted.
Otherwise this edition had no changes of consequences. It
still included Henkel's preface of April 11, 1811.

The resolution of the North Carolina Synod speaks for
itself. Henkel's Christian Catechism had won official recognition for the instruction of the youth in a wider circle than
had been anticipated.

THE GERMAN CHRISTIAN CATECHISM (1811-1816)

> Der Christliche Catechismus, Verfasst zum Unter-
> richt der Jugend in der Erkenntniss der Christlichen
> Religion, samt Morgen- und Abend- Lieder, und
> Gebete. 1st ed. New Market: Ambrosius Henkel
> und Co., 1811.[24]

The year 1811 was a busy year for Paul Henkel and
his press. Der Christliche Catechismus was his third catechism to appear in print. The signed preface was more explicit in stating the purpose Henkel had in mind for his new
rendition. He had, he wrote, been asked by many Christian
parents of different denominations to prepare a catechism or
a book of instruction of this kind for the instruction of the
young. He realized, of course, that there were many different German catechisms for the youth but they were all written to meet the religious viewpoints of their denomination,
bearing also the name of the same. He believed there was a

need for a catechism that was more general in its thrust and
for this reason he had prepared this book.   He had made
every effort to have this catechism conform to the Holy Scriptures.   He had taken pains also to keep the text as simple
and clear as possible.   Since he had recently prepared a
similar catechism in English, which had been well received,
he thought he should all the more prepare one for the Germans in their own language.   The preface was dated October
1, 1811.

In the main the German rendition was the same as the
English, though with some minor differences.   The English
removed the Bible references in the Chief Parts; these were
included in the German.   The explanation to the Third Commandment (his Fourth) was an improvement.   It read in part,
"that we should fear and love God that we may not despise
preaching (the Gospel) and his Word."   He not only defined
preaching, he also omitted the reference, "especially on the
sabbath day" (p. 6).[25]

He changed some of the Bible references in the Order
of Salvation, which otherwise remained the same.   The German had many of the same hymns though there were some
differences probably because the German hymnals offered a
better selection than the English.   In the Table of Duties,
Henkel remained faithful to the Luther text, leaving Of Rulers
or Magistrates unchanged and omitting the addition in the
English on Of Aged Men and Of Aged Women.

In 1816, a second edition appeared with an enlarged
title the same as his English rendition of 1816.   This edition
was registered with the clerk of the District of Virginia the
same day, January 9, 1816, as the fourth English edition.
In most instances it was a translation of that revision, including all the additions.   There were two minor additions,
however.   On the page facing the preface, Henkel listed five
Bible passages, each one setting forth the importance of
Christian instruction, especially of children by their parents.

The selection of hymns was augmented to include several to be sung at meal time.   The Table of Duties was augmented by the two paragraphs in the English, Of Aged Men
and Of Aged Women.

Like the Christian Catechism, the German rendition
sold well.   Laurentz Wartmann, head printer for Ambrose
Henkel and Co., wrote to Paul Henkel January 28, 1812,

that he had printed and finished 1500 English catechisms since
Paul had left, and then added, "The sale for the German and
English Catechism is very large."[26] Recognition to both
Christian Catechisms was given by the North Carolina Synod
in 1812, when it addressed the question which catechism
should be normative. "It was unanimously resolved that Luther's Smaller Catechism must ever be the basis of catechetical instruction; and the catechisms of Ambrosius Henkel, explaining Luther's catechism may be used, but this is left to
each pastor to do as he pleases."[27] Similarly permissive
use was accorded to the two catechisms by the Tennessee
Synod at its organization meeting in 1820. Speaking of Luther's Small Catechism the synod said it "shall always be the
chief catechism of our churches. But the Catechism styled
the Christian Catechism which was published in the German
and English languages, in New Market, Shenandoah County,
Virginia, may also be used in connection to explain Luther's
Catechism."[28]

Chapter VIII

INDEPENDENT GERMAN CATECHISMS, 1805-1834

With the exception of those congregations which were influenced by Paul Henkel's catechisms, only five new catechisms, one of doubtful character, are known to have been published independently for German speaking Lutherans during a period of almost 30 years, 1805-1834. Most congregations in need of a German catechism used the official catechism of the Pennsylvania Ministerium of which some 28 editions were printed during this time. The use of the authorized catechism was being strongly urged by the leaders of the Ministerium. So when the North Carolina Synod in 1812 addressed a letter to the Ministerium suggesting close cooperation between the two groups, Pres. Helmuth in his reply urged the North Carolina Synod, as one instance for closer ties, that they use the catechism "as it is printed in most places in Pennsylvania" and they introduce no new catechism unless both parties agreed to it.[1]

In addition to the Pennsylvania catechism, however, there was still some demand for Lochman's catechism also, since as noted earlier, three additional prints were made during the first two decades of this period.[2]

Unlike the English speaking Lutherans, the Germans, especially those in the rural areas, were somewhat insulated against the prevailing Deism that was undermining many of the churches of the day. In a number of instances where it was feared that the current spirit might affect the German Lutherans, pastors were strongly urged to place greater emphasis on the daily Christian life in their sermons and instruction, and with it encourage the "mutual edification" of one another.[3] In fact the Ministerium, as early as 1792, had made such "experimental religion," as it was called, a constitutional requirement for its clergy.[4] The moderately Pietistic thrust of the Pennsylvania catechism seemed to have served well for this purpose.

146

However, this emphasis on "experimental religion" in time paved the way for revivalism, or New Measures, which were already threatening some of the English speaking Lutherans, especially along the frontier where there were few resident pastors. When, therefore, Paul Henkel was reassigned as a traveling preacher in 1811 to Ohio, Kentucky, Virginia, and Pennsylvania, Pres. Helmuth was instructed to advise him "to have no dealings with camp meetings, if he should find such departures from our Evangelical ways."[5] One of the serious problems that arose in connection with New Measures was, as we shall see later, the decline of catechetical instruction which proved too tame when compared to the "instant" religion that was "gotten" in the revivals.

CONRAD F. TEMME'S CATECHISM, 1816

The five German catechisms printed during this period varied considerably in their faithfulness to the Lutheran witness. The earliest of these catechisms was prepared for Canadian Lutherans in 1816 by Conrad Ferdinand Temme of Lüneburg, Nova Scotia. Printed in Philadelphia it made its appearance under the title,

> Dr. Martin Luther's Catechism explained and provided with the Principal Prooftexts from Holy Scriptures, together with an Appendix for Evangelical Lutheran Christians in British North America. Philadelphia: Conrad Zentler, 1816.[6]

Temme was pastor of a congregation that, although primarily Lutheran, had strong ties with the Reformed as well as the Anglican Church. In fact while calling himself Lutheran, Temme was at the same time a member of the Society for the Propagation of the Gospel in Foreign Parts, and like other Canadian pastors of this period, had been ordained by the Anglicans in order to be recognized as a minister by the English authorities.

The German and Reformed settlers of Lüneburg had a long history together, having come to this area around 1750. In this somewhat isolated region from the rest of the Lutherans in America they at first experienced great difficulty in obtaining a pastor. They appealed to their fellow Germans in Europe and in Pennsylvania, often to no avail. In June 1768, they made a direct appeal to Mühlenberg. At that time they said they had about 150 families in the area and lamented the fact that their youth, some already in their second generation, had not yet been confirmed. [7]

At the time Mühlenberg was unable to help them. Eventually, in October 1772 the somewhat aged Friedrich Schultz of New York did come and served them for about ten years. [8]

After the war there was a greater influx of Lutherans and Reformed from the States, most of whom had been Tories during the war. The appeals for help were then directed to Halle and to Helmstädt. Through Halle they got Johann Schmeisser who served almost 25 years. He was followed by F. C. Temme in 1808, who had been directed to them by Helmstädt. He too was to remain in this area for some 25 years.

The congregation at first had been a union church but later the groups separated, though retaining close ties over the years.

Temme, who was a graduate of Helmstädt, dedicated his catechism to the theological faculty of the Helmstädt Academy in recognition of its support and service in providing pastors for the North American provinces.

Temme said he had a threefold purpose in mind when he wrote this catechism. 1) It was to serve as a summary of Christian religious truths for the adults of his congregation. The catechism was to be a means to keep these truths before their eyes and thus shield them from errors. Parents could use the book also to teach their children in the event there were no schools. 2) Children and young people could use the catechism as a text for instruction in school and church and so provide each confirmand with a catechism for life. 3) Hopefully, the catechism might serve also as a reader, in which children could practice spelling and reading.

The catechism was composed of the Five Chief Parts of Luther's catechism with a detailed explanation. Added were five appendices: 1) The Seven Penitential Psalms; 2) A Universal Confession of Faith for a Protestant Christian; 3) Morning- Evening- and Table- Prayers for Children; 4) A Confession of Faith at One's Confirmation; and 5) A daily Prayer of Pious Parents for their Children.

The catechism had some sound Lutheran emphases, but it nevertheless frequently displayed a strange mixture of Lutheran and Reformed views blended with Pietistic and Rationalistic leanings that were disturbing from a Lutheran viewpoint.

In the introductory section to Luther's catechism, Temme minimized the differences between the Lutherans and the Reformed, as well as with the Anglicans. Of the latter he stated, "The English church separated from the Roman Catholics and may be regarded as a sister church to the Lutherans because it fully agreed with in the essentials or in the main things." (p. 42).

From the outset the catechism magnified the importance of human reason and experience. Frequently reason and Scripture were paired together in judging doctrinal matters. Thus, Temme stated from these two sources we can believe that there is only one God (p. 32). In practice, however, much was set forth that was not "reasonable," yet very Scriptural, e.g. the Trinity (p. 85) and the angels (pp. 87f.).

Christ's descent into hell was enumerated and explained under his state of humiliation. In explaining it, Temme admitted that this article of faith was too deep for our human reason and must await our arrival in heaven. This much, he said, was clear, the descent was closely associated with Christ's burial and was the deepest depth of his humiliation (pp. 107f.).

Furthermore, Temme's explanation weakened the vicarious atonement, particularly when he allowed room for man's cooperation as essential to his redemption. While he listed the means of grace as the Word of God, prayer and the sacraments, his concept of the means was quite unusual. The Word of God was explained to be the means and opportunity wherein God, as it were, speaks or makes his will known to us. These means and opportunities were said to be human reason, the conscience, fortune and misfortune, the Holy Scriptures and the office of preaching (Q. 208-210, p. 121).

According to Temme, the laying on of hands by a pastor or bishop was essential to confirmation for thereby the promised Spirit was given to strengthen the faith and confirm one's baptismal covenant (p. 149).

The treatment of Baptism was meager and even some of this was questionable. For example, Temme maintained that Baptism must be performed by a certified pastor to be valid.

The explanation to the Lord's Supper was somewhat more carefully done but it too had some aberrations. Local circumstances probably prompted the advice that, while Jesus

did not state how often one should commune, the fact that
the Lord's Supper replaced the Passover suggested that one
should commune at least once a year. The true Christian
as a friend and venerator of Jesus would commune several
times a year if the opportunity were given him.

The Universal Confession of Faith for a Protestant
Christian, purportedly drawn from Scripture and the Augsburg Confession, continued in the same theological vein. It
was a mixture of human reason and Scripture. The second
paragraph already gave the setting for this "confession of
faith,"

> I believe in a true God, according to the principles
> of sound reason from nature and according to the
> revealed doctrinal statements from the Holy Scrip-
> tures, whom I, according to Jesus' direction am
> to confess as a triune God, in the Father, in the
> Son, and in the Holy Spirit. [p. 193]

Two other instances may be cited to reflect the viewpoint Temme was attempting to bring across.

> I believe that he who would be born again must be
> baptized by an ordained preacher of the Christian
> Church in the name of the Father, the Son, and
> the Holy Ghost; must be instructed in the doctrine
> of Jesus; and be confirmed and so of his own con-
> viction must join Jesus' institution of grace. [pp.
> 195f.]

Temme further stated that infant Baptism without confirmation was only half of a Baptism for the mature years
and thus would not be sufficient for an adult to be accepted
as a subject in Jesus' kingdom (pp. 196ff.).

The catechism contained a number of such strange
mixtures of Pietism and Rationalism, though one may unex-
pectedly also meet up with a series of sound doctrinal statement.

STECK'S BRIEF INSTRUCTION, 1817.

About the time that Temme published his somewhat rationalistic catechism in Canada, John Michael Steck, pastor
at Grünsburg, Pa. was preparing a modification of the Penn-

sylvania catechism in an attempt to simplify it for confirmation instruction, without changing its confessional basis and
evangelical spirit.   He titled it,

> A Brief Instruction in the Christian Doctrine and
> an Examination for Confirmation.   1st ed.   Grüns-
> burg [Pa.]:   Johannes Armbrust & Companie, 1817.[9]

Speck included Luther's catechism according to the
text of the Pennsylvania edition, omitting, however, the Table of Duties and Luther's Prayers.   Obviously Steck felt
that the tabular form of presenting catechetical material was
too difficult to handle for confirmation instruction.   He therefore recast the Pennsylvania Analysis of the Catechism in the
form of questions and answers, but restricted himself to the
Ten Commandments.   The section was titled, Introduction to
the Holy Ten Commandments.   Interestingly, Steck followed
Luther's spirit more closely in the Third Commandment than
did the Pennsylvania catechism by avoiding the usual Reformed
emphasis for which Lutherans with a Pietistic orientation were
noted.

The second part was titled, In Short Questions and Answers.   Here in a more ambitious vein Steck combined the
73 questions and answers of the Würtembergische Kinder-
Examen with the 169 in Starcke's Order of Salvation in Questions and Answers, using the former as the basis for his
new structure, some questions from Freylinghausen's Order
and part of Starcke's table, The Order of Salvation in Nine
Statements were interspersed.   What might have been an awkward hodgepodge turned out, with a few exceptions, to be a
fairly smooth presentation.   Here and there a rough spot
shows through, but by and large it was suitable for its purpose (e.g. Q. 306-07, p. 46 and Q. 334-37, p. 49).

Steck's third part, titled The Explanation of the Four
States of Man, was a conversion of Starcke's Order of Salvation in a Short Table into 188 questions and answers.   It
began with the second part of Starcke's Table which dealt
with man, using his fourfold divisions as a pattern: man's
state of innocence, of sin, of grace, and of glory.   This
part contained a fuzzy section concerning man's will wherein
the author said God gave man a free will either to be saved
or to be lost (p. 63), but added that man cannot himself believe for this was worked alone in him by the Holy Spirit (p. 64).

At the close of these three sections, Steck added Some

Important Stanzas which Occur in the Examination. He concluded with the Würtembergische form for the confession of
sin and three hymns, two from the Pennsylvania catechism
and one his own selection.

We may well concur with Schmucker's evaluation of
this instruction book, "The whole catechism leaves on an ex-
aminer a strong impression of the excellence, earnestness
and diligence in his work of the author."[10]

"CARLISLE" CATECHISM, 1820

title,
In 1820, an anonymous catechism appeared under the

> The Lutheran Catechism for the Youth, especially
> for those who wish to be Confirmed. Carlisle:
> John M. Farland, 1820.[11]

Though the title implied that this booklet was prepared also
for the youth in general in mind, the level of the material
would likely limit it to those immediately preparing for confirmation. From the distance from which one must necessarily judge this catechism, it would appear that the level
was, in fact more suitable even for somewhat younger children.

The first part, called Introduction to the Catechism,
dealt only with the first three Chief Parts of Luther's catechism. The questions and answers were limited to dissect-
ing the wording of Luther's catechism into smaller bits. The
second part, The Questions and Answers for Those Preparing
for the Sacrament, was cast much in the same way. Part
three dealt with Starcke's Order of Salvation in a Short Table. It was recast in the form of questions and answers.
The sacrament of Baptism was treated only in this section
and then in a very brief manner. The Lord's Supper, which
had received some attention under the Christian Questions
and Answers, was given minimal emphasis in this part.

The final section, Special Questions, was directed to
those about to be confirmed. It emphasized the need to confess and apply the instruction given, to one's life. But at
this point the author regrettably allowed the importance of
reason to slip in. To the question, "What gives you the assurance and why do you confess this? [i. e. your certainty

that the Christian doctrine is true], the answer given was, "Because it agrees with my experience and is grounded in the Holy Scriptures" (p. 29).

JÄGER'S CATECHISM, 1833

Gottlieb F. J. Jäger, pastor of the Pennsylvania Ministerium serving congregations in Berks County, Pennsylvania, [12] prepared a catechism of his own in 1833, bearing the title,

> A Catechism of Christian Doctrine in Questions and Answers. Kutztaun [Pa.]: Hawrecht and Wink, 1833. [13]

The catechism was arranged in two uneven parts, Concerning the Doctrines (pp. 5-37) and The Duties of the Christian Life (pp. 38-43). The material and form of the part on Doctrines was largely based on Starcke's Order of Salvation in Questions and Answers. Luther's catechism was used only in the explanations of the Second Article of the Creed and for the definition of Baptism.

The second part on the Duties was in fact Luther's explanation of the Ten Commandments.

The appendix contained two hymn stanzas as prayers and the Hymn of Faith. These were followed by Questions after the Examination and before the Rite of Confirmation and the Confession of Sins to a Pastor. The final section was a hymn for the children partaking of the Lord's Supper for the first time (ten stanzas), closing with four stanzas to be sung by the congregation.

Since the author did not make full use of Luther's catechism he did not always catch the deeper evangelical meaning. On one point Jäger was somewhat unique. In the introductory section he had enumerated the four world religions, Judaism, Christianity, Mohammedanism, and Heathenism and stated that the Christian religion was the best. This was followed by the question, "Are, however, the other religions therefore damned and lost?", to which the answer was, "No! for Jesus said, Matt. 8:11, 'many will come etc.'" (p. 3). Under the same means of grace, Jäger further asked, "Are the means of grace necessary for salvation for all people?" The answer given was "No; only for those who can have them" (p. 25).

The catechism did not include prayer among the means of grace as other catechisms frequently had done. Even the Word of God as a means of grace was not equated with the Bible. Jäger clearly stated that the Word of God was contained in the Holy Scriptures (p. 25), though he allowed later that the Bible may be called the Word of God because it came from Him (p. 26).

According to B. M. Schmucker, Jäger's catechism appeared in several editions. He cited the 4th edition printed in 1853 in Hamburg. He further cited an edition by his son, T. T. Jäger, in which the catechism was appended to the Ministerium catechism. Whether this was a new catechism or a revision of his father's is not clear. It was given the title,

> An Explanation of the Catechism for Use in Confirmation Instruction, by G. F. J. Jäger, Allentown: Brobst, Diehl & Co. 14

It is likely that this edition was printed after 1850 but the writer has not seen it, nor any of the editions beyond the 1833 copy.

H. WM. SCRIBA'S "ANFANGSGRÜNDE," 1834

Whether Scriba's Anfangsgründe [Rudiments] should be considered in a study of Luther's catechisms may seriously be doubted on several counts. First is the fact that the book makes no reference to Luther's catechism nor was it intended to be used alongside of it. Secondly, and this is probably the most important reason, is the fact that it was not even Lutheran in its theological witness. It was translated, according to Scriba, from the French, though he mentioned neither the author nor the title of the original text. Since it was a French book, we have a strong clue of its Reformed origin. Since, however, Anfangsgründe has been listed as a Lutheran catechism in several Lutheran bibliographies, it has been included in this study. 15

No doubt the book has been listed as a Lutheran text because Scriba was a Lutheran pastor and ministered to a Lutheran congregation in Strassburg, Franklin County, Pa., when the book was published. At the time he was a member of the West Pennsylvania Synod and remained on its roll until 1839. What happened after that has not been determined. 16

Scriba's translation appeared under the title,

Rudiments of Christianity or a Brief Summary of
the Truths and Duties of the Christian Religion.
Chämberburg, [Pa.]: Heinrich Ruby, 1834.17

There was frequently a strange blending or confusion of the
law and the Gospel, as well as the use of reason in support
of a biblical truth.   To the question, for instance, "How can
we be certain that the Christian religion is the true religion?"
the answer given was, "Through its author, which is Jesus
Christ, the Son of God, through the marvelous deeds which
he performed, and the establishment of a very reasonable
worship" (p. 3).

The catechism does set forth clearly that mankind was
redeemed by Jesus Christ (p. 23).   The Spirit saves us, "in
that he reveals to our spirit our duties and inclines our will
to do them" (p. 47).   The catechism points out that it is not
sufficient to know and believe that Jesus Christ is the Redeemer of the world, that through his death he attained the
forgiveness of our sins and eternal salvation, but one must
accompany that faith with a sincere effort to live a good life
(pp. 61f.).   The emphasis thereafter is on the ethical duties
of a true Christian, as had already been indicated by Scriba
in his preface.

Such an effective, living faith is produced by the Word
of God through the Holy Spirit.   This the Spirit effects
through reading and meditating on the Word and by prayer
in which we ask God that he give us this faith (p. 63).   Nothing is said at this point about the sacraments.

The catechism thereafter presents the Ten Commandments, dividing them in the Reformed manner.   The Sabbath
is said to be binding upon us for God requires a day of rest
after six working days.   Christians have chosen Sunday as
their Sabbath (pp. 77f.), and this day is observed not only
by attending worship but in spending the day in meditation
and prayer and in only the most necessary tasks.

In addition to believing the truths of God and exercis-
ing his Christian duties the true believer is to observe the
sacraments (p. 114).

In treating Baptism, the emphasis is placed on man's
action rather than the gracious activity of God.   In Baptism,

it is said, we enter the Christian Church and dedicate ourselves to the Triune God, for Baptism represents to us the
cleansing of our sins and our regeneration (p. 115).

The Lord's Supper is likewise explained as a symbol
for the bread represents for us the body and the wine, the
blood of Christ (pp. 118f.). As bread and wine together
nourish us, so the body and blood of Christ nourish us in
the hope of eternal life (p. 119). It is not the natural body
and blood of Christ that feeds our soul, for that would be
impossible. We are offered the redemptive work of Jesus
Christ in the sacrament for it is a seal to assure us that
we have been redeemed. Thus the Lord's Supper is not a
mere representation of the death of Christ, but a means by
which we become partakers of the benefits of his death in
order to have a true fellowship with him. Thus the catechism denies the real or sacramental presence but yet the
sacrament is regarded as a means whereby we receive the
benefits of his redemption (pp. 120f.).

Much is made of the fellowship in the Lord's Supper.
The reverent communicant therein unites in fellowship with
Christ and he with him and therein we have a fellowship, a
special relationship, with all believers.

The catechism closes with a series of short prayers
for one's devotion as one partakes of Holy Communion and
for use in one's daily worship at home.

Chapter IX

ENGLISH CATECHISMS DURING THE RISE OF
"AMERICAN LUTHERANISM, " 1820-1828

The writers of English catechisms did not surrender
to the type of Rationalism which Quitman had unsuccessfully
fostered, although they did reflect a strong reaction to this
threat by manifesting a closer tie with the English Protestant
denominations about them. Unlike the German Lutherans who
rallied to the generally accepted Pennsylvania Ministerium
catechism, the English Lutherans had no catechism of official standing in the 1820's to which they might turn. The
catechism of the New York Ministerium had not taken hold
over the long period and the Paul Henkel catechisms were
acceptable only in limited areas. Consequently English-
speaking Lutherans found a closer kinship with other Protestant communities about them and made common cause with
them against Rationalism and the general religious indifference
of the day. The failure of the German-speaking Lutherans of
an earlier generation was now taking its full toll. When the
rising German immigration toward the end of the 1820's and
in the early 1830's absorbed most of their resources, the
losses to the English denominations and to a non-Lutheran
stance did not seem to be a serious problem.

The English catechisms produced during this period
reflected the general influence of the Protestant denominations' religious viewpoint. More and more of the catechisms
surrendered Luther's evangelical freedom in the interpretation of the Decalog and reverted to an Old Testament version.
Equally evident was the loss of the Lutheran witness concerning the sacraments. The explanation of both Baptism and the
Lord's Supper took on more generally a symbolical meaning,
their power as a means of grace thereby was lost. Only the
practice of infant Baptism was not surrendered. In fact, it
was singled out as a sound practice over against the Baptists
who were particularly active at this time and who attempted
to proselyte among the Protestants, especially on the frontier.

157

The surrender of the uniquely Lutheran witness had
to be squared with Luther's catechism as well as with the
other symbols of the Lutheran Church.   Under the leadership of S. S. Schmucker and assisted by likeminded leaders
such as John G. Lochman and Ernest L. Hazelius, the binding nature of the Confessions was consequently denied.   To
alter Luther's catechism, especially concerning the Lord's
Supper, was therefore not deemed non-Lutheran but rather
an adjustment to changing times.

One other element may be seen in the English catechisms of this period.   The popularity of the New Measures
also in many quarters of English-speaking Lutherans had its
effect on confirmation instruction.   Catechetical classes were
said to encourage a rote Christianity, lacking the warmth
and excitement of camp meetings.   Consequently there was
a growing tendency to drop formal instruction and rely more
on New Measures.   The catechisms prepared during this
decade were in many instances meant to counteract this growing neglect in favor of the revivals. [1]

F. C. SCHAEFFER'S CATECHISM, 1820

Luther's Short Catechism, New York: E. Conrad,
1820.

Friedrich C. Schaeffer (1792-1831), pastor of the
United Congregations in New York, produced a catechism in
1820, that was unusual in several respects. [2]   It reversed
the order of the first two Chief Parts of Luther's catechism
and based the catechism on the wording of Exodus 20.   Thus
the catechism began with the Apostolic Creed.   The Third
Article was changed to read, "I believe in the Holy Ghost,
the holy Catholic (universal) Church."

The use of Exodus 20, for the wording of the Ten
Commandments instead of Luther's became, as stated earlier, a common practice during this decade and the next.
This was done to accommodate the growing custom of even
closer fraternization with other Protestant churches in a
common cause during the time when the confessional stance
of Lutherans was weakening.

By using the Exodus version, Schaeffer found it necessary to write his own explanation for the new Second Commandment:

What is more particularly enjoined in this commandment?

That we should so fear and love God, as not to
represent him or his attributes under any figure
or form, with an intention to direct our devotion
to it [p. 9].

While the translation of the catechism was not the
same as Kuntze-Strebeck's, there were some striking simi-
larities. Schaeffer was more faithful to the Luther text in
the Lord's Supper.

The Office of the Keys consisted of the three Bible
passages frequently substituted for the more traditional
verses. It was followed by Luther's Confession of Sins.

An unusual feature of this catechism was the inclusion of a section called Extracts from Luther's Larger Catechism, taken from his Brief Exhortation to Confession.[3]

Following this was The Christian Doctrine Systematically Arranged. This was Starcke's Order of Salvation in
a Short Table, but not rendered in outline or tabular form,
but in paragraphs and thus made more meaningful for the
youth. The contents were basically the same.

LOCHMAN'S PRINCIPLES OF THE CHRISTIAN RELIGION, 1822-1834

John George Lochman (1773-1826), already the author
of a German catechism, published an English one while pastor at Harrisburg, Pa., and president of the newly formed
General Synod (1821).[4] His lack of confessional concern
came through more clearly in his English publication than
in his German one. At the time his catechism appeared he
was on the catechism committee of the General Synod.
Strictly speaking, it was not a Luther catechism since it
did not include his text, though occasionally it was cited but
without any reference to the author. The catechism was important for the non-confessional stance it represented during
that critical period when the spirit of the Proposed Plan
(Plan Entwurf) and later, S. S. Schmucker's American Lutheranism, fostered by the General Synod, threatened to de-
stroy the unique evangelical witness of the Lutheran Church
in many parts of this country.[5]

Lochman's catechism first appeared in 1822, under the title,

> Principles of the Christian Religion, in Questions and Answers, designed for the Instruction of Youth in Evangelical Churches. Harrisburg: John S. Wiestling, 1822.

The title reflected the spirit of the author, lacking as it does any reference to "Lutheran," and stating that it was designed for Evangelical Churches. In fact, the preface made it clear that the more correct name for the denomination was "The Evangelical Church," the designation "Lutheran," having been given to it by its opponents.

A striking example of Lochman's non-Lutheran stance may be found in the same preface, in which he stated that the leading principles of this church were,

> That the Holy Scriptures, and not human authority, are the only source from whence we are to draw our religious sentiments, whether they relate to faith or practice.

> That Christians are accountable to God alone for their religious principles, and that therefore no person should be punished by the civil authority, for his religious principles, as long as he makes no attempt to disturb the peace and order of civil society. And

> That Christ has left no record, no express injunction with respect to the external regulation and form, which is to be observed in his Church, and consequently, that every society has a right to establish such a form, as seemeth conducive to the interests, and adapted to the peculiar state, circumstances and exigencies of the community; provided that such regulations be in no respect prejudicial to truth, or favorable to the revival of superstition. Hence some of the Lutheran Churches have an Episcopalian form of government, as in Denmark, Sweden, etc.; and others have more of a Presbyterian form, as in many parts of Germany, Prussia and America.

Thus we see no reference to the confessionally strong Lutheran emphasis on the centrality of the Gospel. The last two principles were obviously of secondary importance and were probably brought to the fore by some of the discussion current during the formation and early years of the General Synod.

Among the introductory questions of the catechism there was already a telling statement that reflected much of its blandness or ambiguity.

> 4. What does the Gospel principally teach?
>
>> What we are to believe and what we are to do, in order to live right and die happy.

The catechism itself was composed of five parts followed by several orders of salvation and a section of hymns and prayers. The five parts were, The Christian Creed; the Ten Commandments; an Order of Salvation, or the Terms on which Sinners are Saved; the Means of Grace; and A Future State.

Lochman also felt constrained to abandon the traditional Lutheran division of the Ten Commandments and reverted, in the spirit of the time, to the Exodus rendition. In a footnote he offered some background for the change and listed the Lutheran division, after which he said,

> To this division the Lutherans adhered at the time of the Reformation, and the greatest part of them adhere to it yet. But finding, that some take offence at this division, and not wishing to dispute about trifles, the compilers of this catechism have given it up, and adopted the division made by other protestant churches. [p. 19]

The ceremonial and civil emphasis of the Old Testament Sabbath were not mentioned in his Fourth Commandment, though this explanation was given,

> The Sabbath with the Jews was the seventh day of the week, called Saturday; but the Christians set apart the first day of the week, called Sunday or Lord's day; because on that day, Jesus arose from the dead, and because the Apostles set it apart for divine worship. 1 Cor. 16,2. [p. 20]

The general Protestant view of the Sabbath was thus

retained and the evangelical freedom of the New Testament, reflected in Col. 2:16.17, as set forth in Luther's Third Commandment, was ignored.

Part III, The Terms on which Sinners are Saved, often missed the mark and dulled the meaning and importance of the Gospel. For example, the evidence of true repentance were explained to be,

> A knowledge of our sins, a hearty concern and sorrow on account of them, ardent prayers for pardon, renouncing every evil principle and practice, and an unreserved dedication of ourselves to God. [p. 26]

This loss was retrieved somewhat in later answers, without removing the ambiguity entirely.

Part IV, The Means of Grace, in the current explanation of that day were said to be, "The reading and hearing of his word--prayer--and the holy Sacraments" (p. 29). This was contradicted later in the Order of Salvation in Systematical Connection, where the means of grace were said to be Word of God and the sacraments (p. 50).

While the sacraments were explained to be ordinances wherein "the benefits of Christ's redemption are not only represented, but also really communicated and applied to penitent believers" (p. 30), this did not come through clearly in the presentation of the individual sacraments. As a matter of fact the above explanation put in question whether the sacraments were valid in the case of unbelievers.

In a footnote, Lochman amplified the necessity for baptizing children with the following interesting observation.

> All who have a right to the end, for the communication of which, means were instituted, must also have a right to the means. Now, according to Scripture, children are entitled to the end or grace which baptism confers, therefore they are entitled to the means, viz, baptism.
>
> Besides, parents have a right to make contracts for their children, as long as they are not come to years of discretion [p. 32].

Nothing was said of the sacramental presence of our

Lord in the Supper. Furthermore the purpose of this sacrament was stated in a bland manner to be,

> Not only to put us in mind of his great love to sinners; but also to offer unto us an interest in his sacrifice, and to assure us, that all penitent and believing souls should be partakers of it, as surely as they partook of the consecrated bread and wine. [p. 33]

Following his major five parts of the catechism, The Duties, Comforts and Hopes of Christians are given, expressed in the words of Scripture. These duties were shaped somewhat by Luther's Table of Duties, though a variety of different Bible passages were included. As the title indicated, it included two subsections on comforts and hopes of a Christian.

This was followed by the Principles of Religion in Short Sentences. They were the altered form of Starcke's Order of Salvation in Nine Sentences, as found in the Pennsylvania catechism. [6]

Another of Starcke's order followed, The Order of Salvation in Systematical Connections. The translation appears to be original, differing somewhat from that of the New York Ministerium catechism of 1804.

The catechism closed with several prayers and hymns taken from Philip Mayer's 1806 catechism. In addition the closing hymn was a translation of the popular Glaubenslied as it had been translated by Christian Endress for Mühlenberg's Table of Gospel Instruction. [7]

Lochman's catechism obviously met a favorable response in some quarters of the Lutheran Church. At least four reprints were made, some with minor changes.

Hagers-town, Md.: Gruber and May, 1823.

This edition added a number of hymns for several occasions and persons: before catechizing, at communion, saying the catechism, early piety, the young convert's prayer [sic], young persons worshiping God, and to remember the creator. In all there were 14 hymns.

2nd ed. Harrisburg: John S. Wiestling, 1825.

This copy was identical with the 1822 copy.

The next two editions were published after Lochman's death:

Germantown: M. Billmeyer, 1827.

This copy was also identical with the first edition.

4th ed. Harrisburg: Jacob Baab, 1834.

This was the only issue, printed seven years later, that mentioned the name of the author. It contained some minor changes. The Duties, Comforts and Hopes of a Christian was shortened by including only the Bible references. It omitted the prayers at the end of the catechism but included a new set of five hymns, dealing with catechetical instruction and confirmation. They were deeply emotional and may have reflected the influence of the New Measures on confirmation.

E. L. HAZELIUS' MANUAL FOR CATECHIZATION, 1823

Much in the manner of Lochman, Ernest Lewis Hazelius (1777-1853) represented a group of influential leaders in the Lutheran Church who raised their voices against Rationalism which was threatening the very life of the church. In a common approach to a common enemy, Hazelius was willing like many others in his day, to gloss over many of the theological differences between Lutherans and other Protestants. In that spirit, he was in fact ordained in September 1809 by the New York Ministerium.

Hazelius had been born in Germany and educated in Moravian schools. He came to America in 1800 and taught until 1809 in the Moravian academy in Nazareth, Pa. For a very brief period he taught in the school of St. John's in Philadelphia and still in the same year he was ordained and accepted a call to New Germantown (present Oldwick), N. J. During his stay there, in 1813, he published a translation of the Augsburg Confession, which clearly reflected his non-confessional bias. Among other matters he translated Article X on the Lord's Supper, to read that the true body and blood of Christ were "spiritually present," instead of "really present" (German, "wahrhaftiglich"). [8]

Years later Hazelius was to criticize David Henkel severely for his confessional stance on the power of regeneration of Baptism and for believing in the sacramental presence of our Lord in the Eucharist.[9]

Even though he lacked a confessional consciousness, Hazelius strongly favored catechetical instruction and the retention of confirmation, both of which tended to be eroded by that sector of the Lutheran Church that was involved in the New Measures of the revivalists.[10]

In 1815, Hazelius was appointed president of the newly formed Hartwick Seminary in western New York. While there, he prepared a catechetical manual for pastors called,

> Material for Catechization, on Passages of the Scripture, containing the Doctrines of Christian Faith and Morality. For the Instruction of Youth, especially in the Evangelical Lutheran Church. Cooperstown: Printed for the Theological Society of Hartwick Seminary, by H. & E. Phinney, 1823.

As the title implied, Hazelius believed that the manual could be used beyond the Lutheran Church since it was not based on any denominational text. Hazelius did intend that his manual be used by those who based their instruction on Luther's catechism for in the index he outlined how it might thus be used.

The manual consisted of Bible passages arranged in logical order under a series of topics. It consisted of two major parts. The first was titled, Passages or the Holy Bible containing the Doctrines of the Christian Religion, under which were listed such topics as, Concerning the Divinity of the Christian Religion; The Effects of the Religion of Jesus; Nature Demonstrates that there is a God; and God is the only Uncreated and Perfect Spirit, and Cannot be Seen. The "doctrines" were set forth in 32 sections. The second part consisted of passages containing the Christian Duties, toward God (sec. 34-39); toward particular persons (sec. 40-47); toward all others without distinction of office (sec. 48-56) and to ourselves (sec. 57-68). The final section listed passages containing comfort for the afflicted (sec. 69).

The grouping of the topics revealed a disproportionate amount of space to duties, while the means of grace, the Gospel and sacraments, received minimal treatment. Important passages, such as Romans 6:3-8 for Baptism were omitted. Like so many others before and after him, Hazelius

equated "Word of God" with the Bible and thus lost much of
the Lutheran thrust necessary to put the Gospel in its proper
setting.   No mention was made of the church as an article
of faith.

By preparing his manual in this manner, Hazelius
avoided making precise theological distinctions, allowing each
teacher the liberty to express himself in a manner most com-
fortable to him. [11]

THE GENERAL SYNOD CATECHISM, 1826-1893

The proliferation of many synods during the early decades of the nineteenth century created a renewed interest in
having Lutherans work together in a common cause, perhaps
even as a common church body.   One of the attempts took
the form of the Proposed Plan (Plan Entwurf) adopted by the
Pennsylvania Ministerium in 1819, and submitted to other interested synods.

After a prolonged discussion, considerable bitterness,
and a number of emendations to the plan, the movement
brought about the adoption of a constitution for a General
Synod in 1820.   Among other things, the proposed constitution authorized the general body to pass on all books, including catechisms, before they were issued by a member synod,
the General Synod reserving for itself the right also to publish such books for "common or public use."[12]

The constitution had no confessional clause, though in
its original proposal it had the very general statement allowing membership to Lutheran synods "holding the fundamental
doctrines of the Bible as taught by our Church."[13]

As one might expect, considering the proponents of
the new organization, the amended constitution expressed interest in cooperative work with other Christian denominations,
saying,

> The General Synod shall be sedulously and inces-
> santly regardful of the circumstances of the times,
> and of every casual rise and progress of unity of
> sentiment among Christians in general, of whatever
> kind or denomination, in order that the blessed op-
> portunities to heal the wounds and schisms already
> existing in the Church of Christ and to promote

general concord and unity, may not pass by neglected and unavailing. [14]

Three of the four synods with representation at the
constituting meeting had ratified the constitution (North Carolina, Maryland, and Pennsylvania) by the time the synod met
for its first official meeting in 1821.   One of the first points
of business was to appoint a committee "to compose an English catechism and to offer it to the consideration of the next
General Synod. "[15]

The committee for this task was C. Endress, J. G.
Schmucker, George Lochman, G. Shober and D. F. Schaeffer.
At its next meeting in 1823 the committee submitted its draft
which was in turn given to another committee for review. [16]
This committee was composed of G. Shober, D. F. Schaeffer,
John Herbst and S. S. Schmucker. [17]   According to S. S.
Schmucker,

> This committee, principally through our own ef-
> forts, resolved to retain Luther's Catechism for
> the present, and to report an improved translation
> of the questions, What is your state by nature?
> etc., with explanatory additions on the decalogue,
> infant baptism and the eucharist, which were fur-
> nished by ourself, ... [18]

By this time the Synod had been reduced to two member synods since the Pennsylvania Ministerium had withdrawn
in the face of opposition within, particularly from its German
rural constituency that feared membership might interfere
with its relationship with the German Reformed churches. [19]

While the General Synod was considering the issuance
of a new catechism, the North Carolina Synod, one of the
two remaining synods, was having internal problems of its
own.   Already in 1820, it had lost a significant number of
pastors and congregations from Tennessee for doctrinal reasons.   These had formed the Tennessee Synod.   A few years
later, in 1824, more were lost in the organization of the
South Carolina Synod.   Apparently conscious of the criticism
concerning its doctrinal position, the North Carolina Synod
resolved in 1825,

> As the complaint is universal, that so many differ-
> ent English catechisms are circulating under the
> name of Lutheran, and which are partly abridged

or not well translated, it was unanimously Resolved,
That none of our ministers can receive any catechism, thereby to instruct children, which in the
articles of faith or doctrinals departs from Dr. Luther's Small Catechism; because we are bound by
the constitution of the General Synod of our Church,
to make no change in the doctrine of the Church.[20]

Finally, later that same year, the General Synod resolved to publish the submitted catechism without, however,
following the recommendation of its reviewing committee. It
arranged with the firm of Gruber and May to have it printed.
The catechism was copyrighted by the firm on March 13,
1827.   There is some question when the first edition appeared
since an uncopyrighted edition was already published by the
firm of Charles Nagle of Frederick, Md. in 1826, under the
title,

> The Smaller Catechism, of Dr. M. Luther.   Fred-
> erick, Md.:   Charles Nagle, 1826.

The catechism was divided into nine sections: The
Five Chief Parts of Luther's Catechism, the Order of Salvation in Short Questions and Answers, the Order of Salvation
in Systematic Connexion, Questions and Answers for those
who would Prepare themselves to Receive the Lord's Supper,
and a final section of Prayers and Hymns.

Luther's Catechism was identical with the text of Mayer
in his Instruction in the Principles and Duties.   It was, however, heavily interspersed with Bible references, but made
no concessions to the reviewing committee suggestions.

Starcke's Order of Salvation in Short Questions and
Answers was taken from the catechism of the Pennsylvania
Ministerium in what appears to be an original translation,
differing from earlier translations in the catechisms of Endress, Bardstown, and Paul Henkel.

The next order of salvation, also from Starcke, was
taken from Lochman's Principles of the Christian Religion.
It was set forth in paragraphs rather than as a table, as it
originally appeared, thus making it somewhat difficult to read
and find through.

The Questions and Answers for those Preparing for the
Lord's Supper was given in a slightly altered form, though

interestingly enough it was not attributed to Luther. The
prayers and hymns were taken from Mayer's and Lochman's
catechisms, with some minor changes.

As stated earlier, a copyrighted edition appeared the
following year with a minor change in the title,

> Luther's Smaller Catechism.   Hagers-Town, Md.:
> Gruber and May, 1827.

With the exception of a few other minor changes in wording,
this catechism was identical with the earlier one.

There seemed to have been some disagreement between
the synod and the printer concerning the cost of the catechism.   The synod in 1827 tried to regain the copyright so
that the catechism could be printed elsewhere and be sold at
12 1/2 cents per copy.   Some agreement must have been
reached since the next three issues continued to be printed
by the same firm or its successor.

> Hagers-Town, Md.:   Gruber and May, 1828.
>
> 3rd ed. Hagers-Town, Md.:   Gruber and May, 1829.
>
> 4th ed. York, Pa.:   Daniel May, 1831.

Some minor changes were made in these three prints.
With the 1828 edition, the Order of Salvation in Systematic
Connexion was printed again in tabular form for easier reading.   Two hymns were added in 1828 for a total of 30.   For
some reason the 1829 edition changed the order of the sections
in the final part of the catechism.   This change was retained
in the 1831 edition.

At the 1831 meeting of the General Synod it was resolved that the catechism be stereotyped and printed by Lucas
and Deaver of Baltimore.   Four thousand copies were to be
printed. [21]

> Luther's Smaller Catechism, 3rd ed. published at
> Gettysburg for sale by Lucas & Deaver, Baltimore,
> 1832.

How the edition number was determined is not known.
With the new print a number of major changes were made in
the catechism, some obviously in accord with the recommen-
dations made earlier by the reviewing committee.   The influ-

ence of S. S. Schmucker, president of the General Synod, was much in evidence. Five questions were added to serve as an introduction to Luther's catechism, four of which were taken from Lochman's Principles. However, some changes were made here also. Lochman had written that the Christian derived his knowledge of religion chiefly from the Gospel, but this was revised to read, "from the New Testament."

The wording of the Ten Commandments was taken from Exodus 20, though the Lutheran division of the commandments was retained and explained in a footnote. The Third Commandment was expanded to include all of Exodus 20:8-11.

An asterisk was inserted in the Creed to explain that "descended into hell" meant "the Place of departed spirits."

Under the question, "What are the benefits of Baptism?" the answer, "It causes forgiveness of sins," was explained, "That is, it is one of the appointments for obtaining those blessings."

At the end of the part on Baptism, a lengthy explanation in the form of questions and answers was appended concerning the mode of baptism and particularly, infant baptism. The final question dealt with confirmation, stating that it was required of those baptized as infants "that they should make a personal profession of religion, that is, should 'confirm' the vows made for them at their baptism, so soon as they attain the years of discretion" (pp. 19f.).

Finally, in connection with the Lord's Supper a footnote elaborated on the presence of our Lord in the sacrament:

> "The Lutheran church," says the celebrated Dr. Mosheim, "does not believe in impanation, nor in subpanation, nor in consubstantiation; nor in a physical or material presence of the body and blood of the Saviour." Elementa Theol. Dog. in loc.
>
> But she maintains that the Saviour fulfills his promise, and is actually present, especially present, at the holy supper, in a manner incomprehensible to us, and not defined in scripture. And why should it be thought a thing impossible, that he, who fills immensity with his presence, should be there where his disciples meet to celebrate his dying love? [p. 20]

The order of the subsequent parts was changed about and, here and there, several minor revisions were made to simplify the text. Isaac Watt's, The Historical Catechism, was added from Mayer's Instruction, toward the end of the catechism.

However, one major revision was made. In the Questions and Answers for those who would Prepare themselves to Receive the Lord's Supper, the following serious omission was made in reference to the real or sacramental presence of the Lord:

> Dost thou believe that the body and blood of Christ are in the sacrament?
>
> Yes, I believe it.
>
> What induces thee to believe it?
>
> The words of Christ, "take and eat, this is my body; take and drink all of this, this is my blood."

This omission was made in all subsequent editions of the catechism.

The catechism appears to have been well received for by 1833, it was reported that some 2650 copies had been sold. [22] However, the leaders were far from satisfied. Dr. D. F. Schaeffer, president of the Synod complained bitterly, "some of the church members are not even acquainted with the distinguishing principles and doctrine of their own Church," and urged that the catechism be introduced in every family of the General Synod. [23]

The South Carolina Synod, though not as yet a member, had adopted the catechism as its own in 1827, but it did not enjoy the popularity expected. Consequently, in 1833 Morris' Catechetical Exercises became the official text. [24]

At the meeting of the Synod in 1837, the printing of the catechism was transferred to its own publication office. Thus the next edition appeared with the same title, bearing the following imprint,

3rd ed. Baltimore: Publication Rooms, 1840.

Since the catechism was a stereotyped reprint, there

were no changes in the text.   Among the later editions of
this reprint are:

> 3 ed. Baltimore: Publication Rooms, 1842.
>
> 8 ed. Baltimore: Publication Rooms of the Evan-
> gelical Lutheran Church, 1847.
>
> Rev. ed. Philadelphia: Lutheran Board of Publica-
> tion, Baltimore, T. Newton Kurtz, n.d.
>
> Rev. ed. Philadelphia: Lutheran Publication Soci-
> ety, n.d.

The edition above was reprinted innumerable times
over the years until the Synod adopted a new catechism at
a much later date.

In spite of the wave of revivalism that had struck
many of the member congregations of the General Synod, the
catechism continued to be used extensively.   Between 1833
and 1835 more than 3000 copies were sold.   From 1837
through 1839 another 5400 were reported sold.[25] However,
by 1848 it was felt that a revision was needed.   A committee
consisting of Henry L. Baugher, S. W. Harkey and V. L.
Conrad was chosen to study the matter.[26]

The committee drew up a set of rules which they
thought should guide the Synod in making the proposed revision:

> (1) To place Luther's Small Catechism as found in
> the present edition at the beginning of the work.
>
> (2) To frame a few additional questions and answers,
> in order to render more nearly complete the truths
> contained in the original without adhering strictly
> to the letter of Luther's answers.
>
> (3) To arrange the whole in a systematic form by
> the use of questions and answers of the order of
> salvation, not repeating those which have been in
> substance already presented in the illustrations of
> Luther's, and inserting those which have not at
> their proper place, thus forming one systematic,
> and not five catechisms.
>
> (4) To print in full but one passage, to prove each
> distinct idea contained in each answer.

> To secure unity both in design and style, they pro-
> pose that after the work shall have been completed
> by the whole committee, it shall be carefully re-
> vised by one of them and again submitted for ap-
> proval to the whole. [27]

The question of revising the catechism created a great
deal of attention because the Synod wished to find the most
effective means that were needed to counteract the "supra-
Lutheran" tendencies of the recently organized Buffalo (1845)
and the Missouri (1847) synods and the spirit of indifference
toward religion by a large number of the people.   In addition
they needed to offset the encroachments of those who fostered
New Measures within its member congregations. [28]

In fact the divisions with the General Synod were so
strong that the committee did not succeed with its plans.
After reporting verbally they were discharged.

In 1857, the Synod instructed J. A. Seiss of Baltimore
to correct the many typographical errors in the many Bible
references of the catechisms. [29]

Seiss complied and reported the corrections to T. Newton Kurtz of Baltimore who at this time was printing the catechism.   But he paid no attention to the list.   Instead he
printed on his own 10,000 copies of the old catechism when
he learned of the Synod's intention to make the revisions. [30]

So the matter rocked on.   Resolutions were passed,
committees were appointed, but no new catechism was printed.
The delay reflected the different trends within the church
body, each fearing the influence of the other in a final revision.   In the meanwhile the old catechism continued to be
printed or other English catechisms were substituted. [31]   Finally, in 1893 the Synod instructed its committee to print a
new catechism which appeared as,

> Luther's Small Catechism Developed and Explained.
> Philadelphia: Lutheran Publication Society, c. 1893.

H. N. POHLMAN'S CATECHISM, 1826

In 1826, a catechism prepared by Heinrich Newman
Pohlman (1800-1874), was published in Morristown, N.J.
Pohlman was the first graduate of the recently founded Hart-

wick Seminary, where his family's friend Hazelius was president.   Pohlman was ordained by the New York Ministerium
in May of 1821.   After a brief ministry in Saddle River, N.J.,
he was called in 1822 to the former parish of Hazelius, Zion
Church in New Germantown (Oldwick), N.J.   He remained
there for 21 years. [32]

While at Zion Church, the trustees at Pohlman's suggestion authorized him to prepare a catechism.   After "crit-
ically examining" his finished manuscript in April of 1825,
they unanimously resolved that 1000 copies "be published for
the use of our congregations."[33]

The title of Pohlman's catechism was

Catechism for the Use of Evangelical Lutheran
Churches.   Morris-Town, N.J.:   Jacob Mann, 1826.

The catechism contained the following parts: Luther's Five
Chief Parts, followed by Fundamental Questions, the True
Way to Salvation, an order of salvation, and an Analysis of
the Principles of Religion.

The first two Chief Parts of the Luther text were based
largely on the rendition found in Lochman's Principles.   It
contained no Bible references nor any questions that might
serve as additional helps.   Like Lochman, Pohlman began
with the Creed.   The interpretation "descended into hell" was
explained parenthetically to mean "or place of departed spirits."   So with the term "Catholic" in the Third Article, which
was explained to mean "universal."

Pohlman followed Lochman's example in giving up the
traditional division of the Ten Commandments and followed
the wording of Exodus 20, except in the new Fourth Commandment.   He used the same explanation for the new Second Commandment as Schaeffer did. [34]

Since Lochman did not use the Luther text for the
Lord's Prayer, Pohlman largely made use of the wording
which was similar to Mayer's 1811 catechism.   The same
was done for the sacraments, though a few minor changes
were made.

The Fundamental Questions were based on the New
York Ministerium Catechism of 1804, though Pohlman often
went on his own and so reduced the total number of questions

to 84.   While the New York catechism had departed from
Kuntze's original in the latter's "Question 94,"[35] Pohlman
changed the wording somewhat to allow for the sacramental
presence of Christ in the Lord's Supper.

Q. 75:   What do we receive in the Lord's Supper?

A.   The body and blood of Jesus Christ under the
external signs of bread and wine.

The True Way of Salvation comes from a source unknown to the writer.   It may have been original with Pohlman, though this is doubtful since nothing was said of Baptism, and the Lord's Supper was referred to only in passing.
Its weakness lies mainly in its omissions.

The title of the next section is not known to the writer since the page bearing the title was missing in the copy
consulted (p. 28).   It appears to be an order of salvation.
Though much was said about repentance and faith, it did not
treat the means of grace.   It did say that God's heavenly
grace was obtained in answer to fervent prayer and that one
must "be diligent in reading the Bible," for it contained the
words of eternal life, and was sufficient, "by the help of
God's Holy Spirit, to make me wise unto salvation."

The final section was Starcke's Short Table in a con-
densed form bearing the title, Analysis of the Principles of
Religion.

THE "CANAJOHARIE" CATECHISM, 1827

An anonymous catechism, whose author's identity has
not yet been determined, appeared in 1827, under the title,

The Lutheran Catechism; or, An Exposition of the
Fundamental Doctrines of Christianity, as contained
in the Shorter Catechism, of Dr. Martin Luther.
Canajoharie, [N.Y.]:   H. Hooghkerk, 1827.[36]

The catechism contained Luther's catechism (called
The Lutheran Catechism), including the Office of the Keys
and the Christian Questions and Answers; the Fundamental
Questions; the True Way to Salvation; the Order of Salvation
in Systematical Connection; and a few miscellaneous parts to
be described later.

The text of the Ten Commandments was based on Exodus 20, but set forth differently than in previous catechisms.
The First Commandment was the traditional Exodus 20:3 with
Luther's explanation but the Second Commandment was altered
in a number of ways.   The commandment itself was from Exodus 20:4-6, but the explanation was an altered form of Pohlman's, [37] to which was added Luther's explanation of his summary of all the commandments ("God threatens to punish, "
etc.).   The Third Commandment was Exodus 20:7, and a
modified Luther explanation.   The Fourth Commandment was
from Exodus 20:8-11, and explained with Luther's exposition
of his Third Commandment.   The remainder was from Luther's text with some modification.   Since the Ninth and Tenth
Commandments were combined, Luther's expositions were also
combined.   Thus the rendition was an awkward effort to com-
bine Luther's rendition with Exodus 20.

The remainder of the Five Chief Parts was in the traditional wording of Luther with some slight changes.   The
Office of the Keys consisted of the three Bible passages commonly substituted.

The Fundamental Questions and the True Way of Salvation were the same as Pohlman had used.   The order of
salvation from Starcke was also the same as had been frequently used during this period.

The final section containing a number of items, is of
considerable interest.   It began with a two-and-a-half-page
treatise on the Lord's Supper in which the author succeeded
in presenting a Lutheran view of the sacrament.   After explaining some of the Lutheran practices in connection with
the sacrament, he set forth his explanation.   Accordingly,
it was stated, the elements in the Lord's Supper (bread and
wine; body and blood) were more "than a signification or
mere symbols."   Lutherans do not believe in transubstantia-
tion nor was it a "mere spiritual enjoyment."   Yet they are
"far from believing in consubstantiation, " nor in a natural
nor spiritual presence.   It was a sacramental presence,
which the author then explained from 1 Cor. 10:16 and from
Luther's catechism.

In a second topic, the author explained the Lutheran
custom of catechising publicly children and young people.   In
addition, he explained the steps leading to confirmation.

A special section was devoted to confirmation, a mix-

ture of Pietism and sacramentalism, with stress on the laying on of hands and on conversion.

> By confirmation we mean a solemn renewal and
> ratification of our baptismal vow, accompanied by
> prayer, and the laying on of the hands of the pas-
> tor of the congregation.
>
> The holy rite of confirmation, it is believed, is
> derived from the practice of the Apostles, and was
> customary in the primitive church. The following
> passages show that it was practiced by the Apostles;
> Acts viii. 14-27--Acts xix. 6--Heb. vi. 2. In this
> passage Paul considers confirmation, or the laying
> on of hands, as one of the fundamental rites of the
> Church.
>
> From these authorities, our Church hath been in-
> duced to retain this rite of confirmation. However,
> we do not consider it a sacrament; because it was
> not ordained by Christ himself, but we do consider
> it an useful and edifying custom, from which many
> can date the beginning of their real conversion to
> God. [p. 34]

The concluding section was on Baptism with special
emphasis on infant baptism.

Apparently the writer was ready to concede to his
Protestant neighbors the Mosaic division of the Law but he
was unwilling to surrender in any way the sacraments, holding firm to a Lutheran confessional emphasis. Nevertheless,
he revealed the effect that the New Measures were having in
reference to confirmation.

"GETTYSBURG" CATECHISM, 1828

Robert C. Wiederaenders lists both an English and a
German Luther catechism without titles, as having been printed
by H. C. Neinstedt of Gettysburg for 1828. [38] The German
catechism we have found. It was a reprint of the Pennsylvania catechism and was listed above. [39] No copy of an English catechism of that date and publisher has, however, been
found by the writer, nor has any other mention of it been
found.

Chapter **X**

CATECHISMS REFLECTING THE BEGINNING OF A
NEW CONFESSIONALISM, 1828-1850

The years between 1828 and 1850 saw a gradual reaction to the doctrinal looseness of the previous decades. It
was not a complete reversal, to be sure, for the non-
confessional movement led by the General Synod, known as
American Lutheranism, was still very much alive and would
continue to make itself felt through the 1860's. But a return to a more confessional Lutheranism was becoming evident.

One of the major factors that accelerated the return
to a more conservative approach was the marked increase
in immigration from Lutheran areas who favored a more
confessional theology.

During the 1830's the number of immigrants from
Germany had risen to 152,454; in the 1840's it had grown
to 434,626; and peaked in the 1850's at 951,667.[1] Obviously
not all these were Lutherans, but a considerable number
were. They came to America chiefly for economic reasons
though some had fled their homeland because of their political views. A few did come for religious reasons in the late
1830's and early 1840's. In addition to the Germans another
35,000 Scandinavians arrived in the 1840's and 1850's, most
of whom were Lutherans.

This striking addition of German Lutherans tended in
time to isolate the Lutheran Church from other denominations
and arrested the swing to the English language. One posi-
tive factor, however, was that in time it established more
firmly a confessional mark on Lutheranism and contributed
immensely in the eventual defeat of Schmucker's American
Lutheranism.

As one may expect, the large number of Lutherans

among these immigrants taxed the resources of the church
in every part of the country, particularly on the frontier.
The number of Lutheran churches jumped from 800 in 1800,
to some 1217 in 1850, and by 1860 the number had reached
2128. [2]

The beginning trend toward a more confessional stance
was reflected in many of the catechisms published during the
period 1828-1850, though some still revealed a tendency to
obliterate the differences between Lutherans and their Protestant neighbors and to favor the so-called American Lutheranism.

The catechism of the Pennsylvania Ministerium continued to be the one catechism most commonly used.   Some
30 editions were printed during this period.   Three of these
editions, printed by Heinrich Ludwig of New York, added the
Augsburg Confession in an appendix.   Of the 19 catechisms
that were first printed during this period, seven included the
Augsburg Confession after 1840, clearly indicating that a confessional interest was beginning to take hold.   In addition to
this, several of these catechisms were in some way indebted
to the Pennsylvania catechism.

The direct influence of the 19th-century European theology on the catechisms of this period may be seen in the
reprint of three very confessional catechisms that had their
origin in Europe, one in Germany and two in Norway and
Denmark.   All three had been brought over in the 1840's by
confessionally conservative groups.   As in the case of the
immigrants during Mühlenberg's day, the Germans and Norwegian Lutherans brought a variety of catechisms with them,
which in time were replaced by American editions or reprints. [3]

On the other end of the confessional scale was Wm.
Sharts' catechism of 1846, prepared for Canadian Lutherans,
which was doctrinally very open.   Ironically, it was one of
the seven catechisms that included the Augsburg Confession,
but which the author characterized as only "substantially correct." Another catechism, Smith's Guide, was also weak
though the young pastor was sincerely attempting to offset the
damage that the New Measures were creating.   Unfortunately
his proposed solution was at the expense of a confessionally
Lutheran witness concerning several important articles of
faith.

DAVID HENKEL'S ENGLISH CATECHISM
1828-1841

By 1826, the demand for a more accurate English
translation of Luther's Small Catechism prompted the Tennessee Synod in September of that year to resolve to publish
a catechism "in an English dress" and authorized Ambrose
Henkel, a son of Paul, to "have the matter receive the proper attention."[4]   He in turn asked his brother David (1795-
1831), pastor in Lincoln County, N.C., to make the translation.

The following year Ambrose submitted the manuscript
to the synod which then spent a day examining it and finally
requested that it be published together with the preliminary
observations that David had prepared.[5]   The list of the 21
persons who participated in the examination, dated September
7, 1827, was given in the forepart of the catechism.   The
catechism was published early in 1828, under the title,

> Doct. Martin Luther's Smaller Catechism, trans-
> lated from the German; with Preliminary Observa-
> tions by the Translator.   Revised and published by
> Order of the Evangelical Lutheran Tennessee Synod.
> To which are added Sundry Hymns and Prayers.
> New Market: Solomon Henkel's Office, 1828.

David Henkel in his Preliminary Observations stated
that he had based his translation on the current German edition in the Pennsylvania Ministerium's catechism, after com-
paring it with Luther's text found in the 1580 edition of the
Book of Concord.   While he found a few variations, "Notwith-
standing, as the text of the American edition, has been for
some considerable length of time in vogue among [us], and
is more familiar to the Lutheran community in the United
States, it is thereby preferred" (p. 5).   He then listed the
variations in two columns.

Henkel further explained that he had also omitted the
form of confession because conditions had changed since Luther's time, "living in Europe under monarchical governments;
hence is not adapted to the people in the United States, under
republican government.   Its language is also obsolete.   For
these reasons, and because it is only a form, it was in all
probability omitted in the American edition."

He clarified at length why Luther's text for the Ten

Commandments differed from that of Exodus 20, particularly
the difference between the Sabbath observance in the Old Testament as compared to that of the New Testament (pp. 7-14).

The basis for Henkel's rendition was Philip F. Mayer's translation in his Instruction, which, however, he did
not hesitate to change if he thought the wording needed to be
improved.   In line with his explanation of the Third Commandment in the Preliminary Observations, he translated it,
"Thou shalt sanctify the Sabbath Day."   In the exposition of
the Ten Commandments he avoided Mayer's variations of Luther's "Was ist das?" to a consistent, "What does this imply?"   He retained the transitional questions between the
Chief Parts, as well as the Bible references found in the
Pennsylvania catechism text.   In the Lord's Supper he again
inserted the word "true," to have it read, "It is the true
body and blood of our Lord."   Following the Lord's Supper
he did not have the traditional Office of the Keys, but instead, he followed the Pennsylvania catechism in using only
the three Bible passages.   He retained the Confession of
Sins, the Christian Questions and Answers (called Godly
Questions and Answers), the Table of Duties, and Luther's
Prayers.

For use in home devotions and church instructions,
Henkel added a considerable number of hymns and prayers
for various purposes, including confirmation.   At the end of
the catechism he included the three ecumenical creeds, the
Lord's Prayer and the Confession of Sins based on the Württemberg Children's Examination.

David Henkel's catechism proved popular in the areas
served by the Tennessee Synod and there were frequent requests for additional copies.   A reprint with some slight revisions appeared already a year after the first edition:

2nd ed.   New-Market: S. Henkel's Office, 1829.

Besides a few editorial changes, mostly in the prayers,
a few new prayers were added for morning and evening devotions.   The Confession of Sins at the close of the catechism
was changed materially by detailing a number of sins to be
confessed, as it had been in the original version.

Even after David's death in 1831, the demands for
English catechisms continued to the extent that, in 1835, the
Synod requested its secretary write Dr. Solomon Henkel of

the New Market Press to prepare additional English books, including his brother David's catechism. [6] A third edition, identical with the second, was finally printed in 1841.

> 3rd ed.   New-Market: S. Henkel's Office, 1841.

To show its concern for confessional theology and its opposition to the General Synod, the Indiana Synod resolved to recommend among other books published by the Tennessee, Luther's Small Catechism, "as containing the Lutheran doctrine in its purity. "[7]

When the first American edition of the Book of Concord was authorized by the Tennessee Synod and published in 1851, the Small Catechism "was copied mainly from the translation" by David Henkel. [8] The two catechisms of Luther were printed separately in 1852 by the Henkel Press. The text of the 1851 Book of Concord was used. However, before the second edition of the Book of Concord was published in 1854, the various confessions were carefully reexamined, the catechisms being revised by Dr. J. G. Morris of Baltimore. [9]

DAVID HENKEL'S GERMAN CATECHISM, 1829

In 1829, the year in which David's second edition of his English translation appeared, he issued a German text of Luther's catechism, reprinted also from the Pennsylvania catechism. Following the Luther text, he further included, as in the English edition, a number of prayers and hymns. The concluding parts were again the ecumenical creeds, the Lord's Prayer, and the Confession of Sins from the Württemberg Children's Examination as it had appeared in the Pennsylvania text.

Henkel's Preliminary Observations were included also in the German edition.

The title of this catechism was,

> Dr. Martin Luther's Smaller Catechism; with Preliminary Observations. Together with a Supplement of Sundry Prayers and Hymns. New-Market: Solomon Henkel's Press, 1829. [10]

David Henkel's German-English Catechism, 1829

In 1829, the Henkel Press published David Henkel's German and English catechisms side by side under the title,

> Doct. Martin Luther's Small Catechism, in the Original German, accompanied by an English Translation; with Preliminary Observations by the Translator. Revised and Published by Order of the Evangelical Lutheran Tennessee Synod. To which are added Sundry Hymns and Prayers. New-Market: S. Henkel's Office, 1829.

JOHN G. MORRIS' CATECHETICAL EXERCISES, 1832-1835

John G. Morris (1803-1895), while pastor in Baltimore, felt the need to prepare a book for use with Luther's catechism that would serve, in his words, as "a more minute development of the christian system" and contain not merely Scripture references but "scripture proofs fully inserted" (Preface, p. iii). The manual was published during January 1832, under the title,

> Catechetical Exercises; or a Familiar Illustration of the Five Principal Articles of Luther's Smaller Catechism, Altered from the German. Baltimore: Joel Wright, 1832.

Morris was ordained by the Maryland Synod in 1827, after having received his theological training under S. S. Schmucker. He had been a member of the first class at the Gettysburg seminary. Morris entered the ministry at a time when denominational consciousness was at a low ebb and unionism was rampant. During the early years of his ministry he was very much a part of the spirit of his day and in time became a leader of the non-confessional elements of his synod, as well as that of the General Synod. [11]

Consistent with his theological stance, for instance, were the comments he made while founding editor of the Lutheran Observer in 1832. A contributor had defended the Lutheran witness of Holy Baptism, to which Morris responded that he would not participate in a controversy regarding the "long exploded doctrine of baptismal regeneration. "[12]

With others of his day, he was open to the revivalis-
tic movement, the New Measures, though he was not an ex-
tremist. The very fact that he favored catechetical instruction was evidence of that. He saw confirmation instruction,
however, as an opportunity for the confirmand to "appropriate
and apply Jesus Christ and his righteousness, and all the
fruits of his redemption anew and personally" for himself.13
Since the book was intended to be used alongside Luther's
catechism, his text was not printed out in the book.

The introductory section of his Catechetical Exercises,
in which he set up the background material, already manifested Morris' confusion in reference to such basic terms as
"doctrine," "gospel," "Word of God" and the "Bible." There
was a frequent mixture of Law and Gospel in the confessional
meaning of these terms.

In the interest of not offending his Protestant neighbors
with whom he worked he, like most of the English catechetical writers of this period, presented the Ten Commandments
in the words of Exodus 20, with no reference to the traditional
Lutheran wording. Ironically, he exposed his background by
speaking of three commandments belonging to the first Table
of the Law (p. 13). This slip was corrected in his next edition.

Morris was one of the first American catechetical writers to make a distinction between the visible and the invisible
church. This may be due to an unnamed German book that he
had run across while preparing his text and which he adopted
as the basis for his manual (Preface, pp. iii-iv). The distinction was applied later when he stated that Baptism made
one "a member of the visible church."

In his Catechumen's Companion, printed about the same
time, he reiterated this, saying, "By this ordinance [i.e.
Baptism], I was solemnly initiated into the society of christians."14

His section on the sacraments further revealed how
non-confessional his theology was at the time. For him,
Baptism only "represents the washing (or purifying) of our
souls by the Holy Ghost, and exhibits the blessings of salvation" (pp. 64 and 66). One of the blessings of the sacrament
was that it "sets forth the forgiveness of sin" (p. 65).

Similarly, the major purpose of the Lord's Supper was

to be "a perpetual remembrance of the death of Christ, and of the benefits we receive thereby" (p. 69). This "remembrance" was the major thrust of his explanation and from this "remembrance" the benefits flowed.

The sacramental presence was bluntly denied with the parenthetical addition to Matt. 26:28, "For this is (or represents) my blood of the New Testament." Similarly in 1 Cor. 11:24, where the parenthetical additions appeared twice. The body and blood of Christ were nowhere explained.

To help the catechumen apply in his life what he had learned during his confirmation instruction and to avoid, what the proponents of New Measures called mere "head religion," he prepared, as already mentioned, The Catechumen's and Communicant's Companion, about the same time as his Catechetical Exercises.15

Though Morris' catechetical manual was so obviously non-confessional, it nevertheless became the official catechism of the South Carolina Synod in 1833, replacing the General Synod's catechism, which had not been well received. If the adopted catechism was intended to stem the tide of New Measures, it failed. By 1846, catechetical instruction was "nearly entirely abandoned by most of our [South Carolina] congregations."16

With only minor changes Morris' book was reprinted in 1835 under the same title.

Baltimore: Lucas and Deaver, 1835.

CHARLES A. SMITH'S CATECHUMEN'S
GUIDE, 1837

Charles A. Smith, a young pastor at Palatine, N.Y., produced a lengthy and formidable volume of some 112 pages which he intended as an aid to catechumens in their preparations for the "lecture rooms."17 It was based on Luther's catechism and included his text at the appropriate places. The book bore the title,

The Catechumen's Guide, prepared with a special reference to the wants of the Evangelical Lutheran Church in the United States. Albany: Joel Munsell, 1837.

Two years before the appearance of this volume, Smith had expressed great concern about the inroads the New Measures were having on the instruction of the young.[18] It was apparently this fear that prompted him to write this book and which, therefore, also helped shape the author's theological stance reflected in the guide.

The heart of the book was written in the form of a series of lectures consisting of explanations of the doctrines laid down in Luther's catechism. At the bottom of each page in fine print, there were questions for the catechumen to answer to determine whether he understood what he had read and learned in class. This procedure, Smith explained, was intended to help combat the prevailing rote learning often associated with confirmation instruction. It was his hope that the questions would "exercise, as much as possible, the reflective powers of the reader," and thus offset the teaching "often too well established" merely to receive answers from memory and that "consequently, they are not to be regarded as expressive of the real sentiments and conviction of the heart."

In contrast to the easy and often emotional "conversion" brought about by the New Measures and the frequent defections that followed, Smith wished also to assist the catechumen "to count the cost" of becoming "soldiers of the cross." He maintained, and this was a basic principle of the book, "that no one should be received into the church, whilst ignorant of the doctrines taught, and the moral obligation enforced in the word of God" (italics in original, p. 7).

His approach also shared the common view concerning confirmation, namely that it was an ordinance whereby one became a member of the church. This was elaborated on at length in pages 293-300.

Smith's lengthy 28-page introduction was clearly a defense of the practice he had in mind, namely to combat New Measures as well as the custom of admitting persons to church membership "without the evidence of genuine piety." These concerns were reflected throughout the book.

The very fact that Smith devoted almost half of the 312 pages of lecture material to the Ten Commandments told much, not only about his concern for piety but also the reason why he lost the evangelical spirit in the process.

While he used the words of Exodus 20, for the Ten

Commandments, he nevertheless followed the Lutheran division of the commandments, explaining his reasons for his
arrangement in a footnote. His rigid view of the Sabbath observance lost much of Luther's evangelical emphasis in the
keeping of the "holy day" (pp. 98-120).

Smith's imbalance of the subject matter may be seen
in the fact that he devoted fewer than 20 pages each to the
Second and Third Articles, only about one page being re-
served to explain the Holy Spirit's work in reference to the
church.

The treatment of the sacraments continued to reflect
a non-confessional view. Holy Baptism was simply a di-
vinely instituted ordinance that served as an initiatory ordinance to receive persons "into communion with the visible
church" (p. 278). He rejected the "very strange misappre-
hension" that prevailed in the minds of many parents who
believed that Baptism was "necessarily invested with a saving efficacy" (p. 287).

One objection Smith had to the view that Baptism had
regenerative power was that parents often neglected the instruction of their children because of it, believing that Baptism was all that was needed (pp. 288f.).

Similarly Smith frowned on the use of sponsors at
Baptism. He regarded the custom to be "wrong, and worse
than useless." The reason for his stand was that it tended
to relieve parents of their responsibilities and, what was
worse, sponsors were "frequently young, thoughtless, and
utterly ignorant of the nature of the relation into which they
enter" (p. 286). It was such abuses that colored much of
Smith's theology.

From a practical viewpoint, Smith placed as much, if
not greater importance on confirmation for it was "the act of
admitting adult believers to all the privileges of church membership, after a public profession of faith" (p. 293).

The Lord's Supper, like Baptism, was regarded as
symbolical.

> Nor is it necessary, in order to attribute to this
> sacrament the peculiar efficacy assigned to it, to
> suppose, as some have supposed, (erroneously) that
> the actual body and blood of Christ are present in
> the bread and wine [p. 302].

It again became evident that Smith was moved, at
least in part, to his view by the fear that to regard the sacrament as a means of conferring God's grace, would naturally result in a mechanical religion.

From the vantage point of more than a century later,
it is difficult to imagine how the average catechumen might
have understood much of what Smith had in mind, to say
nothing about leading him to a genuine evangelical piety.
Certainly the use of Greek terms (e.g., p. 237) could do
little to reach the young adolescent mind. The ponderous
volume might have been more helpful as a guide to the pastor than to the catechumens. It does demonstrate, however,
an overreaction or a wrong solution, on the part of a young
pastor in his first charge, to a prevailing condition.

Yet it should not go unnoticed that Smith's Guide was
included in the book depository of the South Carolina Synod
in 1837, and made available to member congregations. 19

ELLING EIELSEN'S ENGLISH
CATECHISM, 1841

A most remarkable print of Luther's catechism in
English was published by the Norwegian lay preacher Elling
Eielsen. A man of boundless enthusiasm engendered in him
by his participation in the Haugean movement in Norway, 20
he was also a controversial figure in Lutheranism. He had
arrived in New York, September 3, 1839, and continued to
the Fox River settlement in Illinois, to preach to scattered
Norwegian immigrants who had settled there. 21

Probably much to his surprise, he there met a few
Norwegian families who, while interested in religious instruction, were unwilling that it be done in the Norwegian
language. Eielsen soon realized, what few other Lutherans
had been willing to admit so quickly, particularly among the
Germans, that if Lutheranism was to survive in America
among his Norwegian compatriots they would need to adapt
themselves to the language of the land. Consequently, Eielsen proceeded to prepare an English translation though he
himself was still a stranger to the language. In a letter
"he explained that he obtained the assistance of a believing
friend to translate those parts of the catechism which American Lutherans had not included in their versions. "22

By 1841 the manuscript was completed and Eielsen set

out for New York to have it printed.   The title of the catechism was,

> Doctor Martin Luther's Small Catechism with Plain
> Instruction for Children, and Sentences from the
> Word of God to Strengthen the Faith of the Meek,
> Translated from the Danish, and published by El-
> ling Elielsen [sic].   New York: n.p., 1841.23

The catechism contained Luther's Five Chief Parts
without his paragraphs on Confession.   The first three commandments in the Decalog followed the wording of Exodus
20:3-4 and 7-8.   The second part was an Analysis of the
Principles of Religion similar to Starcke's Short Table.   This
was followed by eleven prayers for the use of children.   In
place of the Table of Duties there was a listing of Bible passages following the main material of the Table.   The catechism concluded with a series of Bible passages on God,
Creation, Sin, Laws, Grace, closing with a collection of
miscellaneous passages appropriate for memorizing.   In all
the catechism comprised 36 pages.

ERIK PONTOPPIDAN'S CATECHISM, 1842/43

Elling Eielsen, who had shown such remarkable vision
in the publication of an English translation of Luther's catechism, was to have another "first" by publishing the first
Norwegian book in America, and that was the popular but
presently controversial catechism of the Danish Bishop Erik
Pontoppidan (1698-1764).

Bishop Pontoppidan had issued his catechism in 1737
to undergird the revival of instruction that had come to Denmark and Norway with the wave of Pietism originating in
Halle, Germany.   Confirmation had already been officially
instituted in 1736.   The new catechism, which in its original
edition contained 759 questions and answers, was a major
factor in putting the Pietistic stamp on the young for decades.   It was the official textbook in Denmark till 1791, [24]
though in Norway it never went completely out of use.

After a brief period of decline during Rationalism,
Pietism revived largely through the efforts of Hans N. Hauge,
who placed less emphasis on the emotions, which the extreme
Pietists had fostered, and more on Christian service.   For
him the call to be a Christian was a call to serve the Lord.[25]
As noted earlier, Eielsen was a devout follower of Hauge.

During the 1820's and 1830's, N. F. S. Grundtvig was
beginning to have a profound effect on Lutherans in Denmark
with his emphasis on the spoken and sacramental word rather
than the written words of Scripture. As one might expect,
his views clashed strongly with the Haugeans and when in 1839
the government authorized a commission to prepare a new
Explanation in place of Pontoppidan's there was a great out-
cry from among the Haugeans. While the revised catechism
was not as radical as had been feared, the Haugeans missed
the clear distinction between Christianity and the world and
the so-called "Explanation" controversy followed in the
1840's. [26]

Eielsen had come to America while the controversy
was still raging at home and he was very much concerned
that the Pontoppidan catechism he saw in need of publication
and distribution among his fellow Norwegians would be faithful to the original Explanation. He was therefore prompted
to go to New York again in August 1842 to have a supply of
his favorite catechism printed. Unfortunately the printer did
not have the kind of type Eielsen wanted to reproduce an exact copy. His Haugean Lutheranism required that the Pontoppidan catechism be faithfully reproduced not only in content
but even in its form and that required the same Gothic type
to allay any suspicion that his publication differed from the
original text. The Gothic type he wanted was available only
in distant Philadelphia, but he waited till it was procured.
This delay, however, postponed his return to the Midwest
until the rivers and the lakes were icebound. Now he had
to choose to wait until spring or return on foot. Eielsen decided on the latter and set out for Illinois, his knapsack filled
with copies of his beloved Pontoppidan strapped on his back. [27]

The complete title of his catechism was,

> Truth unto the Fear of God, in a simple and as
> short as possible, yet sufficient Explanation of
> Blessed Dr. Martin Luther's Small Catechism.
> New York: Henry Ludvig, 1842. [28]

The catechism included all of Pontoppidan's 759 Questions
and Answers, followed by a Brief Summary of the Saving
Truth (pp. 150-154); morning and evening prayers (pp. 154-
156); the three Ecumenical Creeds (pp. 157-161); and the 21
Articles of the Augsburg Confession (pp. 161-179).

The catechism presented Lutheran theology in a blend

of Orthodoxy and Pietism that was a mark of Norwegian Lutheranism at home and in America. In Norway the attempt to have Pontoppidan replaced after 1848, failed and the government order was rescinded, though the controversy continued for another two decades. [29]

In America the catechism became a focus during the election controversy among Lutherans because of Question 548, which explained God's election with the answer,

> God has appointed all those to eternal life who He from eternity has foreseen would accept the offered grace, believe in Christ, and remain constant in this faith unto the end. [30]

An abbreviated edition of Pontoppidan was published in 1864, and translated by E. Belfour in 1877. Both editions have become a standard for most Norwegian Lutherans in America.

As for Eielsen, he organized the first Norwegian Lutheran synod in America, April 13-14, 1843, officially called the Evangelical Lutheran Church in America, but generally known as the Eielsen Synod. He was its president 1846-1883. Eielsen had been ordained October 3, 1843.

THE JOINT OHIO SYNOD CATECHISMS OF
1831 AND 1842

As early as 1831, the Synod of Ohio had authorized the publication of an English translation of Luther's catechism. [31] The initial order was for a 1000 copies to be sold for 12 1/2 cents each. A second 1000 copies were to include the Augsburg Confession. These were to be sold at 18 3/4 cents. [32] We have been unable to locate copies of either catechisms, though a photocopy of the title page is in the Concordia Historical Institute, St. Louis. The title of this new issue was

> Luther's Smaller Catechism, correctly translated from the original. Published under the auspices of the Ev. Lutheran Synod of Ohio. First edition. Greensburgh [Pa.]: Jacob S. Sieck, 1831.

In 1842, the Ohio Synod again issued a Luther catechism but one that was based largely on the later catechism

of the General Synod (1832 and thereafter), but with some
notable differences. The title read,

> Luther's Smaller Catechism; New Philadelphia [O.]:
> Lutheran Standard Office, 1842.

The Ohio catechism omitted Isaac Watts' Historical
Catechism and restored in the Christian Questions and Answers, the two questions on the sacramental presence in the
Lord's Supper.[33] In fact it was because the General Synod
catechisms had omitted the questions that the Eastern District
of the Ohio Synod had called for the publication of an "un-
mutilated catechism."[34] However, the catechism still omitted
Luther's "true" in the explanation of the Lord's Supper. This
was in harmony with the agenda currently in use which had
adopted the formula of the Prussian Union that had, "Christ
says: 'This is my body.'"

The catechism furthermore added the 21 Articles of
the Augsburg Confessions, to give a clear witness of its own
confessional stand.[35] Four hymns in the supplement were
also omitted for a total of 18.

The synod in accepting the catechism had ordered an
initial edition of 3000 copies.[36]

JOHN G. MORRIS' CATECHISM, 1844-1850

Some twelve years after the appearance of his Catechetical Exercises, John G. Morris prepared an entirely new
catechism under the title,

> Luther's Shorter Catechism, Illustrated by Additional
> Questions and Answers. Baltimore: Publication
> Rooms of the Evangelical Lutheran Church, 1844.

This book had a similar purpose to that of Morris'
first manual but this time he included Luther's text at the
appropriate places. Instead of beginning with the Ten Commandments, he introduced his instruction with an overview
of the Bible--its origin, proofs for its inspiration, its contents by books, and its division into Law and Gospel.

This was followed by the Ten Commandments. These
were again set forth according to Exodus 20. With the exception of his Second and Tenth Commandments, he followed
Mayer's translation in giving Luther's explanation. His ex-

position of the Fourth Commandment, while using Luther's explanation for the Third, lost some of its evangelical thrust by his Protestant approach to the Sabbath.

Under the Creed, there was a strange omission in Luther's explanation of the Second Article. The catechism omitted "and also true man born of the Virgin Mary." This error was not corrected in the later editions examined (2nd ed. of 1844, and the 3rd ed. of 1850). Yet the omission must have been unintentional since the humanity and the virgin birth were clearly acknowledged in Morris' explanation. Both the deity and the humanity of Christ were regarded as necessary for man's redemption (pp. 61f.).

The meaning of the term "church" in the Third Article was explained somewhat better in this catechism than in his earlier one, yet not without a degree of ambiguity. He gave four different meanings to the term: 1) "a building set apart for the public worship"; 2) a congregation of people who meet together for worship; 3) "a society of christians distinguished by place, doctrines, government and form of worship. As the churches of Judea, Samaria, Galilee, the Lutheran church, the church of England, etc."; 4) "the whole christian society ..., called the body of Christ" (p. 76).

Of interest are his reasons for preferring "the Lutheran branch of the Holy Catholic Church over others";

I.   Because her doctrine, government, discipline and mode of worship are truly scriptural and apostolic.

II.   Because she is the church of the Reformation, from which all other Protestant churches have had their origin.

III. Because, whilst other Protestant churches have divided into various minor sects, the Lutheran church has continued one [sic].

IV.   Because the Lutheran church allows the right of private judgment in matters of faith and insists on uniformity only in fundamental doctrines.

V.   Because the Lutheran church vests all ecclesiastical power in the people and not in the ministry.

VI. Because each congregation has the right of
     electing and deposing its ministers without the
     permission of any Synod [p. 78].

The sacraments were described as means of awakening and strengthening of faith (p. 94). While Morris ascribed
the power of accomplishing this to the Holy Ghost, he made
no reference to the Gospel as the means. He spoke of there
being two parts to the sacraments, the outward sign and the
inward spiritual grace. This "inward grace" is "the spiritual
benefit which the soul receives from the Holy Ghost and communion with Christ" (p. 95).

Luther's meaning of Baptism was amplified and then
explained:

> That baptism is not mere water (or a mere human
> ceremony) but it is that water which the command-
> ment of God enjoins and which is connected with
> God's word (that is, it is a divine institution).

> What does he mean by this?

> That baptism is not a mere external ceremony, but
> a solemn divine institution in which as often as it
> is administered, the great doctrine of the purifica-
> tion of the heart by the words of God, is set forth
> (p. 96).

Luther's explanation of the benefits of Baptism are introduced with the question,

> What are the benefits of baptism in the opinion of
> Luther?

> It causes the forgiveness of sins, delivers from
> death and the devil and gives everlasting salvation
> to those that believe, as the word and promise of
> God declare.

> Did he mean that the bare act of baptism secures
> these blessings?

> No; but that baptism is one of the ordinances
> through which believers appropriate the promise
> of these blessings to themselves (p. 96).

Nowhere does Morris confess the regenerative power

of Baptism.   Even in connection with infant Baptism he
avoided a statement to that effect.   To the question, "How
can infants perform the duties incumbent on baptized persons?" he said,

> They promise to do them by their parents or spon-
> sors, who are bound to bring them up in the nur-
> ture of the Lord, and infants are also bound by en-
> gagements entered into by their parents for them
> [p. 98].

In the Lord's Supper one comes to a surprising addition.   There Morris inserted the word "true" to Mayer's Luther text, "It is the true body and blood of our Lord."   In
his 1832 catechism, the "inward part" of the sacrament was
simply "the body and blood of Christ," but in this revision
he explained that the "inward part or thing" signified was
"the body and blood of Christ which are spiritually taken,
and received by the believers in the Lord's Supper" (p. 100).

Even though Morris was not as forthright in his denial
of the sacramental presence in the Lord's Supper as he previously had been, he still was not clear in his witness of it.
He said, in the sacrament we make this profession,

> By eating this bread and drinking this cup, we de-
> clare our conviction that our souls are as dependent
> on the atonement of Christ for salvation, as our
> bodies are on our daily bread for support, and as
> our bodies would not be supported unless food were
> eaten, so our souls will receive no benefit from the
> atonement of Christ, unless by faith we receive and
> enjoy it [p. 100].

While no change took place in the sacramental elements, Scripture had nowhere specified the mode of Christ's
presence in the sacrament, "hence every person should be
left to the free exercise of his judgment on that subject."

In reference to Luther's explanation how such bodily
eating and drinking can produce the great effect attributed to
the sacrament, Morris further explained,

> He [Luther] means that the believer is really a par-
> taker of Christ and of the benefits of his death, and
> that his interest herein is sealed in this ordinance,
> in other words, that in this sacrament, the true be-

liever appropriates to himself the benefits of redemption [p. 103].

Parts of Morris' catechism in reference to the sacraments may be ambiguous, but there was no doubt as to where
he stood at this time in his ministry.   The year following
the publication of this catechism he, together with some other
leaders of the General Synod, 37 addressed a revealing letter
to the United Lutheran and Reformed Church of Germany de-
scribing the stand of the Lutherans they represented.   Among
other things they wrote, "The peculiar view of Luther on the
bodily presence of the Lord in the Lord's Supper has been
abandoned long ago by the great majority of our preachers."38

B. M. Schmucker gives this evaluation of Morris' catechism,

> Its great defects are that it failed to grasp the
> meaning of Luther; that the added questions often
> do not grow out of, or bring out the meaning of the
> text; that in consequence of this failure to grasp
> Luther's meaning, important subjects are introduced
> separately, and not where Luther's explanation would
> place them, as repentance and faith after the Com-
> mandments.   The failure to grasp the true sense,
> force and scope of the text is most marked in the
> treatment of the second and third articles of the
> Creed.   In the treatment of the Sacraments, the
> added matter is in another spirit and, teaches
> another doctrine from the text.   This Catechism is
> interesting as a sign of its times, when it was held
> to be very excellent, but the author and the church
> have fortunately outgrown it. 39

Yet the catechism was accepted by many and a second
edition appeared the same year.

> 2nd ed.   Baltimore: Publication Rooms of the
> Evangelical Lutheran Church, 1844.

A third edition appeared a few years later,

> 3rd ed.   Baltimore: T. Newton Kurtz, 1850. 40

Yet there is something that must be said in defense
of Morris.   As time went on he was swept up by the confessional movement in the Lutheran Church and became a staunch

witness of it.   He voted against the Definite Platform when
it was submitted to the Maryland Synod in 1855.   As a member of the committee he opposed any new confession of faith
and renewed his declaration of adherance to that contained in
his ordination service, "which embraces the fundamental doctrines of the Word of God, as correctly taught in the doctrinal articles of the Augsburg Confession."[41]

As time went on, Morris became even more loyal to
the Lutheran Symbols.   Speaking of those later years,
Schmucker said, "Dr. Morris could not now [in 1886] write,
publish or circulate his catechisms, for they no longer express his deep convictions."[42]   As Ferm put it, Morris
"reeled completely over to a confessional type of Lutheranism."[43]

Perhaps the crowning statement attesting to Morris'
change comes from the conservative Tennessee Synod which
invited Morris to revise the translation of Luther's Small
and Large Catechism for its second edition of the Book of
Concord in 1852.[44]

DRESDNER KREUTZ CATECHISM, 1845

With the rise of confessional consciousness among the
Lutherans in Germany during the early nineteenth century and
as a further reaction to earlier Rationalism, some of the old
catechisms once popular among the conservative Lutherans,
were revived.   One of these was the Dresdner Kreutz, or
Dresden Cross Catechism of 1688, so called because it had
originally been prepared by the pastors of Holy Cross Church
in Dresden.   They had been commissioned to do so by John
George III, elector of Saxony, in 1663.   Wishing to raise the
level of religious instruction in his territory, the elector had
authorized the pastors to prepare an explanation of Luther's
catechism and to corroborate it by citing Scripture passages
in support.   According to the elector, the final copy received
the stamp of approval from the theological faculties of the
universities of Leipzig and Wittenberg as well as from the
Church Council of Saxony, and was now to be the official catechism of his electorate (Preface, ii-iii).

During the catechism's revival it had been widely used
also in Prussia.   So it was not surprising that when a group
of Old Lutherans decided to leave Germany in 1839 under the
leadership of John A. A. Grabau, in protest to the Prussian

Union, the Cross Catechism was very much in evidence among
the emigrants.   Before leaving Germany and later again in
the United States they were joined by others from Silesia,
Pomerania, and other areas of Germany.   Contingencies of
the different groups settled chiefly in Buffalo, N. Y. and Milwaukee, Wisc., with a sizable group also in the nearby settlement of Freistadt.   The Wisconsin settlers were under the
leadership of L. F. E. Krause who declared the Dresden
Cross Catechism to be the official text of the two congregations. 45

The Dresden Cross Catechism was used also in the
Buffalo congregation where it became an additional irritant
between the Silesian and the Prussian members, who had
been quarreling much of the time they had been brought together.   Two school teachers sided with the Silesian faction
claiming with them that the catechism taught falsely concerning the person of Christ.   The outcome of that controversy
was that late in 1840, the teachers were removed from office
and a number of Silesians left to form a separate congregation after they had been excommunicated. 46

On June 25, 1845, the several congregations in New
York and Wisconsin, under the leadership of Grabau and
Krause, organized The Synod of the Lutheran Church Emigrated from Prussia during a meeting in Milwaukee.   The
group was generally known as the Buffalo Synod.   Four pastors and 18 lay delegates were in attendance.

One of the first actions of the newly organized synod
was to make the Cross Catechism the official text and to authorize a reprint of it under its original title,

> Dr. Martin Luther's Small Catechism by the Gra-
> cious Order of the Elector of Saxony, Explained by
> the Ministers of Holy Cross in Dresden by Ques-
> tions and Answers, and further Corroborated with
> Passages cited from Holy Scripture.   Buffalo: G.
> Zahm, 1845. 47

The catechism comprised 1) the Five Chief Parts of
Luther's Small Catechism, including his introduction, the Office of the Keys and the Christian Questions and Answers;
2) a lengthy explanation of it in the form of questions and answers; and 3) a list of Bible references to passages to be
learned by the catechumens.   The list was grouped according
to the church year.

The Cross Catechism was undoubtedly the most extensive catechism for children published in America up to this
time, comprising some 550 pages. Some of the bulk resulted
from the large number of Bible passages that were written
out to illustrate, deepen, and prove the answers given. Often
the passage included an additional verse from the context to
help clarify the meaning. One may well question whether
the large number of passages were always needed for the
purpose intended.

Furthermore, the questions went into great detail. For
Luther's explanation of the Ten Commandments, practically
every word was explained and applied in detail. This in effect circumvented the simplicity Luther had in mind.

Consistently throughout the catechism the authors
sought to apply the Scriptural truths to the lives of the catechumens. Two stereotyped questions were usually used to
assist in this purpose: "How does this [truth] serve as a
great comfort?" and "How does this serve us for a godly
life?"

While the catechism was confessionally sound, even to
satisfy such an ultraconservative group as the Buffalo Synod,
here and there an answer was given that seemed to take in
more territory than was warranted and so lacked precision
by failing to highlight the Gospel and its centrality. Thus to
the question, "What is the Christian doctrine?" the answer
was, "It is the doctrine of the triune, true God and of his
beneficial acts which a Christian must necessarily know and
believe if he would be saved" (p. 141).

The authors strove to make the catechism applicable
to the lives of the children, though the sheer bulk must have
been frightening. Yet it was warmly received by the pastors
of the Buffalo Synod.

About the same time that Grabau and his followers
came to America, another conservative Lutheran group came
from Saxony under the leadership of Martin Stephan who settled in Missouri. This group had purchased in 1838 900
copies of the Cross Catechism for use in their future homeland. [48] When these, together with likeminded Lutherans from
Franconia who settled in Michigan, organized into a synod in
1847, generally known as the Missouri Synod, many continued
to use the Cross Catechism. When the original supply was exhausted or was not available, they purchased the Buffalo edi-

tion. But this soon came to an end as the doctrinal controversy between the Missouri Synod and the Buffalo Synod became more bitter.   The leaders of the Buffalo Synod would
not place their publication on the open market.[49] This forced
the Missouri Synod to turn elsewhere and later to prepare
catechetical material of its own.[50] Still later, in 1858, in
preparing a revision of the catechism of Johann Conrad Die-
trich for its first official catechism,[51] the Missouri Synod
made use of some parts of the Cross Catechism.[52]

In the meantime, in 1852, Henry Ludwig reprinted the
Cross Catechism for the Buffalo Synod. While the Missouri
Synod never published its own Cross Catechism, the Wisconsin Synod (organized in 1850) did.   The catechism was undated and was printed by Geo. Brumder in Milwaukee.

WEST PENNSYLVANIA SYNOD
CATECHISM, 1845-1850

In 1845, the West Pennsylvania Synod[53] authorized the
publication of a catechism prepared by C. G. Weyl, pastor
of Trinity Church in Baltimore, entitled,

> Dr. Luther's Small Catechism, to which is added
> the Orders of Salvation, together with the Form for
> the Administration and Management of the Evangeli-
> cal Lutheran Church in North America.   Baltimore:
> Lutherische Buchhandlung, 1845.[54]

Weyl had compiled his catechism partly from the General Synod's revised catechism of 1832 and that of the Pennsylvania Ministerium.   The introductory questions and the
text for the Commandments were drawn from the former.
The explanatory notes and the series of questions concerning
Baptism were translated and retained by Weyl.[55]

Weyl did, however, include the major portions of the
Luther text of the catechism of the Ministerium, including the
three Bible passages which comprised the Office of the Keys.
This was followed by the Christian Questions and Answers.
He further inserted the Confession of Sins from the Württem-
berg Children's Examination in place of Luther's Confession.
Thereafter Weyl followed the Ministerium catechism, including
not only the Table of Duties and Luther's prayers but also
the four orders of salvation by Starcke, the Württemberg
Children's Examination and the Analysis of the Catechism.[56]

He did not retain Freylinghausen's Order of Salvation, the List of Most Important Key Passages, and a Short Explanation of the Ten Commandments in Verses, the Golden A B C, the seven Penitential Psalms, and the multiplication table. Weyl retained the hymns but added three of his own choice to be sung at confirmation, all of them quite subjective and somewhat emotional. The catechism closed with a form for the administration and management of a congregation as required by the synod.

The catechism served not only the West Pennsylvania Synod but was used extensively also in the General Synod since it did not have a German catechism of its own.

While the original edition did not carry Weyl's name, a second edition published the same year did have his name, though it gave his initials as C. J. The new edition was identical in every respect except that it added the A B C's, Aids to Reading and the multiplication table. Obviously this print was intended also for school use.

Another edition, revised and enlarged, was published in 1850 by T. Newton Kurtz of Baltimore. This print omitted the helps for schools but added the Augsburg Confession, indicating that the confessional movement among German Lutherans in this part of the country was having its impact here also.

E. PEIXOTO'S "LEITFADEN" FOR
THE USE OF LUTHER'S
CATECHISM, 1845-52

The material for this Leitfaden, or Guide, though first published in 1845, had been in use for over 50 years in the United Congregations of Alt-Goschenhoppen, Indianfeld and Toheck, Pa., when Engelbert Peixoto became their pastor in 1840. The original Guide had first been prepared by Conrad Roeller some time during his pastorate there from 1772 to 1796. He had been followed by his son J. G. Roeller, who served from 1798 until shortly before Peixoto assumed the pastorate. [57] Very likely he made some changes during his long ministry in this combined parish. At any rate, when Peixoto became pastor, the wish was expressed by some of the members that he continue to use the Guide in the instruction of the children for confirmation. Though Peixoto was ready to comply, he was confronted with two problems. First,

the Guide had never been published and was found only in the
handwritten copies widely scattered among his members. The
copies, as one might expect, contained many errors because
they had been written by the children from dictation or directly from a sample. Another problem was, according to
Peixoto, that the Guide was dated. While he found no fault
with the contents, it bore the stamp of the previous century
(Preface). Since no manuscript copy is now available, it is
impossible to determine to what extent the Guide was in fact
altered by Peixoto. At any rate, he published it under the
title,

> A Guide according to which Dr. Martin Luther's
> Small Catechism is Explained while conducting Con-
> firmation Instruction in the United Evangelical Lu-
> theran Congregations in Alt-Goschenhoppen, Indian-
> feld, and Toheck. Sumnytaun, Pa.: E. Benner,
> 1845. 58

The catechumens were expected to use the Guide alongside of Luther's catechism, as may be seen from the fact
that the questions referred them to the text as the Guide proceeded through the Five Chief Parts.

In assessing the Guide one must agree with B. M.
Schmucker that the subjects were treated somewhat super-
ficially, "their deeper meaning not being brought out."59
For instance, in speaking of Jesus' redemption of mankind,
the Guide stated that He redeemed us from the Law by re-
pealing the Mosaic ceremonial regulations; from the power
of sin by his teaching, his example, and through the outpour-
ing of the Holy Spirit; and from the punishment of sin by taking it upon Himself in our stead (p. 21).

The Guide's treatment of Baptism was somewhat weak,
due to a degree, because of the omissions. On the other
hand the section on the Lord's Supper clearly taught the real
or sacramental presence and otherwise gave the sacrament
extensive coverage. Another plus was that the Guide made
no mention of prayer as being a means of grace, as several
other catechisms had stated.

Apparently Peixoto's rendition of Roeller's material
was well received so that the Guide was reprinted in 1852 in
a copyrighted form by the same printer. The new edition
was identical to the first except that subheads were added for
the Five Chief Parts and a confirmation hymn was added.

However, Ludwig Walz, the next pastor refused to use the Guide and with that it was discontinued. 60

OHIO SYNOD, EASTERN DISTRICT, CATECHISM, C. 1846

Some time during 1840-1846, when the Lutherische Kirchenzeitung of the Joint Ohio Synod was first published in Pittsburgh by Fred Schmidt, the Eastern District of the Joint Ohio Synod issued an undated catechism from that press, titled,

> The Small Catechism of the Blessed Dr. Martin Luther, to which is added the Order of Salvation, an Analysis of the Catechism, the Württemberg Children's Examination, the 21 Articles of the Augsburg Confession, together with Hymns, etc. Pittsburgh: Printery of the Luth. Kirchenzeitung, n. d. 61

The title gives the contents of the catechism. The orders of salvation were Starcke's Short and Simple Questions and Answers and the Short Table.

In addition to the Augsburg Confession, the catechism contained the Nicene Creed and the Athanasian Creed. It closed with the Seven Penitential Psalms.

As the contents indicated, the catechism strongly reflected the confessionalism of this branch of Lutherans in America.

WILLIAM SHARTS' CATECHISM, 1846

A catechism strongly influenced by the theology of S. S. Schmucker was published by William Sharts [Shartz], pastor at Williamsburgh, Dundas County, Ontario, Canada, in 1846. 62 It was called,

> A Catechism Designed for the Young in the Evangelical Lutheran churches, in the Eastern District, C. W. Ogdensburgh, N. Y.: Frontier Sentinal Office, 1846.

Strictly speaking this catechism was not directly re-

lated to Luther's catechism nor does it in any way imply that
it was intended to be used alongside of it.   However, in a
few instances Luther's catechism was quoted, though in no
way was it identified.   It may therefore be questioned whether
the catechism belongs in this study.

A unique feature of the catechism was that it contained
the Twenty-One articles of the Augsburg Confession, "taken
almost entire" from Dr. S. S. Schmucker's Doctrinal Theology, according to a notice at the beginning of the book.
However, this should not be misconstrued to mean that Sharts
had accepted the Confession as a witness of his own theological commitment.   A better clue to that was the name of
Schmucker, for it was his influence that normed the doctrinal
contents of the catechism.   This was clearly seen in the answer to the question later in the catechism,

> Are we bound to believe every sentiment contained
> in this confession [Augsburg Confession]?
>
> A.   We are not; but that the fundamental doctrines
> of the word of God, are taught in it in a manner
> substantially correct [pp. 10f.].

The catechism comprised three parts: 1) Ten Commandments, Creed and the Lord's Prayer, p. 3; 2) Sacraments and Church (including Judgment and Sundry Duties),
p. 4; 3) The Augsburg Confession, p. 16, with a closing section containing four prayers for the use of children.   The
second part received the major attention.

The Ten Commandments were given according to Exodus 20 and were divided according to the Protestant enumeration.   No further explanation was given of the commandments, the Creed, and the Lord's Prayer.

The sacraments were explained in the following manner,

> A sacrament is an ordinance appointed of God, by
> which the benefits purchased by the Savior are not
> only symbolically represented to the senses, but
> spiritual blessing is also actually conferred on
> those who faithfully use them [p. 4].

They were instituted

That the means may be afforded us for membership

in his visible church on earth:--that we may remember forcibly the passion of our blessed Lord:
--be redeemed from the power of death and the
devil:--receive such blessings as can be imparted
to us in the sacraments only, and to become fitted
for heaven [p. 5].

The specific advantage of Baptism was,

Union with Christ's visible church, the influences
of the Holy Spirit, assurance of God's favor, the promise of the pardon of sin, and of eternal life [p. 6].

Concerning the Lord's Supper Sharts clearly denied
the real presence of Christ in the sacrament.   It was only
a spiritual presence (p. 6).

Confirmation was described as "the ceremony of admitting persons to the full privileges of the church" (p. 7).

In treating the church, only the visible church was
given attention and of it, he said it was not "possible for any
one body of Christians; for any particular branch of Christ's
church to be the one only true church" (p. 10).

Obviously Sharts had a very broad view of what the
means of grace were.   He explained,

Means of grace are all those things which have a
tendency to impress the mind with divine truth,
and in the right use of which we have reason to
expect the influence of the holy spirit. [p. 12]

The principal means of grace were, "Preaching, reading of the holy scriptures, prayers and the sacraments.   To
these may be added likewise, self-examination, catechization,
and confirmation" (p. 12).

Sharts' catechism may be regarded as an example of
both the best and the worst in the non-confessional theology
espoused in behalf of what later was to be called American
Lutheranism by Schmucker and his adherents.

THE SOUTH CAROLINA SYNOD
CATECHISM OF 1846

The South Carolina Synod had had some difficulty in

authorizing a catechism suitable for confirmation instruction. In 1827 it had adopted the General Synod's catechism but when this did not meet with general acceptance it shifted to Morris' Catechetical Exercises in 1833.   By this time the New Measures had taken a strong hold on the congregations of this Synod so that by 1846, catechism instruction had all been abandoned by most of the congregations.[63] In that year, however, the Synod finally authorized a catechism of its own in the hope that it might be a means to help restore confirmation instruction.   The title of this new catechism was,

> The Smaller Catechism, of Dr. M. Luther.   Columbia, S.C.:   The South Carolinian Office, 1846.

The new catechism was a modified version of the General Synod's earlier catechism (1826) with some important changes.   It contained the Five Chief Parts of Luther's catechism, using the same text as that of the General Synod's catechism, including the Bible references that had been inserted with the commandments and the sacraments.   These were followed by the Order of Salvation in Short Questions and Answers, also from the General Synod's catechism.   The final section was the traditional Questions for those who Intended to Receive the Sacrament with their Answers.   This translation differed from the previous ones and in addition, restored the word "true" in the question dealing with the Lord's presence in the sacrament.   Consequently it differed considerably from the later edition of the General Synod which had omitted the two questions concerning the sacramental presence.

This simplified version did not contain the Order of Salvation in Systematic Connection, the Table of Duties and the prayers and hymns.

THE HENRY LUDWIG CATECHISM, 1847-1850

Henry Ludwig, one of several publishers of the German Pennsylvania Ministerium catechism, had been repeatedly solicited by some of the confessional elements in the Lutheran Church to publish the whole of Luther's catechism and a faithful translation of the Augsburg Confession.   Apparently as early as 1844, Ludwig had already included the Augsburg Confession in his Pennsylvania Catechism in an appendix and the same was now being requested for a new edition in English.[64] Consequently, in 1847 he published a catechism with the title,

Dr. Martin Luther's Smaller Catechism; to which is added The Order of Salvation and An Analysis of the Catechism, with other matters relating to Confirmation, translated from the German, some of which have never appeared in the English language.   To which is added The Augsburg Confession, carefully translated from the German.   New York: Henry Ludwig, 1847. 65

This new English catechism was to a large extent a reprint of the German Pennsylvania catechism with some important changes.   Luther's catechism was largely taken from Mayer's translation with a few minor changes.   The directions to "The Head of the Family," that Luther had placed over each of the Five Chief Parts, were retained only for the Creed and for Baptism.   This may have been an oversight.   Ludwig followed Mayer in omitting the word "true" concerning the body and blood of Christ in the sacrament. B. M. Schmucker, however, stated that the word appeared in later editions. 66   Similarly Ludwig retained Mayer's weakened opening words for the explanation of the Third Article which read, "I believe that I cannot merely by my own reason etc."

Ludwig differed with Mayer in following the wording of the Ten Commandments to Exodus 20, though he retained the Lutheran division of the commandments.

For the Office of the Keys, he followed the Pennsylvania Catechism in giving simply the three Bible passages frequently used.   He omitted Luther's subheading for the Table of Duties, "For Various Holy Orders and Estates...."

Only three of the orders of salvation by Starcke were included, the Hymn of Faith having been omitted.

Ludwig further retained the Analysis and the Württemberg Children's Examination which he translated: A Short Examination, in Questions and Answers, by which Catechumens are to be examined in Church, previous to Confirmation (p. 54).   Its clear statement concerning the sacramental presence of Christ in the sacrament was a definite sign of the confessional change taking place among the Lutheran churches during this decade.

A new translation of Freylinghausen's Order of Salvation found a place in this English catechism. 67   Ludwig fur-

ther included the List of the Most Important Scripture Passages.... (p. 67).

A unique addition to the catechism was Luther's
[Shorter] Preface to his Larger Catechism. [68] This was followed by the Unaltered Augsburg Confession in its entirety.
The closing section was a collection of 29 hymns, all but 12
were taken from the General Synod catechism (1840).

The omissions were, besides the Hymn of Faith, A
Short Explanation of the Ten Commandments in Verses, the
Golden A- B- C-, and the Seven Penitential Psalms.

Ludwig's catechism was well received among those
whose confessional consciousness had been awakened.   It
received formal sanction from the Joint Synod of Ohio. [69]
Two editions appeared in rapid succession, in 1849 and in
1850.   In 1853, Ludwig issued a new revised edition with
some changes and additions: The Nicene and Athanasian
Creeds, the Penitential Psalms, Carlisle's translation of
Ein' feste Burg, and a number of hymns. [70]

ST. JOHN'S EASTON CATECHISM, 1848

An anonymous catechism was published by St. John's
Evangelical Lutheran Sunday School Society of Easton titled,

> Luther's Smaller Catechism, and Principles of the
> Christian Religion, 2nd ed.   Easton: Argus Office,
> 1848. [71]

This catechism was based in part on the 1832 revision of the
General Synod's catechism and in part on Lochman's Principles.

From the General Synod's catechism it took the introductory questions, the Five Chief Parts of Luther's catechism,
Starcke's Order of Salvation in Short Questions and Answers,
the Historical Catechism and the Prayers.   The trend toward
confessional Lutheranism prompted the author here too to in-
sert the word "true," in the explanation to the Lord's Supper
as originally written by Luther.   In the Questions and Answers, the author felt constrained to amplify the answers to
the questions on the Christian's inability to attain "a state of
sinless grace" and the possibility to "relapse and fall from
the state of grace" (pp. 38-40), reflecting no doubt some of

the problems with the "perfectionists" among the sects of his day.

The Historical Catechism was extended to include a list of the apostles and how they died a martyr's death as told by ancient traditions (pp. 67f.).

Lochman was the source for Principles of Religion in Short Sentences, altered slightly from Starcke's Nine Brief Sentences, and the Hymn of Faith.

The most significant addition to the catechism was the inclusion of the Twenty-One Articles of the Augsburg Confession in a translation that has not been identified.

H. LUDWIG'S GERMAN LUTHER TEXT, 1847

The same year in which Henry Ludwig printed his English catechism, he also reproduced the German text of Luther's Small Catechism in a 36-page edition.

> Enchiridion. The Small Catechism for the Ordinary
> Pastors and Preachers by Dr. Martin Luther. New
> York: Heinrich Ludwig, 1847.72

CATECHISM OF CONRAD MILLER, 1849

The catechism by Conrad Miller had a long and involved history before it was finally put into print. B. M. Schmucker has traced it in part and has given this account:

> The question and answers were used by Mr. Miller
> for many years before they were taken down and
> printed by one of his catechumens, and he was thus
> led to revise and issue this Catechism. At how
> early a date he prepared his work we do not know.
> In its preparation, he made use of a series of
> questions used by his older brother, Dr. Jacob
> Miller, with whom he studied. Dr. J. Miller's
> questions were never printed, but were dictated to
> the catechumens. A copy taken down by Dr. H.
> H. Muhlenberg, when he attended instruction, has
> by his courtesy been compared with a printed cate-
> chism of Conrad Miller. All Dr. Miller's questions
> are used, and his order is observed, but a very

great deal of matter has been added to them. The
widow of Rev. Conrad Miller, still living [in 1886]
at a very advanced age, says that the original basis
of this Catechism was prepared by the Rev. Dr. F.
W. Geissenhainer, Sr., and used by him in the
New Hanover charge, so that in its successive
forms it was used in those churches for over a
half a century. [73]

The catechism was published in 1849, sponsored by a
certain Edwin G. Fritz under the title,

Lutheran Catechism, together with an Explanation,
for Use in Confirmation Instruction in the Congregations of Falkner's Swamp [New Hanover], Boyers-
town, Sassaman, Kieler, etc. Sumnytaun, Pa. E.
Benner, 1849. [74]

The catechism contained only the Five Chief Parts of
Luther's text replete with Bible references. These were
followed by two of Starcke's orders of salvation, Short and
Simple Questions and Answers and the Short Table, and the
Confessional Prayer from the Württemberg Children's Exami-
nation. Two hymns were added including Starcke's Hymn of
Faith. The bulk of the catechism was an explanation of Lu-
ther's catechism (pp. 57-106), beginning, however, with the
Creed which was followed by the Decalog and the other Chief
Parts. The explanation closed with a one-page listing of
Bible references, probably indicating which passages were to
be memorized. The catechism concluded with a section of
17 hymns for various occasions at home and at school,
Prayers for the Dying, Bible Passages for the Sick, and
finally a collection of 102 prayers, many of which were simply hymn stanzas. Strangely, among the many prayers, Luther's Morning and Evening Prayers were not included.

Schmucker gave the following high praise to Miller's
catechism,

The text of Luther underlies and shines through the
whole body of the questions, and his spirit pervades
them. There is no foreign inharmonious matter
introduced. The instruction based on this Catechism
must have been very thorough and in its doctrines
very pure. [75]

Schmucker, however, regarded the inversion of the

Creed and the Decalog in the explanation as "a serious blem-
ish, "[76] though one may not agree with him on that score.
Schmucker may have been influenced in his judgment by the
common treatment of Luther's catechism as an order of salvation, which would require a prior explanation of the Decalog.

In spite of Schmucker's high praise, to which one may
be in general agreement, the catechism did have a few statements that might be questioned. As in the case of Peixoto,
Miller's catechism stated that Christ has redeemed us from
1) the Mosaic Law; 2) the rule of sin; 3) the punishment for
sin; and 4) the power of the devil (p. 69). The redemption
from the Mosaic Law was explained to mean that Christ had
repealed it (p. 70). Thus Paul's declaration that we were
redeemed from the power of the whole law (Romans 7), was
overlooked. In spite of Miller's statement concerning the
Mosaic Law, he still imposed it in connection with Sabbath
observance in the Third Commandment (pp. 82f.).

Miller followed the traditional view of confirmation,
placing the stress on the renewal of the baptismal covenant.

FR. WYNEKEN'S "SPRUCHBUCH, " 1849-1852

During its organization meeting in 1847, members of
the Missouri Synod were impressed by a report concerning
Henry Ludwig's tract of Luther's catechism, whereupon it
was recommended to the congregations for general use. [77]

But more than a tract edition was needed. Already
in 1848, the Synod felt the need to publish a companion book
to Luther's catechism which would contain a listing of the
Bible passages which would further support and explain Luther's text. For this task it appointed Fr. K. D. Wyneken,
pastor in Baltimore, as editor, to be assisted by a committee
comprising Pastors Wilhelm Sihler, Ernst G. Wm. Keyl, Fr.
Aug. Crämer, and C. F. W. Walther. [78] Wyneken's book
appeared under the title,

> Book of [Bible] Texts for the Small Catechism of
> Luther.   Baltimore: n.p., 1849. [79]

The Bible passages were grouped according to Luther's
catechism with two introductory sections, one on Revelation
and the other on The Holy Scriptures. The Decalog was in-

troduced with a section on the Law.   The Creed was prefaced
by several sections on the doctrine of God and His attributes.
Appended to Holy Baptism were sections on the Office of the
Keys, Confession and Absolution.

How widespread the use of this Book of Texts was,
has not been determined.   Its use did merit a reprint in
1852, by J. Neuten Kurtz of Baltimore.

H. LUDWIG'S LARGE AND SMALL
CATECHISMS, 1850

Further evidence of the ready market that the growing
confessional movement among German Lutherans offered was
the publication of Luther's two catechisms by Henry Ludwig
in 1850, "reprinted from the Book of Concord."[80]

The Small Catechism was unique in that it included
not only the usual parts of the catechism but also the Marriage Booklet and the Baptismal Booklet that were part of the
original Enchiridion.   Faithful to the Book of Concord, it did
not include the Office of the Keys nor the Christian Questions
and Answers.

SUMMARY

The history of the issues of Luther's Small Catechism printed in and for America before 1850 is primarily a story of this catechism as it was printed in two languages, German and English. The Swedish and Dutch Lutherans of America, largely lost their linguistic identity after their homelands no longer maintained their ties with the colonies. The new generations of Swedes adopted English as their tongue while many of the youth of the Dutch shifted to the German before they too adopted the language of the country. With the Germans it was different. Immigrants continued to come to America and, fostered by their numbers, they for the most part continued to speak German in their adopted country.

Like their Swedish and Dutch counterparts, the Germans came to America largely for economic reasons. A few, as in the case of the Palatinates in the early 18th century, came for political reasons, while the Salzburgers in the 1730's and the Prussians and Saxons around the 1840's came for religious reasons. Coming for religious reasons, they were well supported by pastors, teachers, and catechisms. Consequently, they had a decided advantage over the others as far as their spiritual care was concerned.

By way of contrast, the German Lutherans who came primarily for economic reasons had little or no help beyond the resources of a family Bible, a catechism or a devotional book. After their arrival they, for the most part, received no direct help from the established State churches. The only groups that were interested in them were a few universities, particularly Halle and Helmstedt, and only occasionally a State church like that of Hanover. Consequently, there was always an extreme shortage of pastors and teachers, and many of those who served were frequently limited in their theological training.

As one would expect, the German immigrants stepping on the shores of America did not come out of a vacuum. They brought with them the type of Lutheranism current at

the moment in their State church.   Therefore the development
of Lutheranism in America paralleled somewhat that current
in Germany.

The major common element of their Lutheranism was
the use of Luther's <u>Small Catechism</u>, especially in the instruction of the youth for confirmation.   This practice, as
we have already noted, was retained with the general use of
this catechism in America.   Of the 29 different German catechisms known to have been published in or for Lutherans in
America, 22 contained Luther's catechism and four more were
to be used alongside of it.   At the most only three did not
have Luther's catechism in mind, though even this might be
questioned in the case of one or two of them.

The prominence of Luther's catechism in the English
editions was much the same.   In all, 30 different English
catechisms were prepared by 1850, 23 of which contained Luther's catechism and three more were to be used alongside
of his text.   Two others could have been used also in this
manner if the teacher so desired.   Only two catechisms were
intended to replace Luther's catechism, that of Quitman in
New York and Sharts in Canada.

The high esteem for Luther's catechism was shared
even by the German Moravians who published two different
editions, one including an explanation by Zinzendorf and the
other containing only the Luther text.   The latter was issued
in two different editions.

While both the German and the English Luther catechisms were first published during the same year, 1749,
their subsequent history during the next 50 years was heavily
weighted in favor of the German publications.   This would
be expected to some extent considering the number of German immigrants that continued to shape early American Lutheranism.   The 29 different catechisms mentioned earlier
appeared in no fewer than 173 editions between 1749 and 1850.

Of this number the single most influential one was the
catechism authorized by the Pennsylvania Ministerium which
was printed in at least 73 editions by 1850.   To these we
might add also the four catechisms that helped shape the final
form of the Pennsylvania catechism.   These were printed in
some 23 editions, all bearing some striking resemblances to
the later official catechism.

The continued presence of Luther's catechism among

the German Lutherans was a contributing factor in keeping
a degree of confessional consciousness alive among both
clergy and laity among American Lutherans.   His catechism
served as a defense for many in their struggle against a
host of threats from various forms of neo-Pietism, Rationalism, American Lutheranism, New Measures and just general indifference.

   In this respect the Pennsylvania catechism was no
doubt the strongest single influence not only because of its
wide and long use and the large number of editions but also
because of its influence upon several catechisms published
independently both in the German and English languages.

   But while Luther's catechism was usually the most
important feature in the catechisms published, its influence
was tempered by a variety of orders of salvation that usually
were included, notably those by Starcke and by Freylinghausen.
Starcke's four orders, one or more of which appeared in almost all catechisms originating in America, had a competing
persistence that was surpassed only by Luther's catechism
itself.   The Pietism they reflected often determined the interpretation of the Luther text.

   The most notable effect of the orders of salvation was
the tendency to teach Luther's catechism as another order,
that is, to take the learner through the logical steps of God's
plan of salvation for mankind.   Almost completely forgotten
was the fact that Luther had intended his Small Catechism to
be taught to baptized children by parents who themselves also
were Christians, thus presupposing faith and spiritual life in
both the teacher and the child.   Luther had intended the Decalog to be taught first of all as the New Testament ethic for
the Christian or, to put it another way, how the Gospel-
motivated life expressed its faith through a God-pleasing life.
The young Christian's fear, love, and trust in a gracious God
were the driving forces to live the new life.   To be sure, the
Decalog remained also a divine judgment.   For as the Christian, who knows himself to be simultaneously a sinner and a
saint, examines his life again in the light of that Law, he
would see himself also as one standing accused before God.
But as a Christian, he could and would turn to the Gospel
again for a blessed assurance of his forgiveness.   In contrast, the orders of salvation used the Decalog primarily as
a preparation for the Gospel, as though the learner was still
in his natural state.   Starcke's several orders of salvation
were particularly effective in this regard.   It is interesting to
note that the European catechisms reprinted in America did

not include any orders of salvation.   This may indeed have
been a factor in their selection.

Similarly, the Pietistic concept of confirmation set
forth in many of the catechisms, particularly with the inclusion of the Württemberg Children's Examination, had a prolonged effect on this rite.   The focal point of the rite continued to be the confirmand's renewal of his baptismal covenant.   Were this to mean merely the renewal of the promise
made by the sponsors at the time of the child's baptism, a
promise given in response to the grace of God in the sacrament, there would have been no problem.   But the baptismal
covenant was understood to mean a covenant made jointly by
God and the sponsors.   But such a covenant was never made
at Baptism.   There God made a covenant of grace, one in
which neither child nor sponsors had any part.   That covenant was lifelong.   It needed no renewal.   It was not broken
by God and could not be broken by man.   It could be denied,
ignored or rejected but not broken.   Only the promise made
by the sponsors or the child, made in response to God's
gracious covenant, could be broken and be renewed.   By
failing to place the emphasis on God's covenant of grace
much of the meaning of Baptism was lost.   The emphasis on
the renewal of the baptismal covenant focused the attention
on man's action and with it gave confirmation an exaggerated
place in the life of the Christian, while all but ignoring the
ongoing power of Baptism which had made the child a member of the church, of God's people.   Unfortunately this Pietistic focus is still much a part of Lutheran folklore.

Another effect of Pietism on Luther's catechism in
America was its understanding of the means of grace.   In
addition to the Gospel and the sacraments one frequently
found listed prayer and the cross of affliction, both the fruit
of subjectivity and what often may have been an unhealthy in-
trospection.

At times the meaning of the Word of God, which in
its New Testament sense meant either the Gospel or Jesus
Christ, was used in its secondary or derived meaning to refer to the Bible.   This encouraged a non-biblical understanding of the term "Word."   This error was compounded when
the Bible, including both Law and Gospel, was regarded as
a means of grace.   All these foreign concepts had their origin primarily in German Pietism.

Rationalism in its more crude and radical forms did

not seriously affect the German catechisms in America.   Unhealthy reactions to Rationalism were at times evident.   This
was seen, for instance, in the emphasis on moralism in Velthusen's catechisms, but their use was confined to the Carolinas and then only for a relatively short period.   Lochman's
German catechism and even more so Temme's Canadian catechism, reflected also an unhealthy reaction to Rationalism,
in the one case with a moralistic spirit and in the other, the
use of reason to bolster up articles of faith.

The most harmful influence on the German Luther
catechisms was the tendency to minimize the doctrinal differences with other German denominations.   Too often German Lutherans were first German and then only Lutheran.
Their cultural and linguistic bonds were stronger than their
ties to a Lutheran confessional theology.   This, too, was a
European heritage, elevated in America as they tried to keep
their identity with other Germans alive rather than adapt
themselves to an English-speaking nation.   This led to a
non-confessional spirit in which a German Lutheran felt
closer to a German Reformed than he did to an English-
speaking Lutheran.

Luther's catechism was therefore often explained in
a manner that wiped out the theological differences, particularly in reference to man's ability to contribute to his salvation and in the teaching of the sacraments as primarily
symbolical acts of the Christian.

With the increase of German immigration, especially
after 1840, a confessional awakening finally began to take
place.   This was evidenced in the growing number of catechisms that included, in addition to Luther's Small Catechism,
the first 21 Articles of the Augsburg Confession.

The story of the English catechism was somewhat different.   Since the German Lutherans were so deeply concerned about retaining their German culture and language,
they were not as sympathetic to the needs of the new English
generations coming up.   At first when the English-speaking
Swedish and Dutch Lutherans were still a force, a start was
made to prepare English catechisms.   But this was of short
duration, except in the New York area where early attempts
to equip the youth with Luther's catechism were kept alive.
In all only four English catechisms were published before 1800.

The 30 English catechisms printed before 1850, already

noted above, were printed in a little over 60 editions. Only
the General Synod catechism, first appearing in 1826, had a
somewhat broad coverage, but even this catechism met strong
competition from a number of more conservative catechisms.

The English catechisms in the main reflected the same
Pietistic effects as did the German catechisms, derived particularly by the frequent use of Starcke's orders of salvation
and the Württemberg Children's Examination.

It was different with the effects of Rationalism. Since
the English speaking Lutherans were surrounded by American
denominations, many hurt by Deism, the effects of Rationalism
were felt more deeply than they were by their German counterparts. However, the negative effect has often been exaggerated as when Quitman's catechism is cited as the dire example of Rationalistic influence. Bad as this catechism was,
the truth of the matter is that it was not well received and,
in fact, inspired new catechisms that were more loyal to the
Christian faith.

But one sad effect the transition to English did have.
As their German counterparts wished to blend in with other
German Christians, so the English Lutherans sought to blend
in with American Protestantism. As with the Germans, they
frequently gave up their Lutheran identity in the sacraments
and in their recognition of the total depravity of the unregen-
erate. The desire to be like other Protestants became most
evident in the presentation of the Decalog in Luther's catechism. They, too, surrendered the evangelical spirit which
Luther had fostered and explained the Ten Commandments
with their Old Testament ceremonial and civic applications.
As a reaction to the prevailing Deism about them, they tried
to support many of the articles of faith with human reason.

But as the German Lutherans were held in check by
the Pennsylvania catechism, so, too, did this catechism hold
some of the English Lutherans in check through several catechisms that were strongly influenced by it.

Part of the devastating forces after the 1830's that at-
tacked both the German and English Lutherans were the New
Measures, which seemed to take away the need for confirmation instruction entirely. Where leaders recognized the consequences of the New Measures, they urged congregations and
synods not to surrender their catechisms to this new threat.
Several catechisms were prepared in order to meet the issues
raised by the New Measures.

As the German element was gradually strengthened in its confessional theology by the new tide of immigration, the English, too, began to take note of their Lutheran identity. The Tennessee Synod, largely influenced by David Henkel, was among the first to stress a confessional theology in its Luther catechisms and later with the publication of the Book of Concord in English. In the 1840's a few catechisms were beginning to show greater confessional loyalty but it was to take somewhat longer before S. S. Schmucker's American Lutheranism with its non-confessional bias would finally surrender to the forces of confessionalism.

One interesting discrepancy may be discerned between the German and the English catechisms in the setting in which the section on The Table of Duties was given. Luther's introductory wording to the Table showed a concern that the Christian ministry was not limited to the priesthood and to the monastic orders. Every Christian was to regard his station in life, whatever it might be, as a possible form of ministry, or in Luther's own words, a "Holy Order." His title for this section therefore read,

> Table of Duties, Consisting of Certain Passages of Scripture for Various Holy Orders and stations, Whereby These are to be Admonished, as by a special Lesson, as to Their Office and Service.

The German editions retained Luther's wording, but English translators who included the Table of Duties seemed to have had some difficulty with it. A number omitted everything beyond the simple title Table of Duties, as in the Anthony Braun (1811) and the Henry Ludwig catechisms (1847 and 1850). Others, however, saw fit to make a change. While David Henkel retained Luther's words in his German editions (1829), he had changed the wording in his translation of 1828 to read, "For the several orders and conditions of men." This was retained in the first American edition of the Book of Concord of 1851. Similarly the Endress' English Pennsylvania Catechism (1805) had, "various orders and conditions of life." This discrepancy between the English and the German catechisms at this point has been perpetuated in the Tappert edition of the Book of Concord, which has, "for various estates and conditions of men" (p. 354).

Only two catechisms were issued during this period in a language other than German or English, and these were Campanius' catechism for the Delaware Indians in 1696, and the Norwegian Pontoppidan in 1842/43.

Appendix

CHRONOLOGICAL LISTING OF LUTHER'S CATECHISMS PREPARED IN OR FOR AMERICA THROUGH 1850

Year*	Title	Page	Library Source**
1696	Johan Campanius, Lutheri Catechismus. Ofwērsatt pa American-Virginiske Spraket. Stockholm: J. J. Ganath.	4ff.	CSL (Reprint)
1744	von Zinzendorf. Der kleine Catechismus D. Martin Luthers. Germanton, [Pa.]: Christoph Saur.	40ff.	LCO
1749	[Peter Brunnholtz], Der Kleine Catechismus Des seel. Herrn D. Martin Luthers. Philadelphia: Benjamin Fränklin und Johann Böhm.	47ff.	ZZZ
	[Peter Brunnholtz], Der Kleine Catechismus. Philadelphia: Benjamin Fränklin und Johann Böhm. 2nd ed.	47ff.	UBG
	[Luther's Small Catechism. Tr. by Peter Brunnholtz and Peter Koch. Philadelphia: Benjamin Franklin.]	94f.	ZZZ
1752	[Peter Brunnholtz], Der Kleine Catechismus Des sel. D. Martin Luthers. Germantown, [Pa.]: Christoph Saur. Enlarged and revised.	53ff.	RMC
	[Peter Brunnholtz], Der Kleine Catechismus Des sel. D. Martin Luthers. Germantown, [Pa.]: Christoph Saur. Enlarged and revised.	55	LCO
1757	Vollständiges Marburger Gesang-Buch. Germantown, Pa. Christoph Saur.	59ff.	LC

---

*Dates in brackets have normally been supplied from sources other than the catechism.
**List of library sources can be found on pages 237-238.

Year	Title	Page	Library Source
1759	Vollständiges Marburger Gesang-Buch. Germantown, Pa. Christoph Saur.	60	CHI microfilm
	Der kleine Darmstädtisches Catechismus. Germanton, [Pa.]: Christoph Saur.	61f.	CSL
1761	[The Rudiments of the Lutheran Catechism with an Abridgment of the Principles of the Christian Religion.] Tr. by Carl Magnus de Wrangel. [Philadelphia: Henrich Miller.]	95f.	ZZZ
1762	[Peter Brunnholtz], Der Kleine Catechismus Des sel. D. Martin Luthers. Philadelphia: Anton Armbrüster. Enl. and rev.	55	LC
	Vollständiges Marburger Gesang-Buch. Germantown, Pa. Christoph Saur.	62	ZZZ
1763	Der kleine Darmstädisches Catechismus. Germanton, Pa.: Chr. Saur.	61	LCO
1764	[Peter Brunnholtz], Der Kleine Catechismus Des sel. D. Martin Luthers. Philadelphia: Anton Armbrüster. 5th and enlarged ed.	55	LCO
[1765]	[Henrich Miller revision], Der Kleine Catechismus Des sel. D. Martin Luthers, Nebst Den Gewöhnlichen Morgen- Tisch- und Abend- Gebethern. Philadelphia: Henrich Miller.	62ff.	ZZZ
1766	[Peter Brunnholtz], Der Kleine Catechismus Des sel. D. Martin Luthers. Philadelphia: Anton Armbrüster. 6th and enlarged ed.	55	LCO
[1767]	[Henrich Miller revision], Der Kleine Catechismus Des sel. D. Martin Luthers. Philadelphia: Henrich Miller.	63	ZZZ
1770	Vollständiges Marburger Gesang-Buch. Germantown, Pa., Christoph Saur.	62	GET
	[Henrich Miller revision], Der Kleine Catechismus Des sel. D. Martin Luthers. Philadelphia: Henrich Miller. 7th ed.	63	LCO
1774	Vollständiges Marburger Gesang-Buch. Germantown, Pa.: Christoph Saur.	62	ZZZ

Year	Title	Page	Library Source
	[Henrich Miller revision], Der Kleine Cate- chismus Des sel. D. Martin Luthers. Phil- adelphia: Henrich Miller. 8th ed.	63	ZZZ
1776	[Henrich Miller revision], Der Kleine Cate- chismus Des sel D. Martin Luthers. Phil- adelphia: Henrich Miller. (May not exist.)	63	ZZZ
1777	[Peter Brunnholtz], Der Kleine Catechismus Des sel. D. Martin Luthers, Germantown, [Pa.]: Christoph Saur and Peter Saur. En- larged and revised.	55	LCO
	Vollständiges Marburger Gesang-Buch. Germantown, Pa. Christoph Saur. 5th and enlarged ed.	60	ZZZ
1778	[Peter Brunnholtz], Der Kleine Catechismus Des sel. D. Martin Luthers. Lancaster, Pa.: Francis Bailey.	55	RMC
1781	[John C. Kuntze's Revision], Der Kleine Catechismus des sel. D. Martin Luthers, Nebst den gewöhnlichen Morgen- Tisch- und Abend Gebetern. Philadelphia: Steiner und Cist.	65ff.	YAL
1782	[_____], _____. Philadelphia: Steiner und Cist.	69	ZZZ
	[Peter Brunnholtz], Der Kleine Catechismus Des sel. D. Martin Luthers. Lancaster, Pa.: Francis Bailey.	55	RMC
1784	[Peter Brunnholtz], Der Kleine Catechismus Des sel. D. Martin Luthers. Philadelphia: Carl Cist.	55	LCO
	[Peter Brunnholtz], Der Kleine Catechismus Des sel. D. Martin Luthers. Philadelphia: Klein und Reynolds.	55	GER
1785	[Pennsylvania Ministerium Catechismus], Der Kleine Catechismus des sel. D. Martin Luthers. Nebst Den gewöhnlichen Morgen- Tisch- und Abend- Gebeten. Germanton, [Pa.]: Leibert und Billmeyer. 1st ed.	71ff.	LCO
	[John C. Kuntze], The Rudiments of the Shorter Catechism of Dr. Martin Luther. Philadelphia: M. Steiner.	97f.	PLS

Year	Title	Page	Library Source
1786	[Pennsylvania Ministerium Catechismus]. Germantaun, [Pa.]: Leibert und Bill- meyer. 2nd ed.	76	GET
	[Pennsylvania Ministerium Catechismus]. Philadelphia: Carl Cist.	76	RMC
	Valerius Tscherning, Catechismus, oder kurzer Unterricht heilsamer Seelen-Weyde, mit Zeugnissen Heil. Schrifft erklärt und bestätigt. Philadelphia: E. Ludwig Baisch.	79ff.	GET
1787	[Pennsylvania Ministerium Catechismus]. Philadelphia und Lancaster, n.p. 1st ed.	76	RMC
	Johann Caspar Velthusen, Erster Kate- chismus, mit den Fünf Hauptstücken. Leipzig: Siegfried Lebrecht Crusius.	84	GET
	Johann Caspar Velthusen, Zweyter Kate- chismus, mit Fragen und mit den Fünf Hauptstücken nebst Luthers Erklärung. Leipzig: Siegfried Lebrecht Crucius.	84f.	GET
	Johann Caspar Velthusen, Helmstädtis- cher Katechismus, oder Christlicher Religions-unterricht nach Anleitung der heiligen Schrift. Leipzig: Siegfried Lebrecht Crusius.	85	IAB
	Johann Caspar Velthusen, Fragebuch für Eltern und Lehrer, oder Anleitung zu Fragen und Gesprächen über den Kate- chismus, mit Rücksicht auf die Ver- schiedenheit der Fähigkeiten und des Alters der Jugend. Leipzig: Siegfried Lebrecht Crusius.	86f.	IAB
	Johann Caspar Velthusen, Spruchregister über den Katechismus. Leipzig: Sieg- fried Lebrecht Crusius.	87	GET
1788	Johann Caspar Velthusen, Nordcaro- linischer Katechismus, oder Christlicher Religionsunterricht nach Anleitung der heiligen Schrift. Leipzig: Siegfried Lebrecht Crusius. 2nd ed.	85	GET
1789	[Pennsylvania Ministerium Catechismus]. Germantaun, [Pa.]: Michael Billmeyer. 3rd ed.	76	PSC

Year	Title	Page	Library Source
1790	[Pennsylvania Ministerium Catechismus]. Germantaun, Pa.: Michael Billmeyer. 3rd ed.	76	FMU
1791	[Pennsylvania Ministerium Catechismus]. Philadelphia: Carl Cist.	76	FMU
1792	[Pennsylvania Ministerium Catechismus]. Chestnut Hill, [Pa.]: Samuel Saur.	76	GET
1793	[Pennsylvania Ministerium Catechismus]. Germantaun, [Pa.]: Michael Billmeyer. 4th ed.	76	FMU
	[Pennsylvania Ministerium Catechismus]. Philadelphia: Carl Cist.	76	RMC (inc.) FMU (inc.)
1795	[Pennsylvania Ministerium Catechismus]. Germantaun, [Pa.]: Michael Billmeyer. 4th ed.	76	RMC
	[Pennsylvania Ministerium Catechismus]. Philadelphia: Carl Cist.	76	RMC
	John C. Kunze and George Strebeck, "Catechism" Appendix to A Hymn and Prayer-Book for the Use of the Lutheran Churches as use the English Language. New York: Hurtin and Comardinger.	98ff.	LC
1796	[G. Henry Ernst Mühlenberg], Abriss der christlichen Lehre fur die evangelische Jugend. [Lancaster, Pa.]: n.p.	88f.	ZZZ
1798	[Pennsylvania Ministerium Catechismus], Philadelphia: Henrich Schweitzer.	76	RMC
	[Johann Goehring], Die sogenannte Heils-Ordnung, in Frag' und Antworten, zum Gebrauch der Informanten. York, Pa.: Solomon Mayer.	90f.	GET
1799	Vollständiger Marburger Gesang-Buch. Philadelphia: Carl Cist. New edition.	60	ZZZ
1800	[Pennsylvania Ministerium Catechismus]. Germantaun, [Pa.]: Michael Billmeyer, 5th ed.	76	FMU

Year	Title	Page	Library Source
	[Pennsylvania Ministerium Catechismus]. Philadelphia: Henrich Schweitzer.	76	RMC
1801	[Pennsylvania Ministerium Catechismus]. Germantaun, [Pa.]: Michael Billmeyer. 5th ed.	76	RLS
1802	[Pennsylvania Ministerium Catechismus]. Philadelphia: Henrich Schweitzer.	76	ZZZ
	[Pennsylvania Ministerium Catechismus]. Germantaun, [Pa.]: Michael Billmeyer. 6th ed.	76	FMU
	Der kleine Catechismus D. Martin Luthers. Barby, [Pa.]: Conrad Schilling.	91f.	FMU
	[Christian F. Endress], Dr. Martin Luther's Catechism for Children and Young People. Philadelphia: Henry Sweitzer.	103ff.	PLS
1803	[Pennsylvania Ministerium Catechismus]. Germantaun, [Pa.]: Michael Billmeyer. 7th ed.	76	GET
1804	[Pennsylvania Ministerium Catechismus]. Philadelphia: Henrich Schweitzer.	76	PLS
	[Pennsylvania Ministerium Catechismus]. Germantaun, Pa.: Michael Billmeyer. 8th ed.	76	CSL
	[New York Ministerium Catechism], Dr. Martin Luther's Catechism. Hudson, N.Y.: Henry Croswell.	105ff.	WLC
	[John George Lochman], Kurzer Inbegriff der Christlichen Lehre Nebst einer Kurzgefassten Kirchengeschichte des Alten und Neuen Testaments. Lancaster, Pa.: Johann Albrecht.	92f.	GET
	John George Schmucker, "Catechism for the Use of those who prepare for Confirmation." Ms.	115ff.	EPA
1805	[Pennsylvania Ministerium Catechismus]. Ephrata, [Pa.]: J. and J. Johnston.	76	PLS
	[Pennsylvania Ministerium Catechismus]. Philadelphia: Carl Cist.	76	CTS

Year	Title	Page	Library Source
	[Christian Endress], The Shorter Cate- chism by D. Martin Luther with the customary Family Prayers, To which is added The Order of Salvation in Nine Short Sections and by Questions and An- swers, etc. Easton, Pa.: Jacob Wey- gandt & Co.	108f.	PMS
1806	[Philip F. Mayer], Dr. Martin Luther's Catechism. Philadelphia: John Geyer.	109ff.	ZZZ
1807	[Pennsylvania Ministerium Catechismus]. Germantaun, [Pa.]: Michael Billmeyer. 9th ed.	76	CTS
	[Philip F. Mayer], Dr. Martin Luther's Catechism. Philadelphia: John Geyer.	112	PLS
1808	[Pennsylvania Ministerium Catechismus]. Libanon, [Pa.]: Jacob Schnee. New ed.	76	MTW
	[Pennsylvania Ministerium Catechismus]. Carlisle, [Pa.]: F. Sanno.	76	GER
	[John George Lochman], Haupt-Inhalt der Christlichen Lehre. Nebst einer kurz- gefassten Kirchen Geschichte. Libanon, Pa.: Jacob Schnee. 2nd rev. ed.	93	ZZZ
1809	[Pennsylvania Ministerium Catechismus]. Germantaun, [Pa.]: Michael Billmeyer. 9th ed.	77	PLS
	Paul Henkel, Der kleine Catechismus des sel. D. Martin Luthers. Neumarket, Schenandoah County (Virg.): Ambrosius Henkel.	131ff.	DUK
1810	[Pennsylvania Ministerium Catechismus]. Philadelphia: Jacob Meyer.	77	PLS
	[John George Lochman], Haupt-Inhalt der Christlichen Lehre. Philadelphia: Jacob Schnee. 3rd rev. ed.	93	GET
1811	[Pennsylvania Ministerium Catechismus]. Philadelphia: George W. Mentz.	77	FMU
	[Philip F. Mayer], Dr. Martin Luther's Smaller Catechism. Frederick-Town, [Md.]: Matthias Bartgis and Son.	114f.	GET

Year	Title	Page	Library Source
	Paul Henkel, Der kleine Catechismus des sel. D. Martin Luthers. Neumarket, Schenandoah County (Virg.): Ambrose Henkel and Co. [Rev. and enlarged].	134	PLS
	Paul Henkel, The First Chief Head of the Christian Catechism, for the Instruction of Youth in the Knowledge of the Christian Religion. New Market, [Va.]: Ambrose Henkel & Co.	136	UV
	Paul Henkel, The Christian Catechism, composed for the Instruction of Youth in the Knowledge of the Christian Religion. New Market, [Va.]: Ambrose Henkel & Co. 2nd ed.	135ff.	PLS
	Paul Henkel, Der Christliche Catechismus, Verfasst zum Unterricht der Jugend in der Erkenntniss der Christlichen Religion. Neu Market, [Va.]: Ambrosius Henkel und Co. 1st ed.	143f.	CMI
	[N. N.], Doctor Martin Luther's Shorter Catechism. Bardstown, [Ky.]: William Bard.	117f.	PMS
	Anthony T. Braun, Dr. Martin Luther's Shorter Catechism. Troy, [N.Y.]: R. Schermerhorn.	120	GET
1812	[Pennsylvania Ministerium Catechismus]. Philadelphia: Jacob Meyer.	77	PLS
	[Anthony T. Braun], Dr. Martin Luther's Shorter Catechism. Boston: Lincoln & Edmunds.	120f.	GPS
1813	[John George Lochman], Haupt-Inhalt der Christlichen Lehre. Libanon, Pa.: Jacob Schnee. 4th rev. ed.	93	GET
	Paul Henkel, The Christian Catechism. New Market, [Va.]: Ambrose Henkel and Co. 3rd ed.	141f.	PLS
1814	[Pennsylvania Ministerium Catechismus]. Philadelphia: G. und D. Billmeyer. 10th ed.	77	GET

Year	Title	Page	Library Source
	[Pennsylvania Ministerium Catechismus]. Philadelphia: Jacob Meyer.	77	GET
	[Philip F. Mayer], Dr. Martin Luther's Catechism. Conrad Zentler.	112	LCO
	Frederick Henry Quitman, Evangelical Catechism or A Short Exposition of the Principal Doctrines and Precepts of the Christian Religion, For the Use of the Churches belonging to the Evangelical Synod of the State of New York. Hudson, N.Y.: William E. Norman.	121ff.	ACR
1815	[Pennsylvania Ministerium Catechismus]. Philadelphia: G. und D. Billmeyer. 10th ed.	77	CSL
	[Pennsylvania Ministerium Catechismus]. Baltimore: William Warner. 1st ed.	77	GET
	[Pennsylvania Ministerium Catechismus]. Chamberburg, [Pa.]: Johann Herschberger. 1st ed.	77	FLP
1816	Paul Henkel, The Christian Catechism. New Market, Va.: 4th ed., enlarged and improved.	142	CMI
	Paul Henkel, The Christian Catechism. New Market, Va.: S. Henkel's Printing Office. 5th ed., from the 4th enlarged ed.	143	CMI
	Paul Henkel, Der Christliche Catechismus. Neu-Market, Virg.: S. Henkels Druckerey. 2nd ed., rev. and enlarged.	144	CMI
	Conrad F. Temme, Dr. Martin Luthers Katechismus erklärt und mit den vornehmsten Beweissspruchen der heiligen Schrift versehen. Philadelphia: Conrad Zentler.	147ff.	PLS
	[Philip Fr. Mayer], Instruction in the Principles and Duties of the Christian Religion for Children and Youth. Philadelphia: Daniel Braeutigam.	126ff.	GET
1817	[Pennsylvania Ministerium Catechismus]. Philadelphia: George W. Mentz.	77	CSL

Year	Title	Page	Library Source
	Johann Michael Steck, Kurzer Unterricht Der Christlichen Lehre, und Examen der Confirmation. Grünsburg, [Pa.]: Johannes Armbrust und Companie. 1st ed.	150ff.	LST
1818	Der kleine Catechismus D. Martin Luthers. Philadelphia: Conrad Zentler.	92	SML
1819	[Pennsylvania Ministerium Catechismus]. Hagerstaun, [Md.]: Gruber and May.	77	PMS
	[Pennsylvania Ministerium Catechismus]. Baltimore: Schaffer und Mund.	77	GET
	[Philip F. Mayer], Dr. Martin Luther's Catechism. Hagers-Town, [Md.]: Gruber and May.	115	PMS
1820	[Pennsylvania Ministerium Catechismus]. Lancaster, [Pa.]: n.p.	77	LCO
	N. N. Der Lutherische Catechismus für die Jugend. Carlisle, [Pa.]: John M'Farland.	152	GET
	F. C. S. [Fr. C. Schaeffer], Luther's Short Catechism. New York: E. Conrad.	158f.	CMI
1821	[John George Lochman], Haupt-Inhalt der Christlichen Lehre. Reading, Pa.: Heinrich B. Sage. 5th rev. ed.	93	GET
	[Philip Fr. Mayer], Instruction in the Principles and Duties. Philadelphia: Daniel Braeutigam.	129	GET
1822	[Pennsylvania Ministerium Catechismus]. Canton, O.: Jacob Sala.	77	CMI
	[John G. Lochman], Principles of the Christian Religion, in Questions and Answers, designed for the Instruction of Youth in Evangelical Churches. Harrisburg: John S. Wiestling.	159f.	GET
1823	[John G. Lochman], Principles of the Christian Religion. Hagers-Town, Md.: Gruber and May.	163	GET

Year	Title	Page	Library Source
	Ernest Lewis Hazelius, Materials for Catechisation on Passages of the Scripture, containing the Doctrines of Christian Faith and Morality. Cooperstown, [N.Y.]: Printed for the Theological Society of Hartwick Seminary, by H. & E. Phinney.	164ff.	PLS
1825	[Pennsylvania Ministerium Catechismus]. Philadelphia: George W. Mentz.	77	ZZZ
	[Pennsylvania Ministerium Catechismus]. Lancaster, [Pa.]: Johann Bär.	77	FMU
	[John G. Lochmann], Principles of the Christian Religion. Harrisburg: John S. Wiesling. 2nd ed.	163	PLS
1826	[Pennsylvania Ministerium Catechismus]. Germantaun, [Pa.]: M. Billmeyer. 11th ed.	77	PLS
	General Synod Catechism, The Smaller Catechism, of Dr. M. Luther. Frederick, Md.: Charles Nagle.	166ff.	LTS
	[H. N. Pohlman], Catechism for the Use of Evangelical Lutheran Churches. Morris-Town, N.J.: Jacob Mann.	173ff.	GET
1827	[John G. Lochman], Principles of the Christian Religion. Germantown, [Pa.]: M. Billmeyer.	164	PLS
	General Synod Catechism, Luther's Smaller Catechism. Hagers-Town, Md.: Gruber and May.	169	CHI
	N. N., The Lutheran Catechism; or An Exposition of the Fundamental Doctrines of Christianity, as contained in the Shorter Catechism of Dr. Martin Luther. Canajoharie, [N.Y.]: H. Hooghkerk.	175	GET
1828	[Pennsylvania Ministerium Catechismus]. Philadelphia: Conrad Zentler.	77	CSL
	[Pennsylvania Ministerium Catechismus]. Lancaster, [Pa.]: H. W. Villee.	77	CSL

Year	Title	Page	Library Source
	[Pennsylvania Ministerium Catechismus]. Gettysburg, [Pa.]: Heinrich C. Neinstedt.	77	GET
	[Pennsylvania Ministerium Catechismus]. Lancaster, [Pa.]: Johann Bär.	77	FMU
	[Philip Fr. Mayer], Instruction in the Principles. Philadelphia: Daniel Braeutigam.	129	GET
	General Synod Catechism, Luther's Smaller Catechism. Hagers-Town, Md.: Gruber and May.	169	MIN
	David Henkel, Doct. Martin Luther's Smaller Catechism. New Market, [Va.]: Solomon Henkel's Office.	180f.	GET
1829	[Pennsylvania Ministerium Catechismus]. Reading, [Pa.]: G. A. Sage.	77	GET
	General Synod Catechism, Luther's Smaller Catechism. Hagers-Town, Md.: Gruber and May. 3rd ed.	169	GET
	David Henkel, Doct. Martin Luther's Smaller Catechism. New Market, [Va.]: S. Henkel's Office. 2nd ed.	181	GET
	David Henkel, Dr. Martin Luther's Kleiner Katechismus. New Market, [Va.]: Salomon Henkel's Druckerei.	182f.	CMI
	David Henkel, Doct. Martin Luther's Smaller Catechism and Dr. Martin Luther's kleiner Katechismus. New Market, [Va.]: S. Henkel's Office.	183	GET
1831	[Pennsylvania Ministerium Catechismus]. Harrisburg, [Pa.]: Jacob Baab.	77	CSL
	General Synod Catechism, Luther's Smaller Catechism. York, Pa.: Daniel May. 4th ed.	169	PLS
	Luther's Smaller Catechism, correctly translated from the original. Published under the auspices of the Ev. Lutheran Synod of Ohio. First edition. Greensburgh, [Pa.]: Jacob S. Sieck.	191	ZZZ

Year	Title	Page	Library Source
1832	General Synod Catechism, Luther's Smaller Catechism. Baltimore: Lucas & Deaver. 3rd ed.	169f.	PLS
	John G. Morris, Catechetical Exercises; or a Familiar Illustration of the Five Principal Articles of Luther's Smaller Catechism, Altered from the German. Baltimore: Joel Wright.	183ff.	PLS
1833	[Pennsylvania Ministerium Catechismus]. Philadelphia: G. W. Mentz und Sohn.	77	GET
	G. F. J. Jäger, Catechismus der Christlichen Lehre in Fragen und Antworten. Kutztaun, [Pa.]: Hawrecht und Wink.	153f.	PLS
1834	[Philip Fr. Mayer], Instruction in the Principles. Philadelphia: Printed for the Tract and Book Society of the Evangelical Lutheran Church of St. John.	129	GET
	John G. Lochman, Principles of the Christian Religion, Harrisburg, [Pa.]: Jacob Baab. 4th ed.	164	GET
	H. W. Scriba, Anfangsgründe des Christenthum's oder kurzer Inbegriff der Wahr- und Pflichten der Christlichen Religion. Chämbersburg, [Pa.]: Heinrich Ruby.	154ff.	GET
1835	John G. Morris, Catechetical Exercises. Baltimore: Lucas and Deaver.	185	GET
1836	[Pennsylvania Ministerium Catechismus]. Philadelphia: G. W. Mentz und Sohn.	77	GET
1837	[Pennsylvania Ministerium Catechismus]. New York: Heinrich Ludwig.	77	GET
	[Pennsylvania Ministerium Catechismus]. Philadelphia: G. W. Mentz und Sohn.	77	GET
	Charles A. Smith, The Catechumen's Guide, prepared with a special reference to the wants of the Evangelical Lutheran Church in the United States. Albany: [N.Y.]: Joel Munsell.	185ff.	PLS
1838	[Pennsylvania Ministerium Catechismus]. Philadelphia: G. W. Mentz und Sohn.	77	GET

Year	Title	Page	Library Source
1839	[Pennsylvania Ministerium Catechismus]. Allentaun, [Pa.]: A und W. Blumer.	77	LCO
	[Pennsylvania Ministerium Catechismus]. Lancaster, [Pa.]: Johann Bär.	78	CSL
	[Pennsylvania Ministerium Catechismus]. Philadelphia: G. W. Mentz und Sohn.	78	GET
	[Philip Fr. Mayer]. Instruction in the Principles. Philadelphia: Printed for the Missionary, Tract and Book Society, of the Evangelical Lutheran Congregation of St. John's Church.	129	GET
1840	General Synod Catechism. Luther's Smaller Catechism. Baltimore: Publications Rooms. 3rd ed.	171	PLS
1841	[Pennsylvania Ministerium Catechismus]. Philadelphia: G. W. Mentz und Sohn.	78	GET
	David Henkel, Doct. Martin Luther's Smaller Catechism. New Market, [Va.]: S. Henkel's Office. 3rd ed.	182	DUK
	Elling Eielsen, tr., Doctor Martin Luther's Small Catechism with Plain Instruction for Children and Sentences from the Word of God to Strengthen the Faith of the Meek. New York: n.p.	188f.	CSL (Reprint)
1842	General Synod Catechism, Luther's Smaller Catechism. Baltimore: Publication Rooms. 3rd ed.	172	CSL
	Joint Ohio Synod Catechism, Luther's Smaller Catechism. New Philadelphia, [O.]: Luthern Standard Office.	191f.	PLS
1842-1843	Erik Pontoppidan, Sandhed till Godfrygtighed udi en eenfoldig og efter Mulighed kort, dog tilstrakkelig Forklaring over Sal. Dr. Mort. Luthers Liden Catechismo. New York: Henry Ludvig.	189ff.	LCD
1843	[Pennsylvania Ministerium Catechismus]. Philadelphia: Mentz und Rovoudt.	78	GET
1844	[Pennsylvania Ministerium Catechismus]. Philadelphia: Mentz und Rovoudt.	78	GET

Year	Title	Page	Library Source
	[Pennsylvania Ministerium Catechismus]. New York: Heinrich Ludwig.	78 and 206	PLS
	John G. Morris, Luther's Shorter Catechism, Illustrated by Additional Questions and Answers. Baltimore: Publication Rooms of the Evangelical Lutheran Church.	192ff.	PLS
	John G. Morris, Luther's Shorter Catechism. Baltimore: Publication Rooms of the Evangelical Lutheran Church. 2nd ed.	196	GET
1845	[Pennsylvania Ministerium Catechismus]. New York: Heinrich Ludwig.	78	GET
	[Pennsylvania Ministerium Catechismus]. Philadelphia: Mentz und Rovoudt.	78	CSL
	Dr. Martin Luthers Kleiner Catechismus. Auf Churfl. Durchl. zu Sachsen Gnädigsten Befehl, vom Ministerio z. M. Kreuz in Dresden. Buffalo: G. Zahm.	197ff.	CMI
	West Pennsylvania Synod Catechism. [C. G. Weyl], Dr. Luther's Kleiner Catechismus welchem beigefügt ist Die Ordnung des Heils. Baltimore: Lutherischen Buchhandlung.	200f.	GET
	Engelbert Peixoto, Leitfaden wornach in den verbundenen Evangelisch-Lutherischen Gemeinden von Alt-Goschenhoppen, Indianfield, und Toheck, bei Ertheilung des Confirmations-Unterrichts der Kleine Katechismus Dr. Martin Luthers erklärt wird. Sumnytown, Pa.: E. Benner.	201ff.	GET
	West Pennsylvania Synod Catechism. C. J. [sic] Weyl, Dr. Luther's Kleiner Catechismus. Baltimore: Lutherischen Buchhandlung.	201	MTW
1846	[Pennsylvania Ministerium Catechismus]. Philadelphia: Mentz und Rovoudt.	78	WSL
	[Philip Fr. Mayer], Instruction in the Principles. Philadelphia: Printed for the Tract and Book Society of the Evangelical Lutheran Church of St. John.	129	GET

Year	Title	Page	Library Source
	[South Carolina Synod], The Smaller Catechism of Dr. M. Luther. Columbia, S.C.: The South Carolinian Office.	205f.	GET
	W. Sharts, A Catechism Designed for the Young in the Evangelical Lutheran Churches in the Eastern District C.W. [Canada]. Ogdenburgh, [N.Y.]: Frontier Sentinel Office.	203ff.	GET
1847	[Pennsylvania Ministerium Catechismus]. Philadelphia: Mentz und Rovoudt.	78	GET
	General Synod Catechism, Luther's Smaller Catechism. Baltimore: Publication Rooms of the Evangelical Lutheran Church. 8th ed.	172	PLS
	N.N. Dr. Martin Luther's Smaller Catechism; to which is added The Order of Salvation and an Analysis of the Catechism, with other matters relating to Confirmation.... New York: Henry Ludwig.	207f.	PLS
	Enchiridion. Der kleine Catechismus für die gemeinen Pfarrherren und Prediger durch D. Martin Luther. New York: Henry Ludwig.	209	ZZZ
1848	[Pennsylvania Ministerium Catechismus]. New York: Heinrich Ludwig.	78	GET
	N.N. Luther's Smaller Catechism, and Principles of the Christian Religion. Easton, [Pa.]: Argus Office. 2nd ed. [1st ed. not located]	208f.	PLS
1849	[Pennsylvania Ministerium Catechismus]. Sumnytown, [Pa.]: Enos Benner.	78	ZZZ
	N.N. Dr. Martin Luther's Smaller Catechism;... New York: Henry Ludwig.	208	PLS
	[Conrad Miller], Lutherischer Catechismus nebst Erklärung, zum Gebrauch beym Confirmations-Unterricht.... Zum Druck gefordert durch Edwin G. Fritz. Sumnytaun, [Pa.]: E. Benner.	209f.	GET

Year	Title	Page	Library Source
	Fr. Wyneken, Spruchbuch zum kleinen Catechismus Lutheri. Baltimore: n. p.	209f.	CSL
1850	[Pennsylvania Ministerium Catechismus]. Allentown, [Pa.]: Blumer, Busch, and Leisenring.	78	PLS
	John G. Morris, Luther's Smaller Catechism. Baltimore: T. Newton Kurtz. 3rd ed.	196	PLS
	West Pennsylvania Synod Catechism. C. G. Weyl, Dr. Martin Luther's Kleiner Catechismus. Baltimore: T. Newton Kurtz. Rev. and enlarged.	201	ACR
	N. N. Dr. Martin Luther's Smaller Catechism. New York: Henry Ludwig.	208	PLS
	Der grosse und kleine Catechismus Dr. Martin Luther's. New York: M. Ludwig & Co.	212	CMI
No date	[Pennsylvania Ministerium Catechismus]. Germantaun, [Pa.]: C. Saur.	78	FMU
	[Pennsylvania Ministerium Catechismus]. Pittsburgh: Robert Ferguson and Co. 1st ed.	78	PLS
	[Pennsylvania Ministerium Catechismus]. Philadelphia: Wm. G. Mentz.	78	FMU
	[Pennsylvania Ministerium Catechismus]. Easton [Pa.]: Heinrich und Wilhelm Hütter. 1st ed.	78	GET
	[Pennsylvania Ministerium Catechismus]. Baltimore: J. T. Hanzsche.	78	ZZZ
	[G. Henry Ernst Mühlenberg], Abriss eines Unterrichts in der christlichen Lehre fur die Evangelsiche Jugend. [Lancaster, Pa.]: n. p.	88	PLS
	General Synod Catechism, Luther's Smaller Catechism. Philadelphia: Lutheran Board of Publication; Baltimore: T. Newton Kurtz. Rev. ed.	172	ACR

Year	Title	Page	Library Source
	General Synod Catechism, Luther's Smaller Catechism. Philadelphia: Lutheran Publication Society. Rev. ed.	172	ACR
	[G. Henry Ernst Mühlenberg], Table of Gospel Instruction. [Tr. by Christian F. Endress. Lancaster, Pa.: n. p. [1817 or later]	88f.	PLS
	Ohio Synod, Eastern District, Der Kleine Catechismus des seligen D. Martin Luther, welchem beigefügt ist Die Ordnung des Heils, eine Zergliederung des Catechismus,... Pittsburgh: Druckerei der Luth. Kirchenzeitung.	203	PLS
Date unknown	N. N. Luther's Smaller Catechism, and Principles of the Christian Religion. 1st ed.	208 284, fn. 71	ZZZ

ABBREVIATIONS FOR LIBRARY SOURCES

ACR   Author's library.

CHI   Concordia Historical Institute, St. Louis, Mo.

CSL   Concordia Seminary Library, St. Louis, Mo.

CTS   Concordia Theological Seminary Library, Ft. Wayne, Ind.

DUK   Perkins Library, Duke University, Durham, North Carolina.

EPA   Eastern Pennsylvania Synod Archives, Lutheran Theological Seminary in Philadelphia.

FLP   The Free Library of Philadelphia.

FMU   Fackenthal Library, Unger Collection, Franklin and Marshall College, Lancaster, Pa.

GER   German Society of Pennsylvania, Horner Memorial Library, Philadelphia.

GET   Abdel Ross Wentz Library, Lutheran Theological Seminary, Gettysburg, Pa.

GPS   German Protestant Society, Waldeborough, Maine.

HTW   Hamma Theological Seminary Library, Wittenberg University, Springfield, Ohio.

IAB   Institut für Auslandsbeziehungen Bibliothek, Stuttgart, West Germany.

LC   Library of Congress, Washington, D. C.

LCD   Luther College Library, Decorah, Iowa.

LCO   Library Company of Philadelphia.

LST   Library of the Lutheran School of Theology, Chicago.

LTS   Lutheran Theological Southern Seminary, Columbia, S. C.

MIN   University of Minnesota Library, Minneapolis, Minn.

PHS   Presbyterian Historical Society, Philadelphia.

PLS   Krauth Memorial Library at Lutheran Theological Seminary, Philadelphia.

PSC   Pennsylvania State College Library, University Park, Pa.

RMC   Readex Microprint Corp. Evans Early American Imprints.

SML   Schwenkfelder Library, Pennsburg, Pa.

UBG   Universitätsbibliothek, Goettingen, West Germany.

UV   University of Virginia Library, Charlottesville, Va.

VAS   Virginia State Library, Petersburg, Va.

WLC   Wm. L. Clemens Library, University of Michigan, Ann Arbor, Mich.

WSL   Wartburg Theological Seminary Library, Columbus Collection, Dubuque, Iowa.

YAL   Yale University Divinity Library, New Haven, Conn.

ZZZ   Not located.

BIBLIOGRAPHY

Acrelius, Israel. A History of New Sweden or The Settlements on the River Delaware. Tr. William M. Reynolds. Philadelphia: The Historical Society of Pennsylvania, 1874.

Allbeck, Willard D. A Century of Lutherans in Ohio. Yellow Springs, Ohio: The Antioch Press, 1966.

Anderson, Carl Magnus, tr. and ed. of "Pastor Wrangel's Trip to the Shore." Reprint from New Jersey History, 87, 1, Spring 1969 by New Jersey Historical Society.

Baur, Richard. "Paul Henkel, Pioneer Lutheran Missionary." Unpublished doctoral thesis, University of Iowa, 1968.

Bernheim, G. D., and George M. Cox. The History of the Evangelical Synod and Ministerium of North Carolina. Philadelphia: Lutheran Publication Society, 1902.

Bernheim, G. D. History of the German Settlements and of the Lutheran Church in North and South Carolina. Philadelphia: The Lutheran Book Store, 1872.

Bente, F. American Lutheranism. 2 vols. St. Louis: Concordia Publishing House, 1919.

Beyreuther, Erich. Zinzendorf und die Christenheit, 1732-1760. Marburg an der Lahn: Francke-Buchhandlung GmbM, 1961.

Bodensieck, Julius, ed. The Encyclopedia of the Lutheran Church, 3 vols. Minneapolis: Augsburg Publishing House, c. 1965.

Boyd, William A., and Charles A. Krummel, "German Tracts Concerning the Lutheran Church in North Carolina," in The North Carolina Historical Review, VII (Jan. 1930), 79-147; (April 1930), 225-282.

Bretscher, Paul G. The Sword of the Spirit. St. Louis: Evangelical Lutherans in Mission, 1979.

Cassel, C. W.; W. J. Finck; and Elon O. Henkel, eds. History of the Lutheran Church in Virginia and East Tennessee. Strasburg, Va.: Shenandoah Publishing House, Inc., 1930.

The Christian Book of Concord or Symbolical Books of The Evangeli-

cal Lutheran Church. Newmarket: Solomon D. Henkel and Brs.,
    1851.

Clark, Delber Wallace. The World of Justus Falckner. Philadel-
    phia: The Muhlenberg Press, 1946.

Clay, John Curtis. Annals of the Swedes on the Delaware. Chicago:
    Swedish Historical Society of America, 1914.

Diffenderffer, F. R. "Early German Printers of Lancaster and the
    Issues of their Press." Papers and Addresses of the Lancaster
    County Historical Society, VIII. Lancaster, Pa.: n.p., 1904,
    pp. 53-83.

Documentary History of the Evangelical Lutheran Ministerium of
    Pennsylvania and Adjacent States. Proceedings of the Annual
    Conventions from 1748 to 1821. Philadelphia: Board of Publi-
    cations of the General Council of the Evangelical Lutheran Church
    in North America, 1898.

Edmonds, Albert Sydney. "The Henkel Family of New Market, Va.,
    Early Printers in the Shenandoah Valley," William and Mary
    Quarterly, Second Series, XVI (July 1936), 414-416.

Edmonds, Albert Sydney. "The Henkels, Early Printers in New
    Market, Virginia, with a Bibliography," William and Mary
    Quarterly, 2nd Series, XVIII (1938), 174-195.

Evangelical Lutheran Hymn-Book with Tunes. St. Louis: Concordia
    Publishing House, 1930.

Evans, Charles. American Bibliography. New York: Readex Mi-
    croprint, 1959.

Ferm, Virgilius. The Crisis in American Lutheran Theology. New
    York: The Century Co., c. 1927.

Finck, Wm. J., ed. and trans. "A Chronological Life of Paul Hen-
    kel, From Journals, Letters, Minutes of Synods, etc.," type-
    written copy, New Market, Va.: n.p., 1935-1937. Duplicate
    copy in Concordia Historical Institute, St. Louis, Mo.

Fink, W. J. "Paul Henkel, the Lutheran Pioneer," Lutheran Quar-
    terly, LVI (July 1926), 307-334.

First General Conference of Lutherans in America, held in Phila-
    delphia, Dec. 27-29, 1898. Philadelphia: Lutheran Publication
    Society, 1899.

Flowers Collection (Henkel Papers) in William R. Perkins Library,
    Manuscript Room, Duke University, Durham, N.C.

Fraas, Hans-Jürgen. Katechismus-tradition. Luthers kleiner Katechismus in Kirche und Schule.   Göttingen: Vandenhoeck & Ruprecht, 1971.

Freylinghausen, Johann A.   Compendium, oder Kurtzer Begriff der gantzen Christlichen Lehre, usw.   Halle: n.p., 1726.

Gardner, John B.   "The Synod of the West," Concordia Historical Institute Quarterly, I (Jan. 1929), 84-91.

Gaustad, Edwin Scott.   Historical Atlas of Religions in America. New York: Harper and Row, c. 1976.

Gemeinschaftliches Gesangbuch, zum Gottesdienstlichen Gebrauch der Lutherischen und Reformirten Gemeinden in Nord America, rev. ed.   Reading: G. Adolph Sage, 1827.

Grabau, Johann A.   "Johannes Andreas August Grabau" tr. by E. W. Biegner, Part VI, Concordia Historical Institute Quarterly, XXIV (Oct. 1951), 124-132.

Graebner, A. L.   Geschichte der Lutherischen Kirche in America. St. Louis: Concordia Publishing House, 1892.

Graebner, Theo., ed. "Diary of Paul Henkel, Pioneer Missionary, 1801," Concordia Historical Institute Quarterly, I (April-July, 1928), 16-20; 43-47.

Graebner, Theodore.   "Paul Henkel, An American Lutheran Pioneer in Missions, Organization, and Publicity," Concordia Historical Institute Quarterly, V (July 1932), 58-63.

Gritsch, Eric W., and Robert W. Jenson, Lutheranism, The Theological Movement and Its Confessional Writings.   Philadelphia: Fortress Press, 1976.

[Hallesche] Nachrichten von den vereinigten Deutschen Evangelisch-Lutherischen Gemeinen in Nord-America, ed. by J. L. Schulze, W. J. Mann, B. M. Schmucker, and W. Germann.   I, Allentown: Brobst, Diehl & Co., 1886; II, Philadelphia: Buchhandlung des Waisenhaus, 1895.

Hazelius, Ernest Lewis.   History of the American Lutheran Church from its Commencement in the Year of our Lord 1685, to the Year 1842.   Zanesville, Ohio: Edwin C. Church, 1846.

Henkel, Ambrose.   "Biographical Sketch of Rev. Paul Henkel," 4-page tract.   n.p., n.d.

Henkel, David.   "Diary of Rev. David Henkel, 1812-1830," typewritten copy by L. L. Lohr of Lincolnton, N.C., made in 1915. N.C. Synod Archives, Salisbury, N.C.   (Original not located)

Henkel, Paul.   "Pocket Diary of 1820."   Archives of Concordia Historical Institute, St. Louis, Mo.

Henkel, Philip. Letter to Ambrose Henkel, dated Jan. 29, 1815 in
    Henry I. Tusing Collection, North Carolina Synod Archives,
    Salisbury, N.C.

Henkel, Socrates. History of the Evangelical Lutheran Tennessee
    Synod. New Market, Va.: Henkel & Co., 1890.

"The Henkel Press of New Market, Virginia" in The Henkel Family
    Records (August 1939), No. 14. New Market, Va.: The Henkel
    Press, Inc., 601-628.

Hinke, William J. "Diaries of Missionary Travels among the Ger-
    man Settlers in the American Colonies, 1743-1748." Reprint
    of a paper originally read before the Pennsylvania German So-
    ciety at Bethlehem, Oct. 5, 1923, n.p., n.d.

History of the Evangelical Lutheran Synod of East Pennsylvania with
    Brief Sketches of its Congregations, 1842-1892. Philadelphia:
    Lutheran Publication Society, n.d.

A History of the Lutheran Church in South Carolina. Columbia,
    S.C.: South Carolina Synod of the Lutheran Church in Ameri-
    ca, 1971.

Hocker, Edward W. "The Sower Printing House of Colonial Times,"
    in The Pennsylvania German Society, Part II, LIII, 1948, 1-125.

Jacobs, Henry Esther. A History of the Evangelical Lutheran Church
    in the United States. New York: The Christian Literature Co.,
    1893.

Jacobs, H. E. "The History and Progress of the Lutheran Church
    in the United States" in The First Free Lutheran Diet in Amer-
    ica, 1877, The Essays, Debates and Proceedings. Philadelphia:
    J. Frederick Smith, 1878.

Johnson, Amandus. The Swedish Settlements on the Delaware, 1638-
    1664. 2 vols. New York: D. Appleton & Co., 1911.

Jonas, George Fenwick, ed. Detailed Reports on the Salzburger
    Emigrants who settled in America. Ed. by Samuel Urlsberger.
    II, 1734-1735. Tr. by Hermann J. Lacher. Athens, [Ga.]:
    University of Georgia Press, c. 1969.

Kirchen-Gesangbuch für Evangelisch-Lutherische Gemeinden ungean-
    derter Confession. St. Louis: Concordia Publishing House, c.
    1892.

Klinefelter, Walter. "The A B C Books of the Pennsylvania Ger-
    mans," in Publications of The Pennsylvania German Society,
    VII, 1973, 1-104.

Koch, Karl. "The American Lutheran Scene, 1831-1841 as Reflected in the 'Lutheran Observer,'" Concordia Historical Institute Quarterly, 37 (July 1964), 55-64.

Koenning, Alton Ray. "Henkel Press: A Force for Conservative Theology in Pre-Civil War Southeastern America," Duke University Bulletin, Sept. 1971.

Kraushaar, Chr. Otto. Verfassungsformen der Lutherischen Kirche Amerikas. Gütersloh: C. Bertelsmann, 1911.

Kreider, Harry J. History of the United Lutheran Synod of New York and New England, I, 1786-1860. Philadelphia: Muhlenberg Press, 1954.

Kreider, Harry J. Lutheranism in Colonial New York. New York: Edward Brothers, 1942.

Kreider, Harry J. "Lutheran Church Life in New York City in the First Half of the Eighteenth Century," Bulletin of the New York Public Library, 62 (Dec. 1958), 610-614.

Kretzmann, Karl. "The First Lutheran Synod in America," Concordia Historical Institute Quarterly, VIII (July-October 1935), 33-36; 76-84.

Kretzmann, Karl. "Early Lutherans and Lutheran Churches in America," Concordia Historical Institute Quarterly, I (April-October, 1928), 20-21; 34-39; 59-63; II (April-July, 1929; January 1930), 8-15; 53-55; 116-21; III (July, 1930; January 1931), 53-56; 113-116; IV (July 1931; January 1932), 43-52; 103-108; V (July 1932), 67-74.

Kretzmann, Karl. "The Constitution of the First Lutheran Synod in America," Concordia Historical Institute Quarterly, IX (April-October 1936), 3-9; 83-90.

Kretzmann, Karl. The Atlantic District of the Evangelical Lutheran Synod of Missouri, Ohio, and Other States and Its Antecedents. Erie, Pa.: Erie Printing Co., c. 1932.

Krueger, J. F. "The History of the English Catechism of the General Synod," Lutheran Quarterly XLIII (April 1913), 181-199.

Kurze Auslegung des Kleinen Katechismus Dr. Martin Luthers. St. Louis: Concordia Publishing House, 1896 and later editions.

[Lindemann, Johann C. Wm.] "Dr. M. Luthers Kleiner Katechismus in Nord-America," Evang-Luth. Schulblatt, III (April and May, 1868), 235-37; 274-77.

Lord, Clifford L. Historical Atlas of the United States. New York: Henry Holt & Co., c. 1944.

Lueker, Erwin L. Lutheran Cyclopedia. St. Louis: Concordia Publishing House, 1975.

Lutheran Book of Worship. Minneapolis: Augsburg Publishing House, 1978.

"The Lutheran Church in New York, 1649-1772. Records in the Lutheran Church Archives at Amsterdam, Holland," tr. Arnold F. van Laer. Bulletin of the New York Public Library, 48 (January-November 1944), Numbers 1, 4, 5, 9, 11; 49 (January-November 1945), Numbers 1, 2, 8, 9, 11; 50 (May and November), Numbers 5, 11.

Lutheran Church in New York and New Jersey, 1722-1760. Lutheran Records in the Ministerial Archives of the Staatsarchiv, Hamburg, Germany. Tr. by Simon Hart and Harry J. Kreider. New York: United Lutheran Synods of New York and New England, 1962.

The Lutheran Hymnal. Authorized by the Synods Constituting The Evangelical Lutheran Synodical Conference of North America. St. Louis: Concordia Publishing House, 1941.

The Lutheran Observer, I (New Series), 1834, passim.

The Lutheran Standard. I (1842) and VI (1848), passim.

Der Lutheraner. XIV (June 29, 1858).

Maasel, Richard George. "A History of the Early Catechisms of the Missouri Synod," an unpublished S. T. M. thesis prepared for Concordia Seminary, St. Louis, June 1957.

Mann, W. J. Part I, "Heinrich Melch. Mühlenbergs Leben" in Die lutherische Kirche in Amerika. Leipzig: Theodor Rother, 1892/93.

Mauleshagen, Carl. American Lutheranism Surrenders to Forces of Conservatism. Athens, Ga.: University of Georgia, 1936.

Missouri Synod. Vierter Synodal Bericht der deutschen evangel-lutherische Synode von Missouri, Ohio, und anderen Staaten, 1950. St. Louis: Niedner Printery, 1851.

Morris, John G. Bibliotheca Lutherana. Philadelphia: n.p., 1876.

Morris, John G. The Catechumen's and Communicant's Companion: Designed for the Use of Young Persons of the Lutheran Church Receiving Instructions preparatory for Confirmation and the Lord's Supper. Baltimore: Joel Wright, 1832.

Morris, John G. Fifty Years in the Lutheran Ministry. Baltimore: James Young, 1878.

Nelson, E. Clifford, ed. The Lutherans in North America. Philadelphia: Fortress Press, 1975.

Neve, J. L., and Willard D. Allbeck. History of the Lutheran
Church in America, 3rd ed. Burlington, Iowa: Lutheran Lit-
erary Board, 1934.

Nicum, J. Geschichte des Evangelisch-Lutherischen Ministeriums
vom Staate New York und angrezenden Staaten und Landern.
New York: Verlag des New York Ministeriums, 1888.

North Carolina Synod. Minutes of the Evangelical Lutheran Synod
of North Carolina--From 1803-1826, Twenty-three Conventions.
Trans. from the German Protocol, Rev. F. W. E. Peshau.
(Microfilm Corpus of American Lutheranism, Reel 27).

North Carolina. Verhandlungen der Conferenzen der Vereingten
Evangelisch Lutherische Prediger, und Abgeordneten, in dem
Staat Nord Carolina Vom Jahr 1811 bis zum Jahr 1812. New
Market, Va.: Ambrosius Henkel und Co., 1812.

Padgett, Stanley D. "The Theology of Paul Henkel in Relation to
His Environment" unpublished S. T. M. thesis prepared for
Concordia Seminary, St. Louis, Mo., May 1867.

Pershing, B. H. "Paul Henkel: Frontier Missionary, Organizer,
and Author," Concordia Historical Institute Quarterly, VII (January 1935), 97-120.

Pfatteicher, Helen E. The Ministerium of Pennsylvania. Philadelphia: The Ministerium Press, 1938.

Preus, J. C. K., ed. Norsemen Found a Church. An Old Heritage
in a New Land. Minneapolis: Augsburg Publishing House, c.
1953.

Protocol of The Lutheran Church in New York City, 1702-1750.
Trans. by Simon Hart and Harry J. Kreider. New York: New
York Synod, 1958.

Qualben, Lars P. The Lutheran Church in Colonial America. New
York: Thomas Nelson and Sons, 1940.

Reichmann, Felix. "German Printing in Maryland: A Check List,
1768-1950." Society for the History of the Germans in Maryland, 27th Report, 1950, pp. 9-70.

Repp, Arthur C. Confirmation in the Lutheran Church. St. Louis:
Concordia Publishing House, 1964.

Repp, Arthur C. "The Lutheran Church in America a Century Ago,"
Concordia Historical Institute Quarterly, 20 (July-October, 1947),
63-79; 155-158.

Reu, J. Michael. D. Martin Luthers Kleiner Katechismus. Die Geschichte seiner Entstehung, seiner Verbreitung und seines Gebrauchs. Munich: Chr. Kaiser Verlag, 1929.

Reu, Michael. Dr. Martin Luther's Small Catechism. A History of Its Origin, Its Distribution and Its Use. A Jubilee Offering. Chicago: Wartburg Publishing House, 1929.

Ryden, Ernest. "Olof Joransson Svebilius," in The Encyclopedia of the Lutheran Church, III, ed. by Julius Bodensieck. Minneapolis: Augsburg Publishing House, 1965, p. 2283.

Sachse, J. F. Justus Falckner. Philadelphia: n. p., 1903.

Schaeffer, C. W. Early History of the Lutheran Church in America from the Settlement of the Swedes on the Delaware, to the Middle of the Eighteenth Century. New ed. Philadelphia: Lutheran Book Store, 1868.

Schmucker, B. M. "Luther's Small Catechism," The Lutheran Church Review V (April-July 1886), 87-113; 165-199.

Schmucker, B. M. "The Lutheran Church in New York City," in Lutheran Church Review, III (July-October 1884), 204-222; 276-295, IV (April-July, 1885), 127-151; 187-209.

Schmucker, S. S. The American Lutheran Church, Historically, Doctrinally, and Practically Delineated in Several Occasional Discourses. Philadelphia: E. W. Miller, 1852.

Scholz, Robert F. "Was Muhlenburg a Pietist?", Concordia Historical Institute Quarterly, 52 (Summer 1979), 50-65.

Schuchmann, Heinz. "Notes on the Origins of Joshuah Kocherthal," tr. Frederick S. Weiser, Concordia Historical Institute Quarterly, XLI (November 1968), 147-153.

Schultz, Eric R. W. "Tragedy and Triumph in Canadian Lutheranism," Concordia Historical Institute Quarterly, 38 (July 1965), 55-72.

Seidensticker, Oswald. The First Century of German Printing in America, 1728-1830. Philadelphia: Schaefer and Koradi, 1893.

Shaw, R. R., and R. H. Shoemaker. Early American Imprints, 2nd series. 1801-1819. Readex Microprint.

Shaw, Ralph R., and Richard Shoemaker. American Bibliography, A Preliminary Checklist (1801-1819).

Sheatsley, C. V. History of the Evangelical Lutheran Joint Synod of Ohio and Other States. Columbus, Ohio: Lutheran Book Concern, 1919.

Stange, Douglas C. "Frederick Henry Quitman, D. D. (1760-1832),"
Concordia Historical Institute Quarterly, XXXIX (July 1966), 67-
76.

Starcke, Christoph. Sechsfach-kurtzgefasste Ordnung des Heils,
Das ist Eine sechsfache Art, die Lehre von des Menschen Heil
und Seligkeit den Einfältigen ordentlich und erbaulich vorzutragen.
New and rev. ed. Erfurt: Johann Friedrich Webern, 1756.

Strobel, P. A. The Salzburgers and Their Descendants. Baltimore:
T. Newton Kurtz, 1855.

Suelflow, Roy. "The First Years of Trinity Congregation, Freistadt,
Wisconsin," c. viii-x, Concordia Historical Institute Quarterly,
XVIII (October 1945), 83-95.

Svengalis, Kendall F. "Theological Controversy among Indiana Lutherans, 1835-1870," Concordia Historical Institute Quarterly,
46 (Summer 1973), 70-90.

Tappert, Theodore G., ed. and trans. The Book of Concord. Philadelphia: Muhlenberg Press, c. 1959.

Tappert, Theodore G., and John W. Doberstein, eds. and trans.
The Journals of Henry Melchior Muhlenberg, 3 vols. Philadelphia: Muhlenberg Press, 1942-1948.

Tennessee Synod. Report of the Transactions of the 8th Evangelical
Lutheran Synod of Tennessee, Sept. 3-8, 1827. New Market:
Sol. Henkel, 1827.

Tennessee Synod. Report of the Transactions of the Seventh Evangelical Lutheran Synod of Tennessee, Sept. 4-7, 1826. New
Market, Va.: Sol. Henkel, n.d.

Urlsperger, Samuel. Elfte Continuatio der ausführlichen Nachrichten
von den Salzburgischen Emigranten, die sich in America niedergelassen haben, 1742-. Halle: Verlegung des Waisenhauses,
1745.

Virginia. Bericht von der Special Conferen der Evang. Luth. Prediger und Abgeordeneten im Staat Virginien, Winchester, Okt.
3, 1808. Newmarket, Va.: Ambrosius Henkel, [1808].

Vollständiges Marburger Gesang-Buch, Zur Uebung der Gottseligkeit,
in 649 Christlichen und Trostreichen Psalmen und Gesängen Hm.
D. Martin Luthers, und andrer Gottseliger Lehrer. Germantown: Christoph Saur, 1770.

Weinlick, John R. Count Zinzendorf. New York: Abingdon Press,
c. 1956.

Weis, James. "The Problem of Language Transition Among Lu-

therans in Ohio, 1836-1858." Concordia Historical Institute
Quarterly, 39 (April 1966), 5-19.

Wentz, Abdel Ross. A Basic History of Lutheranism in America.
Philadelphia: Muhlenberg Press, c. 1955.

Wentz, Abdel Ross. History of the Evangelical Lutheran Synod of
Maryland of the United Lutheran Church in America, 1820-1920.
Harrisburg: Evangelical Press, 1920.

Wentz, Abdel Ross. "The Ordination Certificate of Justus Falckner," Concordia Historical Institute Quarterly, XLI (May 1968),
65-86.

Wiederaenders, Robert C. "A Bibliography of American Lutheranism, 1624-1850." Privately mimeographed.

Willkomm, Martin. "Report on the Birth Record of William Christopher Berkkenmeyer," Concordia Historical Institute Quarterly,
VII (October 1934), 95-96.

Wischan, F. "Kurze Geschichte der deutschen evangel-luther.
Gemeinden in und em Philadelphia und der lutherischen Synoden
Amerikas" Part II in Die lutherische Kirche in Amerika. Leip-
zig: Theodor Rother, 1893.

Der Wochentliche Philadelphische Staatsbote. March 7, 1763-Dec.
24, 1764 (60-154); and 3, 1775-May 26, 1779 (466-920).

Wolf, E. J. "History of the General Synod," Lutheran Quarterly,
XIX (October 1889), 420-458.

Wolf, Edmund Eyster. The Lutherans in America. A Story of
Struggle, Progress, Influence and Marvelous Growth. New
York: J. A. Hill and Co., 1890.

Wolf, Edward C. "Lutheran Hymnody and Music Published in America, 1700-1850. A Descriptive Bibliography," Concordia Historical Institute Quarterly, 50 (Winter 1977), 164-185.

Wolf, Richard C. Documents of Lutheran Unity in America. Philadelphia: Fortress Press, 1966.

Wuorinen, John H. The Finns on the Delaware, 1638-1655. New
York: A. M. S. Press, Inc., 1966.

Wust, Klaus. "German Printing in Virginia. A Check List, 1789-
1834." Reprint, pp. 54-66.

Zion Lutheran Church, Oldwick, N.J. "Minutes of the Vestry
Board," April 1825. Congregation's archives.

CHAPTER NOTES

CHAPTER I

1. Finland was an integral part of Sweden until 1809, when the Finns were taken over by Russia.

2. John H. Wuorinen, The Finns on the Delaware, 1638-1655. New York: A.M.S. Press, Inc., 1966, p. 75.

3. Karl Kretzmann, "Early Lutherans and Lutheran Churches in America," Concordia Historical Institute Quarterly, IV (July 1931), 46.

4. Wuorinen, op. cit., p. 54.

5. Israel Acrelius, A History of New Sweden or The Settlements on the River Delaware. Tr. William M. Reynolds. Philadelphia: The Historical Society of Pennsylvania, 1874, p. 39.

6. Ibid., p. 35.

7. J. Michael Reu, Dr. Martin Luther's Small Catechism, A History of Its Origin, Its Distribution and Its Use. Chicago: Wartburg Publishing House, 1929, p. 275. J. Rudbeck, 1581-1648.

8. Ibid. Gothus, 1565-1646. His catechism followed the Nürnberger text of 1531 which added, "I am the Lord, thy God," as opening words to the Ten Commandments. It followed the Danish-Norwegian edition of 1575, in placing the section on Confession after the Lord's Supper. Reu's D. Martin Luther's Kleiner Katechismus. Munich: Chr. Kaiser Verlag, 1929, p. 95.

9. Lutheri Catechismus Öfwersatt på American-Virginiske Språket.

10. Acrelius, op. cit., p. 368, fn.

11. Ibid., p. 283.

12. Kretzmann, op. cit., IV (Jan. 1932), 108.

13. Wuorinen, op. cit., p. 75.

14. Ibid., p. 112.

15. Acrelius, op. cit., p. 178.

16. Ibid., p. 181.

17. Ibid., p. 184.

18. Ibid., pp. 183-184.

19. Ibid., p. 187.

20. Ibid., pp. 190-193.

21. Enfaldig Forklaring Öfwer Lutheri Lille Catechismus, stält genom Sporsmal och Swar.

22. Ernest Ryden in "Olof Jöransson Svebilius," The Encyclopedia of the Lutheran Church, ed. by Julius Bodensieck. Minneapolis: Augsburg Publishing House, 1965, III, p. 2283.

23. Acrelius, op. cit., p. 198.

24. To Dr. Israel Kolmodin, dated Oct. 29, 1697. John Curtis Clay, Annals of the Swedes on the Delaware. Chicago: Swedish Historical Society of America, 1914, p. 62.

25. Acrelius, op. cit., p. 218.

26. Ibid., p. 303.

27. Ibid., pp. 243-244. Reynolds translated the latter "confirmation." But this is an anachronism since Naessmann was anti-Halle or anti-Pietistic and was called an Orthodox or scholastic Lutheran by the Pietists. Acrelius, op. cit., p. 248. The Swedes during this early period referred to the act simply as "catechism." Their liturgy, like most of the Orthodox Lutherans, treated the subject broadly under the general heading, "What is to be done when the youth come, for the first time to the Lord's Supper?", cp. Church Order of 1686. See also Arthur C. Repp, Confirmation in the Lutheran Church. St. Louis: Concordia Publishing House, 1964, for the historical background of confirmation. The process of instruction should therefore not be referred to as "confirmation" since that term at this time was a mark Pietism.

28. Acrelius, op. cit., p. 368. A previous donation of books by King Charles XII had been received in 1705, and again in 1708. However, the lists given do not specifically mention catechisms. They did include Bibles, prayerbooks, primers, and spiritual meditations. Clay, op. cit., pp. 78 and 83.

29. Acrelius, op. cit., p. 338.

30. Wuorinen, op. cit., p. 117.

31. Acrelius, op. cit., pp. 220 and 282. Andreas Sandel in 1715, and Anders Hesselius in 1720.

32. Ibid., p. 303. Israel Acrelius (1714-1800) was a graduate of the University of Upsala at the time when it was a center of Pietism in Sweden. He was a staunch defender of Mühlenberg.

33. Ibid., pp. 304-305.

34. Abdel Ross Wentz, A Basic History of Lutheranism in America. Philadelphia: Muhlenberg Press, c. 1955, p. 6.

35. Theodore G. Tappert in The Lutherans in North America, ed. E. Clifford Nelson, Philadelphia: Fortress Press, 1973, p. 6.

36. B. M. Schmucker, "The Lutheran Church in New York City," The Lutheran Church Review, III (July 1884), 207.

37. Harry Julius Kreider, Lutheranism in Colonial New York. New York: Edward Brothers, 1942, p. 49.

38. Karl Kretzmann, op. cit., II (July 1929), 53.

39. Kreider, op. cit., p. 66.

40. Letter April 25/May 5, 1669, in "The Lutheran Church in New York, 1649-1772," tr. Arnold J. F. van Laer. Bulletin of the New York Public Library, 48 (Sept. 1944), 771.

41. Ibid., pp. 771-772.

42. Ibid.

43. Harry Julius Kreider, History of the United Lutheran Synod of New York and New England. Philadelphia: Muhlenberg Press, 1954, I, 2.

44. Kreider, Colonial New York, p. 66.

45. Ibid., p. 67.

46. Reu, Small Catechism, pp. 131 and 275.

47. Ibid., p. 131. The full title was De Kleyne Catechismus Ofte Onderwysinge in de Christlijcke leere D. Martini Lutheri. Mitegaders het kleyne Corpus Doctrinae: Om de Jonckheydt ende eenvouldige Christenen in de vorseyde Catechismus noch meer te öffenen usw.

48. B. M. Schmucker, "Luther's Small Catechism," The Lutheran
     Church Review, V (April 1886), 89.

49. Supra, p. 6.

50. Tappert, op. cit., p. 13.

51. Delber Wallace Clark, The World of Justus Falckner, Phila-
     delphia: The Muhlenberg Press, 1946, p. 12.

52. Abdel Ross Wentz, "The Ordination Certificate of Justus Falck-
     ner," Concordia Historical Institute Quarterly, XLI (May
     1968), 65-86.

53. Clark, op. cit., p. 55.

54. Ibid., pp. 16-19.

55. Kreider, Colonial New York, p. 32.

56. Letter, Nov. 10, 1705, "The Lutheran Church in New York
     (1649-1772)," Bulletin, 49 (Jan. 1945), p. 4.

57. Ibid., pp. 4-5.

58. Clark, op. cit., p. 68.

59. Ibid., pp. 76-77. The Dutch title is Grondlycke Onderricht
     van Sekere Voorname Hoofd-stucken, der Waren, Loutern,
     Saligmakendon Christelycken Leere, Gegrondet op den Grondt
     van de Apostelen en Propheten, daer Jesus Christus de
     Hoeck-Steen. New York: W. Bradfordt, 1708.

60. Ibid., p. 77. See also Karl Kretzmann, op. cit., XI (Jan.
     1939), 121-124.

61. Henry Eyster Jacobs, A History of the Evangelical Lutheran
     Church in the United States. New York: The Christian Lit-
     erature Co., 1893, p. 21. So also A. L. Graebner, Ges-
     chichte der Lutherischen Kirche in America. St. Louis:
     Concordia Publishing House, 1892, who reproduced the sec-
     tion on "Free Will," pp. 92-93.

62. Letter dated Feb. 17, 1713 acknowledged the receipt of the
     books. Bulletin of the New York Public Library, 49 (Jan.
     1945), 9. The Paradijschofkens was written by Johann Arndt
     in 1612, as one of several works to offset some of the po-
     lemical literature of the day. Arndt had hoped "to lead the
     believers in Christ away from a dead faith to one producing
     the fruits of faith." Reu, Small Catechism, p. 179.

63. Letter dated Oct. 23, 1713. Bulletin, op. cit., p. 12.

64. Some of these are cited by Graebner, op. cit., pp. 96-97; Jacobs, op. cit., pp. 118-120; and F. Bente, American Lutheranism. St. Louis: Concordia Publishing House, 1919, I, 26-27.

65. Bente, op. cit., I, 27. Being a Pietist the word "confirmed" came natural to Falckner.

66. Lars P. Qualben, The Lutheran Church in Colonial America. New York: Thomas Nelson and Sons, 1940, p. 173.

67. Heinz Schuchmann, "Notes on the Origins of Joshuah Kocherthal," Concordia Historical Institute Quarterly, XLI (November 1968), 147-153.

68. Graebner, op. cit., p. 107.

69. Ibid., p. 108.

70. Kreider, Colonial New York, p. 35.

71. Letter October 3, 1715, in Bulletin, op. cit., 49 (January 1945), 14.

72. Kreider, Colonial New York, pp. 36-37.

73. Ibid., p. 39.

74. Martin Willkomm, "Report on the Birth Record of William Christopher Berkkenmeyer," Concordia Historical Institute Quarterly, VII (October 1934), 96.

75. Kreider, Colonial New York, p. 39.

76. Ibid., pp. 39-41.

77. Report of Oct. 21-Nov. 1, 1725. Bulletin, op. cit., 49 (February 1945), 104.

78. Ibid., p. 105.

79. Letter Nov. 18, 1726. Ibid. (Sept. 1945), 655.

80. Letter Nov. 1, 1728. Ibid., p. 659.

81. Catechismus D. Martini Lutheri, door klare Spreucken heylicher Schrifture ende eenige vragen, tot beter verstant des selven dienend, befestiget ende voorgestelt. cp. Protocol of the Lutheran Church in New York City 1702-1750. Tr. Simon Hart and Harry J. Kreider. New York: New York Synod, 1958, p. 34. According to Reu, this catechism originated in Rostock where Taddel had been pastor before he came to Amsterdam in

        1649. The catechism included the Questions and Answers attributed to Luther. Reu, Luther's Catechism, p. 131.

82. Hoofdleerstukken der Christelijke Leere. Protocol, p. 34.

83. Bijbelsche Catechismus School. Ibid. Graebner says that Cordes came from Hamburg as the fourth pastor in Amsterdam in 1641, op. cit., p. 43.

84. Noodige Grondstellingen of Leerpuncten, dewelke tot d'kennisse van den waaren godsdienst behooren, bevattelijk voorgesteld, na de ordre van de Catechismus Lutheri kostelijk verklaard, en uyt de H. Schriftuur bevestigt. Vraags-wijse opgestelt tot oeffeninge voor de Aanwassende jeugt, maer wel voornamentlijk ten dienste van diegene, dewelke haar tot des Heeren H. Avondmaal will begeven. Zeer bekwaam voor all Christelijke Huisgezinnen. Protocol, p. 117.

85. Protocol, p. 151.

86. Kreider, Colonial New York, p. 44.

87. Ibid., pp. 44-45.

88. Ibid., p. 45.

89. Letter to the Amsterdam Consistory, Aug. 1, 1732. Bulletin, op. cit., 49 (November 1945), 815.

90. Ibid.

91. Kreider, Colonial New York, p. 46.

92. Ibid., 84. The three pastors present were Berkenmeyer, Knoll and Wolf. In addition, nine laymen were in attendance.

93. B. M. Schmucker, The Lutheran Church in N.Y., III (October 1884), 284.

94. Karl Kretzmann, "The Constitution of the First Lutheran Synod in America," Concordia Historical Institute Quarterly, IX (April 1936), 7. Kretzmann obviously overstated his case in referring to this meeting as a "Synod."

95. Ibid., IX (October 1936), 85.

96. Ibid., IX (April 1936), 8.

97. Kreider, Lutheran Church in New York and New Jersey, p. 71.

98. Ibid., p. 25.

99. Ibid., pp. 78-79.

100. Ibid., p. 100.

101. Ibid., p. 106.

102. Ibid., pp. 109-110.

103. Ibid., pp. 124-125.

104. Ibid., p. 106.

105. Ibid., p. 107.

106. Theodore G. Tappert and John W. Doberstein, eds. and translators. The Journals of Henry Melchior Mühlenberg. Philadelphia: Muhlenberg Press, 1942, I, 108.

107. Kreider, Colonial New York, p. 59.

108. Ibid., p. 63.

109. Graebner, op. cit., p. 243; Wentz, Basic History, p. 16.

110. Jacobs, op. cit., p. 190.

111. Ibid., p. 189.

112. Whether Mühlenberg may rightly be called a Pietist has been questioned by Robert F. Scholz, "Was Muhlenberg a Pietist?," Concordia Historical Institute Quarterly, 52 (Summer 1979), 50-65. He defends his position by defining Pietism in a narrow sense. Accepting his narrow understanding of Pietism, Mühlenberg could certainly not be classified as a Pietist. Yet many would question Scholz's definition, for it leaves little room for changing circumstances. A similar case could certainly be made for the followers of Lutheran Orthodoxy and even for those who were influenced by Rationalism.

113. Journals, I, 20.

114. Ibid. Entries for May 24, 1742.

115. Ibid., I, 21.

116. Ibid., I, 195.

117. Ibid., I, 101. Rambach (1693-1735) was a Pietist. He had been taught at Halle and Giessen and was the author of a number of hymns.

118. Ibid., I, 98.

119. Ibid., I, 195. Hymn of Faith was the name given to this order in the English catechisms of a later date.

120. Reu, Small Catechism, p. 199. Eric W. Gritsch and Robert
     W. Jenson, Lutheranism, The Theological Movement and
     Its Confessional Writings. Philadelphia: Fortress Press,
     1976, p. 21.

121. Journals, I, 98.

122. Ibid., I, 46.

123. Ibid., I, 327.

124. Ibid., I, 335.

125. Ibid., I, 90, fn. Brunnholtz was born in Niebuhl, Schleswig
     and studied in Halle.

126. Christoph Starcke, Sechsfach-kurtzgefaszte Ordnung des Heils,
     Das ist Eine sechsfache Art, die Lehre von des Menschen
     Heil und Seligkeit den Einfaltigen ordentlich und erbaulich
     vorzutragen. New and revised ed. Erfurt: Johann Fried-
     rich Webern, 1756. Mühlenberg and Brunnholtz had access
     to the earlier edition, 1743.

127. Journals, III, 429.

128. [Hallesche] Nachrichten von den vereinigten Deutschen
     Evangelische-Lutherischen Gemeinen in Nord-America, ed.
     by J. L. Schulze, W. J. Mann, B. M. Schmucker, and W.
     Germann. Allentown, 1886, I, 413.

129. Wentz, op. cit., p. 20.

130. A History of the Lutheran Church in South Carolina. Colum-
     bia, S.C.: The S.C. Synod of the L.C.A., 1971, p. 40.

131. Wentz, op. cit., p. 79.

132. Ibid., p. 19.

133. Jacobs, op. cit., pp. 151-160.

134. For an extended text see Richard C. Wolf, Documents of Lu-
     theran Unity in America. Philadelphia: Fortress Press,
     1966, #7, pp. 17-19.

135. Compendium, oder Kurtzer Begriff der gantzen Christlichen
     Lehre, etc. Halle: n.p. 1726. Entry for August 26 [27],
     1734, in George Fenwick Jones, ed. Detailed Reports on
     the Salzburger Emigrants who Settled in America, edited by
     Samuel Urlsberger. II, 1734-1735. Tr. by Herman J.
     Lacher. Athens, Ga.: University of Georgia Press, v.
     1969, p. 134.

136. Ibid., III, 17-18. III, 1736, ed. by J. and Marie Hahn, c. 1972.

137. Ibid., II, 134. Entry for Aug. 26 [27], 1734.

138. Ibid., II, 8. Entry for Aug. 21, 1734.

139. Ibid., III, 237. Entry for Nov. 5, 1736.

140. Among the authors represented were Joachim Lange (1670-1744), Paul Anton (1661-1730), Johann A. Freylinghausen (1670-1739), Schubart, and Johann Arndt (1555-1621). Arndt, though strictly speaking not a Pietist, was highly regarded by Pietists for his devotional literature. Entries for May 13 and 16 in Samuel Urlsberger, Elfte Continuatio der ausführlichen Emigranten, die sich in America Niedergelassen Haben, 1742-. Halle: Verlegung des Waisenhauses, 1745, pp. 1960 and 1966.

CHAPTER II

1. Abdel Ross Wentz, A Basic History of Lutheranism in America. Philadelphia: Muhlenberg Press, c. 1955, p. 46.

2. Henry Eyster Jacobs, A History of the Evangelical Lutheran Church in the United States. New York: The Christian Literature Co., 1893, pp. 196-197.

3. John R. Weinlick, Count Zinzendorf. New York: Abingdon Press, c. 1956, p. 154.

4. Theodore G. Tappert and John W. Doberstein, eds. and trans. The Journals of Henry Melchior Mühlenberg. Philadelphia: Muhlenberg Press, 1942, I, 76-82.

5. Weinlick, op. cit., p. 178.

6. Der kleine Catechismus D. Martin Luthers. Mit Erläuterungen herausgegeben zum Gebrauch der Lutherische Gemeinen in Pennsylvanien. Germanton: Gedruckt bey Christoph Saur, 1744.

7. Trans. from The Lutheran Hymnal, 311.

8. Ibid., 313.

9. [Hallesche] Nachrichten von den vereinigten Deutschen Evangelische-Lutherischen Gemeinen in Nord-America, ed. by J. L. Schulze, W. J. Mann, B. M. Schmucker, and W. Germann. Allentown, Pa., 1886, I, 413.

10. Ibid., I, 526. To the above, the editors add in Note 120, p.
    673, that two copies of the same were sent to Francke and
    that no known copies exist.

11. Der Kleine Catechismus Des seel. Herrn D. Martin Luthers,
    Nebst Den gewöhnlichen Morgen- Tisch- und Abend- Gebätern.
    Wobey Zum Gebrauch der erwachsenen Jugend hinzugefüget:
    Die Ordnung des Heyls In einem Lied bekant unter dem Name
    Das Glaubens-Lied Und In kurtzen eifältigen Fragen und Ant-
    worten. In Schulen und bey der Kinder-Lehr nützlich zu
    gebrauchen. Die zweyte Auflag. Philadelphia: Druckts und
    verlegts Benjamin Fräncklin und Johann Böhm, 1749.
        This heretofore unknown edition is in the Göttingen Uni-
    versity library and was found there with the assistance of
    Dr. Haas-Jürgen Fraas (Munich), who had listed it in his
    Katechismustradition. Reu who had not seen either 1749
    editions, erred in supposing they were the same as the 1752
    editions. (Dr. Martin Luther's Small Catechism. Chicago:
    Wartburg Publishing House, 1929, p. 277.)

12. III. Den Sabbath halte theur, ich selbst hab ihn gegeben, Zu
    deinem Heil, und deiner Seelen Leben.

13. Reu, op. cit., p. 201. Rambach (1693-1735) was A. H.
    Francke's successor at Halle. His views on teaching were
    set forth in his Wohlunterwiesener Informator, published
    posthumously in 1737.

14. 1764. Journals, II, 93.

15. 1765. Ibid., II, 217. See also Journals, III, 424 for 1781.

16. 1765. Ibid., II, 236.

17. Ibid., II, 60 and 90f.

18. 1782. Ibid., III, 481 and 484f.

19. Reu, op. cit., pp. 39-44.

20. Ibid., pp. 44f.

21. Journals, I, 98. Reu erroneously ascribed the original to
    Ziegenhagen who merely revised it. Op. cit., p. 278.

22. Christoph Starcke. Sechsfach-kurtzgefaszte Ordnung des Heils,
    Das ist Eine sechsfache Art, die Lehre von des Menschen
    Heil und Seligkeit den Einfältigen ordentlich und erbaulich
    vorzutragen. New and revised edition. Erfurt: Johann
    Friedrich Webern, 1756, p. 6.
        This is hymn 29 in Kirchen-Gesangbuch für Evangelische-
    Lutherische Gemeinde ungeänderter Augsburgischer Confes-
    sion. St. Louis: Concordia Publishing House, 1903.

23. Ibid., Hymn 10.

24. Reu, op. cit., p. 278.

25. Starcke, op. cit., pp. 7-22.

26. Der Kleine Catechismus Des sel. D. Martin Luthers, Nebst
     Den gewöhnlichen Morgen- Tisch- und Abend- Gebätern.
     Wobey Die Ordnung des Heils, in einem Liede, in kurtzen
     Sätzen, in Frage und Antwort, und in einer Tabelle, wie
     auch der Inhalt der heiligen Schrift in Versen, hinzugefüget.
     Zum gebrauch der Jugend. Nebst einem Anhang der sieben
     Busz-Psalmen, einem geistlichen Lied und das Einmal Eins.
     Germantown: Gedruckt und zu haben bey Christoph Saur.
     n. d.

27. B. M. Schmucker, "Luther's Small Catechism," The Lutheran
     Church Review, V (April 1886), 93.

28. May 6, 1778. Journals, III, 148.

29. Op. cit., pp. 3f. Reu here also erroneously ascribed the
     original to Ziegenhagen, op. cit., p. 278.

30. So the Rev. John A. Krug of Frederick, Md. wrote to Muhlen-
     berg that he was preaching on the Nine Brief Statements
     (1779), Journals, III, 270.

31. Starcke, op. cit., pp. 23-26.

32. Ibid., p. 24. "Die überbliebenen Kräfte vermögen nichts zur
     Seligkeit. 1 Cor. 2, 14. Der natürliche Mensch vernimmt
     nichts."

33. "Die überbliebene Kräfte sind nicht hinlänglich zur Seligkeit.
     1 Cor. 2, 14.", p. 78.

34. P. 61. See infra, p. 70. The second official edition, 1857,
     included this order of salvation, cp. p. 61.

35. See infra, p. 101. While de Wrangel is known to have trans-
     lated this order in his 1761 catechism, we do not know
     whether he already had made the additional change since no
     copy of his catechism is known to exist.

36. Vollständiges Marburger Gesang-Buch, Germantown, 1770 ed.,
     Hymn 12 in Appendix, p. 465. See also in Kirchen-
     Gesangbuch, op. cit., Hymn 242, slightly modified, and
     The Lutheran Book of Worship, 1978, Hymn 291.

37. The hymn is found also in Gemeinschaftliches Gesangbuch,
     Reading, 1827, used by Lutherans and Reformed. Hymn 141.

38. Marburger Gesang-Buch, Appendix, Hymn 32, pp. 486-488.

39. Article VIII. A History of the Lutheran Church in South Carolina. Columbia, S.C.: S.C. Synod of the L.C.A., 1971, p. 121.

40. E.g. 1759. Journals, I, 410.

41. Ibid., I, 70.

42. Vollständiges Marburger Gesang-Buch, Zur Uebung der Gottseligkeit, in 649 Christlichen und Trostreichen Psalmen und Gesangen Hm D. Martin Luthers. und andrer Gottseliger Lehrer. Germantown: Christoph Saur, 1757.

43. Journals, I, 70.

44. E.g. Ibid., I, 110 (1745); II, 244 (1765).

45. J. Michael Reu, D. Martin Luthers Kleiner Katechismus. Munich: Chr. Kaiser Verlag, 1929, p. 253.

46. Der kleine Darmstadtische Catechismus Herrn D. Martin Luther. Nebst beygefügten Frag-Stücken, fur diejenigen sonderlich, welche Christlichem Gebrauch nach confirmiret werden, und hierauf zum erstenmahl das heilige Abendmahl gebrauchen. Germanton: Chr. Saur, 1759.

47. Marburger Gesang-Buch, Hymn 368. Also in Kirchen Gesang-Buch, op. cit., Hymn 407, and Evangelical Lutheran Hymn-Book, 1930 ed. St. Louis: Concordia Publishing House, Hymn 527.

48. Miller was the publisher of Der Wochentliche Philadelphische Staatsbote. The advertisement was carried frequently thereafter until Oct. 1766.

49. Der Kleine Catechismus Lutheri, mit der Ordnung des Heils und den Würtembergischen Kurzen Kinder Examen etc. wie auch Der Ungeanderten Augspurgischen Confession, etc. Zum Gebrauch der Jugend und Alten; ist nun gebunden zu haben bey Henrich Miller, Buch Drucker in der Zweyten-strasse, zu Philadelphia.

50. Journals, II, 251. July 9, 1765.

51. Ibid., 257.

52. August 17, 1767 carried the same title with the addition of Jan. 6, 1766, as noted above. Subsequent advertisements appeared through mid-October, 1767.

53. Der Kleine Catechismus Des sel. D. Martin Luthers, Nebst

Den Gewöhnlichen Morgen- Tisch- und Abend Gebethern.
Welchem Die Ordnung des Heils, in einem Liede, in kurtzen
Satzen, in Fragen und Antwort, und in einer Tabelle. Wie
auch Das Würtembergische Kurze Kinder-Examen. Die Confirmation. Gebether, Lieder, etc. beygefüget; Und Die un-
geanderte Augspurgische Confession. Imgleichen das Güldene
A-B-C der Jugend angehänget ist. Zum Gebrauch der Jugend
und Alten. Philadelphia: Henrich Miller, 1765.

54. Formed on the basis of Lukas Osiander's Booklet for Communi-
     cants of 1590 and J. V. Andrea's Instruction for Children of
     1621.

55. Also in the prayer of renewal of the covenant with God, p. 101.
     See supra, p. 58.

56. The ambiguity of the meaning of the baptismal covenant, while
     present also in the earlier editions was not as pronounced in
     the Renewal of the Covenant. While they regarded the bap-
     tismal covenant as bilateral also, one in which both God and
     the Christian were involved, they stated clearly that God's
     part of the covenant remained "firm and eternal." Only the
     Christian on his part had daily transgressed the covenant and
     had thereby broken it and become a "slave of sin and Satan."
        This non-Lutheran concept of the renewal of the baptismal
     covenant, a product of Pietism, was generally held among
     Lutherans in America and still is perpetuated in many of the
     agendas printed in the United States, e.g. Liturgy and Agenda.
     St. Louis: Concordia Publishing House, 1921, pp. 331-332.

57. Journals, III, 187. Kuntze was born in Mansfeld, Saxony, and
     came to Philadelphia in 1770, to be appointed second pastor
     of St. Michael's and Zion's congregations, working closely
     with Muhlenberg. He later married his daughter, Margaretha
     Henrietta. In 1784 he was called to the city of New York and
     later became involved in the publication of English catechisms.

58. Journals, III, 187. Sept. 15-18, 1778. See also III, 428, for
     an interesting discussion concerning the contents of the new
     catechism.

59. Der Kleine Catechismus des sel. D. Martin Luthers, den
     gewöhnlichen Morgen- Tisch- und Abend Gebetern. Welchem
     Eine weitere Anweisung zur Christlichen Lehre, für die Weiter
     gekommenen und Confirmanden, beygefüget ist. Zum Gebrauch
     der Jungen und Alten. Philadelphia: Steiner und Cist, 1781.

60. Journals, III, 187.

61. Ibid., 391.

62. Ibid., 408.

63. Ibid., 428.

64. Ibid.

65. Op. cit., pp. 27-37.

66. Freylinghausen (1670-1739) was a renowned German theologian
     known chiefly as a hymnologist. In 1715, he became an as-
     sistant at Halle to his father-in-law, A. H. Francke. Later,
     in 1723, he became a sub-director at the orphanage. Earlier
     in 1723, he had prepared a compend of theology for the chil-
     dren in the upper grades of the high schools. Walter E.
     Buszin, The Encyclopedia of the Lutheran Church, edited by
     Julius Bodensieck, Minneapolis: Augsburg Publishing House,
     c. 1965, II, 889.

67. Ordnung des Heyls, Nebst Einem Verzeichniss der wichstigsten
     Kern Sprüche der Heil. Schrift darin die vornehmsten
     Glaubens-Artikel gegründet sind. Wie auch einem sogenann-
     ten Guldenen A-B-C, und Gebetlein. Denen Einfältigen und
     Unerfahrnen zum Besten herausgegeben von Joh. Anaas.
     Freylinghausen. Philadelphia: Steiner und Cist, 1776. No
     copy of this booklet has been found. The title was taken
     from an advertisement in Henrich Millers' Pennsylvanische
     Staatsbote (formerly the Philadelphische Staatsbote), Oct. 8,
     1776.

68. Dr. Martin Luther's Catechism for Children and Young People.
     Philadelphia: Henry Sweitzer, 1802, pp. 19-24.

69. See supra, fn. 67.

70. Journals, III, 429. June 14, 1781.

CHAPTER III

1. Documentary History of the Evangelical Lutheran Ministeri-
    um of Pennsylvania and Adjacent States, Philadelphia:
    Board of Publications of the General Council of the Evan-
    gelical Lutheran Church in North America, 1898, p. 184.

2. Ibid. The titles of the subsections were determined from the
    1770 edition and compared with the 1785 catechism, since no
    print from 1774 was available.

3. Ibid.

4. Ibid.

5. Ibid.

6. <u>Ibid.</u>, p. 190.

7. Theodore G. Tappert and John W. Doberstein, eds. and trans-
    lators. <u>The Journals of Henry Melchior Mühlenberg</u>, Phila-
    delphia: Muhlenberg Press, 1942-1948, III, 648.

8. <u>Der Kleine Catechismus des sel. D. Martin Luthers. Nebst</u>
    <u>Den gewöhn-lichen Morgen- Tisch- und Abend- Gebeten.</u>
    <u>Welchem Die Ordnung des Heils, in einem Liede, in kurzen</u>
    <u>Sätzen, in Frag und Antwort, und in einer Tabelle; Wie auch</u>
    <u>Eine Zergliederung des Catechismus. Das Würtembergische</u>
    <u>Kurze Kinder-Examen Die Confirmation und Beichte beygefüget;</u>
    <u>Und Etliche Lieder, Freylinghausens Ordnung des Heils, Das</u>
    <u>Güldene A, B, C, der Kinder, und die Sieben Buss-Psalmen,</u>
    <u>angehänget sind.</u> Zum Gebrauch der Jungen und Alten. 1st
    ed. Germanton: Leibert und Billmeyer, 1785.
        Leibert and Billmeyer separated in 1787. The latter's
    sons, George and Daniel, took over their father's business
    around 1812. Though their books continued to be printed in
    Germantown, they were labeled as having been printed at
    Philadelphia. Walter Klinefelter, "The A B C Books of the
    Pennsylvania Germans," in <u>Publications of the Pennsylvania</u>
    <u>German Society</u>, VII, 1973, pp. 22ff.

9. <u>Supra</u>, p. 56.

10. <u>Der Kleine Katechismus Dr. Martin Luthers, nebst verschie-</u>
    <u>denen belehrenden und erbauenden Zusätzen, wie auch beige-</u>
    <u>fügter unveränderter Augsburgischer Confession.</u> Sumnytown,
    Pa.: Enos Benner, 1857.

11. The 1848 print of Ludwig includes the appendix dated 1844.

12. <u>Vierter Synodal Bericht der deutschen evangelisch-lutherische</u>
    <u>Synode von Missouri, Ohio, und anderen Staaten, 1850</u>, St.
    Louis: Niedner Printery, 1851, p. 39.

13. <u>Ibid.</u> That not all members of the Missouri Synod agreed with
    the evaluation, see Richard George Maasel's unpublished
    S. T. M. thesis, "A History of the Early Catechisms of the
    Missouri Synod," June 1957, Concordia Seminary, St. Louis.

14. <u>Ibid.</u> E.g. the so-called "Schwan" catechism, pp. 28-29:
    <u>Kurze Auslegung des Kleinen Katechismus Dr. Martin Lu-</u>
    <u>thers.</u> St. Louis, Mo.: Concordia Publishing House, 1896,
    and later editions.

15. <u>Ibid.</u>, p. 39.

16. Printed by Conrad Zentler for the bookseller George Mentz.
    Zentler had taken over the firm of Carl Cist in 1807 from
    his widow. He continued to print catechisms for Mentz and
    his successors. Klinefelter, <u>op. cit.</u>, p. 23.

17. Printed in 1848 or earlier.　Lindemann purchased a copy in
　　1848.　"Dr. M. Luthers Kleiner Katechismus in Nord-
　　America," Evang-Luth. Schultblatt, III (May 1868), 274f.

CHAPTER IV

1. Catechismus, oder kurzer Unterricht heilsamer Seelen-Weyde,
　mit Zeugnissen Heil.　Schrifft erklärt und bestätigt.

2. William A. Boyd and Charles A. Krummel, "German Tracts
　concerning the Lutheran Church in North Carolina During the
　Eighteenth Century," in The North Carolina Historical Review,
　VII (Jan. 1930), 81.

3. Ibid., 91.

4. Ibid., 143.　Report of Helmstedt Professors.

5. Ibid., 94.

6. Ibid., 93.

7. G. Fr. Seiler of Erlangen had prepared a catechism that included
　Luther's Small Catechism but supplemented by him with sev-
　eral orders.　It did not contain any noticeable curtailments of
　biblical truths though it placed considerable emphasis on moral
　theology.　See Michael Reu, Dr. Martin Luther's Small Cate-
　chism.　Chicago:　Wartburg Publishing House, 1929, pp. 231f.
　A copy of the catechism was left with Mühlenberg a few
　months before he died but he did not comment on it in his
　Journals (Tappert, Theodore G., and John W. Doberstein,
　eds. and trans.　The Journals of Henry Melchior Mühlenberg,
　Philadelphia:　Muhlenberg Press, 1948), III, 698, Jan. 13,
　1786.

8. Boyd and Krummel, op. cit., Jan. 1930, 93.

9. Ibid., 95.　Velthusen's report.　See also his introduction to the
　larger catechism.

10. Report of 1786.　Ibid., 147.

11. Erster Katechismus, mit den Fünf Hauptstücken.

12. Zweyter Katechismus, mit Fragen und mit den Fünf Haupt-
　stücken, nebst Luthers Erklärung.　The preface explicitly
　stated that the text was prepared for the German youth in
　North Carolina but was useful also for the local catechetical
　institute.　The catechism limited itself to the Five Chief
　Parts, omitting also Luther's Confession of Sins.

13. Helmstädtischer Katechismus, oder Christlicher Religionsunterricht nach Anleitung der heiligen Schrift.

14. Question Book, p. 111.

15. Ibid., pp. 108ff.

16. Also in Second Catechism, p. 45.

17. Fragebuch für Eltern und Lehrer, order Anleitung zu Fragen und Gesprächen uber den Katechismus, mit Rücksicht auf die Verschiedenheit der Fahigkeiten und des Alters der Jugend.

18. Boyd and Krummel, op. cit., (April 1930), 238. Velthusen's report.

19. Spruchregister über den Katechismus.

20. Faber served St. John's 1787-1800. See A History of the Lutheran Church in South Carolina, Columbia, S.C.: South Carolina Synod of the L.C.A., 1971, pp. 105f.

21. Sermon printed in Boyd and Krummel, op. cit., (April 1930), 276.

22. G. D. Bernheim, History of the German Settlements and the Lutheran Church in North and South Carolina. Philadelphia: The Lutheran Book Store, 1872, and G. D. Bernheim and George H. Cox, The History of the Evangelical Lutheran Synod and Ministerium in North Carolina. Philadelphia: Lutheran Publication Society, 1902.

23. Abriss der Christlichen Lehre für die evangelische Jugend. He was pastor in Lancaster for 35 years, 1780-1815.

24. B. M. Schmucker, "Luther's Small Catechism," Lutheran Church Review, V (July 1886), 165.

25. Ibid., 171. Baker's first charge as a candidate was in Germantown in 1813. (Documentary History of the Evangelical Lutheran Ministerium of Pennsylvania and Adjacent States, Philadelphia: Bd. of Publications of the General Council, 1898, p. 447.) Trumbauer's early charge as a candidate was in Lancaster Co. Ibid., p. 570. A photocopy of his Abriss is in the possession of the writer.

26. Schmucker, op. cit., p. 171. Wolf classified Endress with the "liberal" party in the Ministerium and a "decided Arminian." He was an aggressive exponent of the use of the English language in the Lutheran churches. (Edmund J. Wolf, The Lutherans in America, New York: J. A. Hill and Co., 1890, p. 302.) The title of the translation was Table of Gospel Instruction.

27. Schmucker, op. cit., p. 172.

28. Ibid., p. 171.

29. The translation was made by Frederick Aug. Muhlenberg (1818-1901), great-grandson of the "patriarch," and professor at Gettysburg College at the time. The pamphlet was printed in Gettysburg by H. C. Neinstedt.

30. Explanation, p. 35.

31. Abriss, 16. Companion, Q. 140, p. 23.

32. Table, 15.

33. Also Gohring or Gering. He was born in the colonies, very likely in Pennsylvania, and was trained for the Lutheran ministry by J. H. C. Helmuth at Lancaster. (Journals, III, 44f.) He was one of the original signers of the Constitution of the Ministerium in 1781. (Documentary History, opposite p. 164, p. 168 and p. 176.) Wolf said of him, "Although he had never entered the precincts of a college he mastered the Latin and Greek languages, the Hebrew and its cognates, became quite proficient in Church History and Patristics, and gathered a vast amount of information on almost every branch of science" (op. cit., pp. 301f.). Of his effective ministry Wolf further said that Goehring preached Christ and him crucified in such a way that "no one could listen to him without being convinced that he had a deep inward experience of every sentiment that he uttered" (Ibid.). Goehring was the author of several polemical works, all written during his pastorate in York.

34. Journals, III, 674.

35. Abdel Ross Wentz, A Basic History of Lutheranism in America. Philadelphia: Muhlenberg Press, c. 1955, p. 83.

36. Die sogenannte Heils-Ordnung, in Frag' und Antworten, zum Gebrauch der Informanten.

37. Auszug aus den ein und zwanzig Lehrartikeln der augspurgischen Confession, zum Gebrauch der Brüdergemeinen, sonderlich der Kinder. Barby: n.p., 1775.

38. Der kleine Catechismus D. Martin Luthers.

39. Following his pastorate at Lebanon, Lochman went to Harrisburg in 1815, where he served until his death in 1826. For a number of years Lochman was secretary and president of the Ministerium and later, in 1821, he was elected the first president of the General Synod. Lochman prepared an English catechism which bore no resemblance to the German one. See

below, p. 159. Neither catechism carried the name of
the author.

40. Kurzer Inbegriff der Christlichen Lehre, Nebst einer Kurzge-
     fassten Kirchengeschichte des Alten und Neuen Testaments.

41. Op. cit., p. 177.

42. Haupt-Inhalt der Christlichen Lehre.

43. A copy of this edition was not available. The title was taken
     from Robert C. Wiederaenders, "A Bibliography of American
     Lutheranism, 1624-1850." Wiederaenders gives neither edi-
     tion nor the name of the printer. The latter was probably
     Joseph Schnee. The edition was supplied elsewhere.

CHAPTER V

1. The estimated number is for 1790. Theodore G. Tappert in
    The Lutherans in North America, ed. by E. Clifford Nelson,
    Philadelphia: Fortress Press, 1973, p. 37.

2. Israel Acrelius, A History of New Sweden or The Settlements
    on the River Delaware. Tr. William M. Reynolds. Phila-
    delphia: The Historical Society of Pennsylvania, 1874, pp.
    245-247. See also Richard C. Wolf, Documents of Lutheran
    Unity in America. Philadelphia: Fortress Press, 1966, #4,
    pp. 11-13.

3. [Hallesche] Nachrichten von den vereinigten Deutsche Evangelisch-
    Lutherischen Gemeinen in Nord-America, absonderlich in
    Pennsylvanien, tr. W. J. Mann, B. M. Schmucker, and W.
    Germann. Allentown, Pa.: Brobst, Diehl & Co., 1886, I,
    p. 670. Translation by B. M. Schmucker in "Luther's Small
    Catechism," The Lutheran Church Review, V (April 1886),
    101.

4. Schmucker, op. cit., 101. Peter Koch died in August, 1749.

5. Wrangel received his doctorate from Goettingen in 1757. Even
    before his ordination he was appointed by the King of Sweden
    to be the court chaplain in 1756. With royal sanction he con-
    tinued his studies in Germany and was ordained in 1758,
    whereupon he was sent to America where he remained until
    1768, when he was recalled to the homeland. Carl Magnus
    Anderson, tr. and ed. of "Pastor Wrangel's Trip to the
    Shore." Reprint from the New Jersey History, 87, 1. Spring
    1969 by the New Jersey Historical Society, p. 5.

6. Schmucker, op. cit., 101.

7. Ibid., pp. 101f.   From a letter of Mühlenberg to Ziegenhagen and Francke.

8. Documentary History of the Evangelical Lutheran Ministerium of Pennsylvania and Adjacent States.   Philadelphia: Bd. of Publications of the General Council, 1898, p. 62.

9. Theodore G. Tappert and John W. Doberstein, eds. and trans., The Journals of Henry Melchior Muhlenberg.   Philadelphia: Muhlenberg Press, 1942-1948, I, 460.

10. Ibid., II, 256f.-1765.

11. Ibid., III, 308.

12. Harry Julius Kreider, Lutheranism in Colonial New York, New York: Edward Brothers, 1942, p. 121.

13. Ibid., p. 123.

14. Journals, III, 655.

15. Ibid., 656.

16. Kreider, op. cit., p. 123.

17. Preface, p. v.   "The translation of the Liturgy, catechism, and Order of Salvation is done by my worthy assistant, Mr. Strebeck."

18. Kreider, op. cit., p. 12.

19. Schmucker, op. cit., 196.

20. Ibid., 104.

21. Supra, p. 56.

22. Op. cit., 171.

23. Supra, p. 57.

24. Op. cit., 194.   See also supra, p. 88 and note 26, Chapter IV.

25. Edmund Eyster Wolf, The Lutherans in America.   New York: J. A. Hill and Co., 1890, p. 302.   Endress was born in Philadelphia.   According to Schmucker, "He was a graduate of the University and had such English culture as no other pastor about Philadelphia had."   Op. cit., 194.   Toward the end of his service in Philadelphia he also served the congregation at Frankford as a licensed candidate for the ministry. Documentary History, p. 317.   He was ordained by the Penn-

sylvania Ministerium in June 1802. Ibid., p. 329. He prepared another catechism while pastor at Easton, Pa. in 1805.
Infra, pp. 108-109.

26. Schmucker, op. cit., p. 194. For additional data on Quitman
see his catechism, Infra, pp. 121-126.

27. J. Nicum, Geschichte des evangelischen Ministerium vom Staate
New York und angrenzenden Staaten und Ländern. New York:
Verlag des New York Ministerium, 1888, p. 84.

28. Preface of the catechism. It was signed by Kuntze as "Senior"
and Quitman as secretary.

29. Mayer was born in New York City April 1, 1781. He gradu-
ated from Columbia College in 1799. He received his theological training under Kuntze whose confessional stand made
a deep impression on him. Nicum, op. cit., pp. 182f.

30. Ibid., p. 91.

31. There were also some linguistic changes based on the 1802
catechism, e.g. the Seventh and Eighth commandments.

32. This writer consulted the copy in the Wm. L. Clements Library
at the University of Michigan.

33. See infra, p. 120.

34. Nicum, op. cit., p. 91.

35. In the Apostles' Creed the statement "forgiveness of sins" had
been omitted, hence the following explanation appeared after
the title page:

> I know not by what accident this short but weighty section
> was omitted in the third article of the creed. Parents
> and teachers will be so good as to add it in its proper
> place, that their children and pupils may not learn the
> article without it.
>
> Having had but a small number struck off, for the use of
> the congregation of Easton and those annexed to it only,
> I am not so uneasy about the omission as I perhaps other-
> wise might have been.
>
>   The translator.

Endress was pastor at Easton at this time.

36. So also in the catechisms of Kuntze-Strebeck, 1795, Endress
of 1802, the New York Ministerium of 1804 and, of course,
Kuntze's 1785.

37. The New York Ministerium recognized English as early as 1797.

Kuntze had opposed the organization of separate English congregations. He preferred that each congregation serve in both languages thus avoiding the fragmentations of the congregations. Later, in 1807, English became the official language in the Ministerium.

38. Documentary History, p. 248. Ironically the revised constitution contained no reference to the Symbolical Books nor even to the Augsburg Confession. It did proclaim its adherance to the German language.

39. Henry Eyster Jacobs, A History of the Evangelical Lutheran Church in the United States. New York: The Christian Literature Co., 1893, p. 314.

40. Peter Mühlenberg had been ordained in the Pennsylvania Ministerium in 1768, but traveled to England to be ordained in the Episcopal Church at which time he subscribed also to the Thirty-Nine Articles. He served as a Lutheran pastor till 1776, when he resigned to join the American forces. Vergilius Ferm, The Crisis in American Lutheran Theology, New York: The Century Co., c. 1927, pp. 19f.

41. Documentary History, pp. 353f.

42. Jacobs, op. cit., p. 328. See also F. Wischan, "Kurze Geschichte der deutschen evangel-luther. Gemeinden in und um Philadelphia und der lutherischen Synoden Amerikas," p. 84. This was by no means the end of the language controversy at St. Michael's-Zion. Another battle with a similar sequence occurred Sept. 26, 1815. Both parties sent letters to the Ministerium in 1816, but the synod felt that the time was too short to give the congregation decisive counsel. (Documentary History, pp. 488 and 491.) Out of this controversy a second English congregation was formed, St. Matthew. Jacobs, op. cit., p. 330.

43. Schmucker, op. cit., p. 197.

44. A. L. Graebner, Geschichte der Lutherischen Kirche in America, St. Louis: Concordia Publishing House, 1892, p. 541.

45. B. M. Schmucker was shown a copy, said to be of 1806, but since the title page was lost he was unable to give the title. His description of the contents, language, and size corresponds with the 1807 edition which the writer has examined. Op. cit., p. 179.

46. Microfilm Corpus of American Lutheranism, reel 4. The notes may have been taken as Mayer dictated them to the class.

47. If the reprint was sponsored by the pastor at Frederick, it was David Frederick Schaeffer who was pastor there from 1806

until his death in 1837. He was also the editor of the first
English Lutheran periodical, the Intelligence. Abdel Ross
Wentz, History of the Evangelical Lutheran Synod of Mary-
land of the United Lutheran Church in America, 1820-1920,
Harrisburg: Evangelical Press, 1920, p. 343.

48. If the catechism was issued by the local pastor in Hagerstown,
it was Benjamin Kurtz, who was pastor at "old St. John's,"
1815-1831. In addition to his pastorate in Hagerstown he
served four Lutheran congregations nearby. He introduced
English preaching and mid-week prayer services and "pro-
tracted" meetings were held. He became editor of The Lutheran Observer in 1833. Ibid., p. 458.

49. A copy was located in the East Pennsylvania Synod Archives
deposited at the Lutheran Seminary in Philadelphia. B. M.
Schmucker assigned his copy to York, 1804, but John
Schmucker was in Hagerstown in that year.
John G. Schmucker (1771-1854) was the father of S. S.
Schmucker. He was ordained to the ministry in the Pennsylvania Ministerium in June 1800 (Documentary History, p.
312). He later helped found the General Synod. He was
known to incline toward a moderate form of the New Measures, without however minimizing the importance of instruction. For additional notes see, The Lutherans in North America, p. 108.

50. B. M. Schmucker thinks it was taken from the German Pennsylvania catechism. Op. cit., p. 173.

51. Christoph Starcke, Sechsfach-kurtzgefasste Ordnung des Heils.
Erfurt Johann Friedrich Webern, 1756, pp. 26-37. "VI
Ordnung des Heils in einer längern Tabelle."

52. Op. cit., p. 173.

53. While a congregation had not been established there at this
time, in 1814, some 72 persons living in the area petitioned
the Pennsylvania Ministerium for a pastor who could "preach
in the English as well as the German language." Documentary History, p. 465.

54. Infra, p. 170, for a similar footnote in the General Synod catechism of 1832 and thereafter.

CHAPTER VI

1. J. Nicum, Geschichte des evangelischen Ministeriums vom
Staate New York und angrezenden Staaten und Ländern. New
York: Verlag des New York Ministerium, 1888, pp. 89 and
91.

2. Ibid., p. 92.

3. Ibid.

4. Braun had joined the Ministerium in 1790, and was pastor at
    the Gilead Church from 1802-1812. He had formerly been a
    Roman Catholic. He died in Brunswick, March 1813. Ibid.,
    pp. 42, 53, 606.

5. Ibid., p. 601.

6. German Protestant Society, Mrs. Esther Gross, curator.

7. Nicum, op. cit., p. 606. The Waldeborough congregation be-
    came a member of the Ministerium in 1812. Ibid., p. 559.
    During the same year Starman published The Order of Con-
    firmation as Observed in the Lutheran Church. Boston: Lin-
    coln & Edmonds, 1812. According to the title page it was
    "published for the use of the German Protestant Congregation
    in Waldeborough, State of Massachusetts."
        Later Starman became deeply involved in New Measures
    and protracted meetings. He was pastor here at this lonely
    outpost till his death in 1854. It was his only pastorate.
    The congregation soon dissolved after his death. Ibid., pp.
    129 and 248.

8. Ibid., pp. 97 and 414.

9. Ibid., p. 98.

10. Henry Eyster Jacobs, A History of the Evangelical Lutheran
    Church in the United States. New York: The Christian Lit-
    erature Co., 1893, p. 317.

11. Nicum, op. cit., p. 594.

12. Ibid., p. 95.

13. Ibid., pp. 99 and 414.

14. Ibid., p. 415.

15. Documentary History of the Evangelical Lutheran Ministerium of
    Pennsylvania and Adjacent States. Philadelphia: Board of
    Publications of the General Council, 1898, p. 490.

16. Date given Jan. 23, 1816; copyright date Jan. 26.

17. B. M. Schmucker, "Luther's Small Catechism," in The Lu-
    theran Church Review V (April 1886), 105. Michael Reu,
    Dr. Martin Luther's Small Catechism, Chicago: Wartburg
    Publishing House, 1929, reprinted Mayer's translation, pp.
    289-293.

CHAPTER VII

1. He was a member of the Pennsylvania Ministerium and helped organize the North Carolina Synod (1803), the German Ohio Synod (1818), and was present at the organization of the Tennessee Synod (1820).

2. He prepared a German hymnal in 1810 (2nd ed. appeared in 1812) and an English hymnal in 1816 (2nd ed. appeared in 1838 and a 4th in 1857). Some 303 hymns were written by Paul Henkel (either translations, paraphrases, or originals). See Edward C. Wolf for complete titles, "Lutheran Hymnody and Music published in America 1700-1850. A Descriptive Bibliography," in Concordia Historical Institute Quarterly, 50 (Winter 1977), 169f.

3. They first settled in Germantown but later Anthony Henkel was called to Virginia. Afterwards he was pastor in Germantown. See supra, pp. 31f.

4. Paul was born in Rowan County, N.C. but later his family moved to the frontier region of the Shenandoah Valley in Virginia. His father's name was Jacob (1733-1779) and his grandfather was John (1706-1778).

5. B. H. Pershing, "Paul Henkel: Frontier Missionary, Organizer, and Author," Concordia Historical Institute Quarterly, 7 (January 1935), 101.

6. Documentary History of the Evangelical Lutheran Ministerium of Pennsylvania and Adjacent States. Philadelphia: Board of Publications of the General Council, 1898, pp. 187-188.

7. Ibid., p. 247.

8. Pershing, op. cit., p. 104.

9. Documentary History, p. 370.

10. E.g., "Diary of Paul Henkel," ed. by Theodore Graebner in Concordia Historical Institute Quarterly, 1 (April-July, 1928), 47. Also William J. Finck, ed. and tr., "Chronological Life of Paul Henkel, from Journals, Letters, Minutes of Synods, etc." New Market, Va.: 1935-1937. Typewritten copy. Aug. 21-Nov. 13, 1809 entry, p. 273. Deposited in Concordia Historical Institute Quarterly, St. Louis, Mo.

11. Der kleine Catechismus des sel. D. Martin Luthers, Worin die fünf Hauptstücke zergliedert und in kurzen Fragen gestellt sind, dass der Inhalt leichter kann gelernt und besser begriffen werden. Nebst andern Fragstücken. Wie auch erbauliche Morgen- Tisch- und Abend- Gebäten, und Liedern, und was sonst nöthig ist. Newmarket, Shenandoah County (Virg.): Ambrosius Henkel, 1809.

12. Bericht von der Special Conferenz der Evang. Luth. Prediger
    und Abgeordenenten im Staat Virginien. Winchester Okt. 3,
    1808. Newmarket: Ambrosius Henkel [1808], p. 3. Original
    in Duke University Library (William R. Perkins Library) as
    MS.

13. Supra, p. 66.

14. The preface bore the date Feb. 8, 1811.

15. As late as 1816 he lamented in a letter to the Ministerium
    "that the German language is fast losing ground" in Virginia.
    Documentary History, p. 488.

16. Infra, p. 144.

17. Stanley D. Padgett in "The Theology of Paul Henkel in Relation
    to His Environment" (S. T. M. Thesis for Concordia Seminary,
    St. Louis, Mo.), came to the opposite conclusion: "By say-
    ing that 'Baptism with faith brings the pardon of sins,' Henkel
    was pointing out to his religious milieu that baptism and faith
    are to be united, that baptism precedes faith, and that faith
    receives the benefits that baptism offers," p. 104f. I take it
    to mean that Baptism of itself has no effective power but
    Baptism with faith brings the pardon of sin. What the cate-
    chism meant to say would in the final analysis depend much
    on the theology of the instructor. The fourth edition improved
    this with "Baptism brings pardon of sin...." (p. 16).

18. 1813, 3rd ed., p. 96.

19. Pp. 54-69. Supra, p. 108.

20. Q. 270 (pp. 68f.) and 287 (p. 72).

21. Vergilius Ferm, The Crisis in American Lutheran Theology,
    New York: The Century Co., c. 1927, p. 31, fn. 64; A. L.
    Graebner, Geschichte der Lutherischen Kirche in America,
    St. Louis: Concordia Publishing House, 1892, p. 619. His
    criticism was of the German edition which was almost identi-
    cal with the English.

22. Fink, "Chronological Life" under the date of June 11, 1811, p.
    283.

23. Schober was an ex-Moravian pastor who joined the Synod of
    North Carolina in 1810. Ibid., p. 294.

24. The title of the German catechism is thus the same as the
    English. Supra, p. 135. A copy of the original draft of
    the title page is in the Flowers Collection (Henkel Papers)
    in the William R. Perkins Library (Manuscript Room) Duke
    University. There is no date on the manuscript so it cannot

be determined whether it was actually used at the time. It closes, however, with "Von Paulus Henkel Evangelischer Lehrer."

25. Supra, p. 137.

26. "The Henkel Press of New Market, Virginia," The Henkel Family Records (August 1939), No. 14, New Market, Va.: The Henkel Press, Inc., 1939, p. 617.

27. Verhandlungen der Conferenzen der Vereinigten Evangelisch Lutherische Prediger, und Abgeordneten, in dem Staat Nord-Carolina Vom Jahr 1811 bis zum Jahr 1812. New Market, Va.: Ambrosius Henkel und Co., 1812, p. 8.

28. Socrates Henkel, History of the Evangelical Lutheran Tennessee Synod, New Market, Va.: Henkel & Co., 1890, p. 26.

CHAPTER VIII

1. H. George Anderson in The Lutherans in North America, ed. Nelson E. Clifford. Philadelphia: Fortress Press, 1973, pp. 99f.

2. Supra, p. 93.

3. Anderson, op. cit., p. 90.

4. Documentary History of the Evangelical Lutheran Ministerium of Pennsylvania and Adjacent States. Philadelphia: Bd. of Publications of the General Council, 1898, pp. 251 (V, I.6); 252 (V, V.10); 257 (V, VII.9).

5. Documentary History, p. 428. Similar advice was given to H. Wm. Scriba who was assigned as traveling preacher in the western and northwestern parts of Pennsylvania. Ibid.

6. Dr. Martin Luthers Katechismus erklärt und mit den vornehmsten Beweissprüchen der heiligen Schrift versehen, nebst einem Anhange für evangelisch-lutherischen Christen in dem englischen Nord-Amerika. Philadelphia: Conrad Zentler, 1816.

7. Documentary History, p. 96; Theodore G. Tappert and John W. Doberstein, eds. and trans. The Journals of Henry Melchior Mühlenberg, Philadelphia: Muhlenberg Press, 1942-1948, II, 370f. See also Journals, II, 441 for May 1770.

8. Journals, II, 511f.

9. Kurzer Unterricht der Christlichen Lehre, und Examen der

Confirmation. 1st ed. Grünsburg [Pa.]: Johannes Armbrust & Companie, 1817. Steck (1756-1830) was ordained in 1806 by the Pennsylvania Ministerium (Documentary History, p. 371). Later he was active in the Ohio Synod (Willard D. Allbeck, A Century of Lutherans in Ohio. Yellow Springs, Ohio: The Antioch Press, 1966, p. 35). Speck or his printer evidently hoped for a later edition but as far as can be determined none was ever printed.

10.   B. M. Schmucker, "Luther's Small Catechism," The Lutheran Church Review, V (July 1886), 178.

11.   Der Lutherische Catechismus Für die Jugend; Insonderheit für solche, Die wünschen confirmiret zu werden. Carlisle: John M'Farland, 1820.

12.   He was licensed as a catechist by the Ministerium in 1819 (Documentary History, p. 539) and at a later date as a pastor.

13.   Catechismus der Christlichen Lehre, in Fragen und Antworten. Kutztaun [Pa.]: Hawrecht und Wink, 1833.

14.   Erklärung des Katechismus, zum Gebrauch beim Confirmanden Unterricht, von G. F. J. Jäger. Allentown: Brobst, Diehl & Co., n.d. Op. cit., pp. 167 and 179.

15.   Robert C. Wiederaenders, "A Bibliography of American Lutheranism, 1624-1850," Privately printed. Listed after "Schott"; B. M. Schmucker, op. cit., p. 167, though he admits that he had not seen a copy (p. 181); J. G. Morris, Bibliotheca Lutherana, Philadelphia: n.p., 1876.

16.   Scriba was a licensed candidate of the Pennsylvania Ministerium by 1803 (Documentary History, p. 332), and served Zion congregation in Manheim (Moheim), Lancaster County in 1807 (Ibid., pp. 386 and 392). He was appointed a traveling preacher in 1811 (Ibid., p. 428) and by 1817, served in Strassburg (Ibid., p. 498), the same year in which he was ordained as deacon (Ibid., p. 522). Soon thereafter he was dismissed by the Scherrer's congregation, near Strassburg, one of the several Scriba had been serving in the area. The records do not indicate the nature of the problem (Ibid., p. 551). Scriba attended the initial meeting of the West Pennsylvania Synod in 1825. In 1836, that synod voted to give him twelve dollars. This might indicate that he had come upon hard times although no explanation was given. He was still located in Strassburg at the time. (Letter dated 8/24/79 to the author from John E. Peterson, archival curator at Krauth Memorial Library, Philadelphia.)

17.   Anfangsgründe des Christenthum's oder kurzer Inbegriff der Wahrheiten und Pflichten der Christlichen Religion. Chämbersburg: Heinrich Ruby, 1834.

CHAPTER IX

1. For additional details on the New Measures see E. Clifford
    Nelson, The Lutherans in North America. Philadelphia:
    Fortress Press, 1973, pp. 135-137.

2. Schaeffer, born in Germantown, Pa., had been licensed by the
    Pennsylvania Ministerium where he had served for a brief
    period. He came to New York in 1815, and was ordained the
    same year by the New York Ministerium. (J. Nicum, Ges-
    chichte des Evangelische-Lutherischen Ministeriums vom Staate
    New York und angrenzenden Staaten und Ländern. New York:
    Verlag des New York Ministerium, 1888, p. 112.) He noti-
    fied the Pennsylvania Ministerium that he wished to remain
    a member with them as well as with New York. (Documen-
    tary History of the Evangelical Lutheran Ministerium of Penn-
    sylvania and Adjacent States. Philadelphia: Bd. of Publica-
    tions of the General Council, 1898, p. 478.) His ordination
    was recognized by Pennsylvania in 1817. (Ibid., p. 507.)
    By a strange coincidence, he was the visiting delegate to
    Pennsylvania in 1816, who had presented Quitman's catechism
    to the Ministerium. (Ibid., 489ff.) Schaeffer succeeded
    Hazelius as president of the New York Ministerium in Sept.
    1830, but died about six months later at the age of 42. (Ni-
    cum, op. cit., pp. 115 and 141.)

3. The extracts began with paragraph 15, Tappert edition of the
    Book of Concord, pp. 460f.

4. Lochman was one of the few who voted against the withdrawal
    of the Pennsylvania Ministerium from the General Synod in
    1823. (Henry Eyster Jacobs, A History of the Evangelical
    Lutheran Church in the United States, New York: The Chris-
    tian Literature Co., 1893, p. 361 fn.)

5. Cp. Vergilius Ferm, The Crisis in American Lutheran Theolo-
    gy, New York: The Century Co., c. 1927, pp. 60-62, for a
    further evaluation of this catechism.

6. Supra, p. 56. Lochman further altered the sentences by divid-
    ing number three, thus making ten sentences.

7. Supra, p. 90.

8. The Confession of Augsburg, which is the Confession of the
    Evangelical Lutheran Church.... New York: James Oran,
    1813. Nicum, op. cit., p. 143.

9. History of the American Lutheran Church from Its Commence-
    ment in the Year of our Lord 1685, to the Year 1842. Zanes-
    ville, Ohio: Edwin C. Church, 1846, pp. 150f.

10. Henry E. Jacobs refers to "some excellent remarks by Dr.

Hazelius on the spiritual desolation resulting from neglect of catechization" in the Minutes of the N. Y. Ministerium, 1830. ("The History and Progress of the Lutheran Church in the United States" in The First Free Lutheran Diet in America, 1877. Philadelphia: J. Frederick Smith, 1878, p. 130.

11. In 1828, Hazelius was elected president of the New York Ministerium and in 1830, he became a theological professor at Gettysburg Seminary, at which time he joined the Pennsylvania Ministerium. Later in 1834, he followed a call to the Southern Seminary in South Carolina. See A History of the Lutheran Church in South Carolina. Columbia, S. C.: South Carolina Synod of the L. C. A., 1971, pp. 175-178.

12. Article III, sec. II, 2 in Richard C. Wolf, Documents of Lutheran Unity in America. Philadelphia: Fortress Press, 1966, p. 68.

13. Article III, Sec. III, Hazelius, History, p. 297.

14. Article III, Sec. VIII, Wolf, Documents, p. 70.

15. Minutes, 1821, p. 5 quoted from J. F. Krueger, "The History of the English Catechism of the General Synod," Lutheran Quarterly, XLIII (April 1913), 181.

16. Minutes, 1823, pp. 4f. cited by Krueger, op. cit., 182.

17. S. S. Schmucker, The American Lutheran Church, Historically, Doctrinally, and Practically Delineated in Several Occasional Discourses. Philadelphia: E. W. Miller, 1852, p. 228.

18. Ibid.

19. Jacobs, History of the Evangelical Lutheran Church, pp. 360ff.

20. Minutes, p. 11 cited by Jacobs in "History and Progress," p. 130, fn. 82a.

21. Krueger, op. cit., 182. Presidential address of 1833.

22. Ibid.

23. Ibid., p. 183.

24. History of the Lutheran Church in South Carolina, p. 228. See infra, pp. 183-185.

25. Krueger, op. cit., p. 183.

26. Minutes, 1848, p. 24 in Krueger, op. cit., p. 187.

27. Minutes, 1850, p. 15 in Krueger, op. cit., pp. 187f.

28. Ibid., p. 188.

29. Minutes, 1857, p. 19 cited by Krueger, op. cit., 188.

30. Ibid., p. 188f.

31. See Krueger, op. cit., for an extensive description of the ten-
     sions and controversies.

32. Nicum, op. cit., p. 185.

33. From a transcript of Zion Lutheran Church, Minutes of the
     Vestry Board, April 1, 1825. Some time later Pohlman be-
     came an ardent revivalist though not, according to Nicum, an
     extremist. (Op. cit., p. 185.) Pohlman was president of
     the New York Ministerium 1840-1848 and 1855-1866. He left
     the Ministerium after it withdrew from the General Synod in
     1867. He was president also of the newly formed New York
     Synod in 1867-1874. He was president of the General Synod
     in 1845, 1868 and 1869. Ibid., p. 186.

34. Supra, pp. 158f.

35. Supra, p. 107.

36. Canajoharie is located on the Mohawk River, some 45 miles
     northwest of Albany and about 25 miles northeast of Hartwick
     Seminary. The first German Lutheran congregation in that
     town was not organized until 1835. (Nicum, op. cit., p. 483)
     An English congregation had been established earlier but noth-
     ing much is known about it. (Ibid., p. 163) The author of
     the catechism was therefore not from the immediate vicinity.

37. Supra, p. 174.

38. "A Bibliography of American Lutheranism, 1624-1850," listed
     by date under "Luther's Small Catechism in English."

39. Supra, p. 77.

CHAPTER X

1. Clifford L. Lord, Historical Atlas of the United States, New
    York: Henry Holt & Co., c. 1944, p. 207.

2. Edwin Scott Gaustad, Historical Atlas of Religions in America,
    New York: Harper and Row, c. 1976, pp. 43 and 168. The
    largest number of Lutheran churches in 1850 were in Penn-
    sylvania, 498; Ohio had 260; New York 81; Indiana 63; and
    Virginia 50. The rest of the states all had less than 50.
    Ibid., p. 168.

3. For an extensive list, including such as were brought over later, through the 1850's-1880's see Michael Reu, Dr. Martin Luther's Small Catechism. Chicago: Wartburg Publishing House, 1929, p. 282.

4. Socrates Henkel, History of the Evangelical Lutheran Tennessee Synod, New Market, Va.: Henkel and Co., 1890, p. 70.

5. Ibid., p. 73.

6. Ibid., p. 87, and again in 1836, p. 89.

7. Proceedings, Evangelical Lutheran Synod of Indiana, 1841, p. 11, cited in Kendall F. Svengalis, "Theological Controversy Among Indiana Lutherans, 1835-1870," Concordia Historical Institute Quarterly, 46 (Summer, 1973), 79.

8. Henkel, History, pp. 129f.

9. Ibid., p. 131.

10. Dr. Martin Luthers kleiner Katechismus; sammt vorläufigen Bemerkung. Nebst einem Anhang verschiedener Gebeter und Lieder, New-Market: Solomon Henkel's Druckerei, 1829.

11. He was president of the General Synod in 1843 and 1883. He served no fewer than eight terms as president of his own synod.

12. I, p. 260 in Karl Koch's "The American Lutheran Scene, 1831-1841 as Reflected in the 'Lutheran Observer,'" Concordia Historical Institute Quarterly, 37 (July 1964), 58.

13. John G. Morris, Catechumen's and Communicant's Companion, Baltimore: Joel Wright, 1832, p. 16.

14. Ibid., p. 63.

15. For Morris' later assessment of New Measures, see his Fifty Years in the Lutheran Ministry, Baltimore: Joel Wright, 1832, p. 16.

16. South Carolina Minutes, 1846, p. 23, quoted in A History of the Lutheran Church in South Carolina, Columbia, S.C.: South Carolina Synod of the L.C.A., 1971, p. 228.

17. Smith was ordained by the New York Ministerium in Sept. 1830. (J. Nicum, Geschichte des Evangelisch-Lutherischen Ministeriums vom Staate New York und angrenzenden Staaten und Ländern. New York: Verlag des New York Ministeriums, 1888, p. 607.) He was one of the few pastors of his conference to protest the formation of the Hartwick Synod a few weeks later. (Ibid., p. 141.) During July 1831, Smith was installed in Stone Arabia-Palatine, N.Y. (Ibid., p. 146.) Later, in 1851, he became pastor of Christ Church, Easton,

Pa., and a member of the East Pennsylvania Synod in 1852. (History of the Evangelical Lutheran Synod of East Pennsylvania with Brief Sketches of Its Congregations, 1842-1892. Philadelphia: Lutheran Publication Society, n.d., p. 363.)

18. Nicum, op. cit., p. 137.

19. History of the Lutheran Church in South Carolina, p. 230.

20. Named after Hans Nielsen Hauge (1771-1824), a Lutheran lay preacher in Norway, who placed an extraordinary emphasis on conversion and sanctification. Hauge had been strongly influenced by Johann Arndt and Erik Pontoppidan. See also J. C. K. Preus, ed., Norsemen Found a Church, Minneapolis: Augsburg Publishing House, c. 1953, pp. 240-247.

21. Preus, op. cit., p. 27. The settlement was in La Salle County, some 50 miles southwest of Chicago.

22. E. Clifford Nelson and Eugene L. Fevold, The Lutheran Church Among Norwegian-Americans. A History of the Evangelical Lutheran Church. Minneapolis: Augsburg Publishing House, c. 1960, I, p. 77.

23. This was the first book printed by the Norwegians in America. Unfortunately Eielsen's name was mispelled on the title page. The catechism was reprinted for a centennial observance in 1925 by Augsburg Publishing House in Minneapolis.

24. Michael Reu, op. cit., p. 207.

25. Preus, op. cit., p. 243.

26. Ibid., p. 256.

27. Nelson-Fevold, op. cit., I, 78. Also Preus, op. cit., p. 28 but on p. 391, the destination was said to be Jefferson Prairie, Wisc.

28. Sandhed til Gudfrygtighed udi en eenfoldig og efter Mulighed kort, dog tilstraekkelig Forklaring over Sal. Dr. Mort. Luthers Liden Catechismo. New York: Henry Ludvig, 1842. The cover has 1843.

29. Preus, op. cit., p. 256.

30. Nelson-Fevold, op. cit., I, pp. 256f.

31. The Ohio Synod became known as the Joint Ohio Synod in 1833 with two districts.

32. Minutes, 1832, pp. 14f., cited by Willard D. Allbeck, A Century of Lutherans in Ohio. Yellow Springs, Ohio: The Antioch Press, 1966, p. 111.

33. Supra, p. 171.

34. Allbeck, op. cit., p. 176.

35. The translation was made by Prof. Charles Frederick Schaef-
     fer of Columbus, formerly pastor at Hagerstown, Md.

36. The Lutheran Standard, I (Nov. 16, 1842), 2.

37. S. S. Schmucker, Henry N. Pohlman, and Benj. Kurtz.

38. Aug. R. Suelflow and E. Clifford Nelson in The Lutherans in
     North America, Philadelphia: Fortress Press, 1973, pp.
     219f.

39. B. M. Schmucker, "Luther's Small Catechism," The Lutheran
     Church Review, V (July 1886), 180.

40. A fourth edition was printed in 1851, and a fifth in 1854. Cop-
     ies continued to be printed beyond 1860.

41. Abdel R. Wentz, History of the Evang. Lutheran Synod of Mary-
     land of the U. L. C. A., 1820-1920, Harrisburg: Evangelical
     Press, 1920, p. 153.

42. B. M. Schmucker, op. cit., p. 179.

43. Vergilius Ferm, The Crisis in American Lutheran Theology,
     New York: The Century Co., c. 1927, p. 170.

44. S. Henkel, History, p. 131.

45. Roy Suelflow, "The First Years of Trinity Congregation, Frei-
     stadt, Wisconsin," c. viii, Concordia Historical Institute
     Quarterly, XVIII (October 1945), 89f.

46. Johann A. Grabau, "Johannes Andreas August Grabau," Part
     VI, Concordia Historical Institute Quarterly, XXIV (October
     1951), 127.

47. Dr. Martin Luthers Kleiner Catechismus auf Churfl. Durchl.
     zu Sachsen Gnädigsten Befehl, von Ministerio H. Kreuz in
     Dresden durch Frag und Antwort erläutert, auch mit ange-
     führten Sprüchen Heil. Schrift bekräftiget. Buffalo: G.
     Zahm, 1845.

48. Richard George Maasel, "A History of the Early Catechism of
     the Missouri Synod," an unpublished S. T. M. thesis prepared
     for Concordia Seminary, St. Louis, June 1957, p. 3.

49. "Das 'Informatorium' und unser Katechismus," Der Lutheraner,
     XIV (June 29, 1858), 180.

50. Maasel, op. cit., p. 30.

51. Originally printed in 1613. It was epitomized in 1627. The
     epitome became the basis of the Missouri Synod's catechism.

52. Dr. Martin Luthers Kleiner Katechisms in Frage und Antwort
     gründlich ausgelegt von Dr. Johann Conrad Dietrich, mit
     Zusätzen aus dem Dresdner Kreuz-Katechismus und den Be-
     kenntniszschriften der ev.-luth. Kirche, und mit Sprüchen
     der heil Schrift versehen. St. Louis: August Wiebusch u.
     Sohn, 1858.

53. The West Pennsylvania Synod was organized in 1825, after a
     number of congregations west of the Susquehanna River de-
     cided to withdraw in protest from the Pennsylvania Ministeri-
     um because the latter had left the General Synod.

54. Dr. Luthers Kleiner Catechismus, welchem beigefügt ist Die
     Ordnung des Heils, sammt dem Formular der Regierung und
     Disciplin der Luth, Kirche von Nord-Amerika. Baltimore:
     Lutherische Buchhandlung, 1845.

55. Supra, p. 170.

56. Supra, pp. 70f.

57. B. M. Schmucker, op. cit., p. 180.

58. · Leitfaden, wornach in den verbunden Evangelisch-Lutherischen
     Gemeinden von Alt-Goschenhoppen, Indianfield und Toheck,
     bei Ertheilung des Confirmations-Unterrichts der kleine Kat-
     echismus Dr. Martin Luthers erklärt wird. Sumnytaun, Pa.:
     E. Benner, 1845.

59. B. M. Schmucker, op. cit., p. 180.

60. Ibid.

61. Der Kleine Catechismus des seligen D. Martin Luther, welchem
     beygefügt ist Die Ordnung des Heils, eine Zergliederung des
     Catechismus, das Würtembergische kurze Kinder-Examen, die
     21 Artikel der A. Confession; nebst Liedern u. s. w. Pitts-
     burgh: Druckerei der Luth. Kirchenzeitung, n.d.

62. Sharts was ordained by the New York Ministerium in 1840 and
     soon thereafter came to Williamsburgh. The same year that
     the catechism was published he left to assume a pastorate in
     the States. J. Nicum, Geschichte des Evangelisch-Lutherischen
     Ministeriums vom Staate New York und angrenzenden Staaten
     und Ländern. New York: Verlag des New York Ministeri-
     ums, 1888, pp. 173 and 608.

63. A History of the Lutheran Church in South Carolina, p. 228.

64. Supra, p. 74.

65. B. M. Schmucker says that the catechism was printed "not
     later than 1846," though he had not seen the earlier prints.
     Op. cit., pp. 108f., The Lutheran Standard, VI (Jan. 3,
     1848), 4, for the first time carried an advertisement of this
     catechism.
          Ludwig, a staunch Lutheran layman, had over the years
     printed the English Luther text in pamphlet form. Thus in
     1834 already, The Lutheran Observer noted that the English
     text had been reprinted by Ludwig at the request of the New
     York Synod's committee on publications and could be obtained
     "at 4 a piece.," I (New Series), April 25, 1834, 260.

66. B. M. Schmucker, op. cit., p. 109.

67. Previously translated by Endress for his 1802 catechism, Supra,
     p. 141.

68. Theodore G. Tappert, ed. and trans., The Book of Concord.
     Philadelphia: Muhlenberg Press, c. 1959, p. 362.

69. B. M. Schmucker, op. cit., p. 109.

70. Ibid.

71. No copy of the first edition has been found nor, as far as the
     writer has been able to determine, has it been previously
     noted.   John Wm. Richards was pastor at St. John's Easton
     (1845-1851), and he may have been the author.   History of
     the Evangelical Lutheran Synod of East Pennsylvania, 1842-
     1892.   Philadelphia: Lutheran Publication Society, n.d., p.
     249 fn.

72. Enchiridion.   Der kleine Catechismus für die gemeinen Pfar-
     rherren und Prediger durch D. Martin Luther.   New York:
     Heinrich Ludwig, 1847.

73. Op. cit., p. 181.   Rev. F. W. Geissenhainer died in 1838.

74. Lutherischer Catechismus, nebst Erklärung, zum Gebrauch
     beym Confirmations-Unterricht in den Gemeinden von Falkner-
     Schwamm, Boyerstaun, Sassaman, Kieler, u.s.w.   Sumny-
     taun, Pa.: E. Benner, 1849.   Edwin G. Fritz probably was
     the catechumen referred to above.

75. Op. cit., p. 181.

76. Ibid.

77. Supra, p. 209.   Erster Synodal Bericht, p. 6 and Maasel, op.
     cit., p. 4.   For the emphasis placed on proper synodical

supervision of catechetical instruction in the congregations
and the general interest in the catechism, see pp. 3-11. See
also supra, pp. 74f. for this synod's reaction to Ludwig's
edition of the catechism of the Pennsylvania Ministerium.

78. Zweiter Synodal Bericht, 1848, p. 26.

79. Spruchbuch zum kleinen Catechismus Lutheri.   Baltimore: n. p.
     1849.

80. Der grosze und kleine Catechismus Dr. Martin Luther's.   Un-
     verändert aus dem Concordienbuche abgedruckt.   New York:
     H. Ludwig & Co., 1850.

INDEX TO SUPPLEMENTS

Supplements to Luther's Five Chief Parts,
except Prayers and Hymns